The Open University

MST124

Essential mathematics 1

Book B

This publication forms part of an Open University module. Details of this and other Open University modules can be obtained from the Student Registration and Enquiry Service, The Open University, PO Box 197, Milton Keynes MK7 6BJ, United Kingdom (tel. +44 (0)845 300 6090; email general-enquiries@open.ac.uk).

Alternatively, you may visit the Open University website at www.open.ac.uk where you can learn more about the wide range of modules and packs offered at all levels by The Open University.

To purchase a selection of Open University materials visit www.ouw.co.uk, or contact Open University Worldwide, Walton Hall, Milton Keynes MK7 6AA, United Kingdom for a brochure (tel. +44 (0)1908 858779; fax +44 (0)1908 858787; email ouw-customer-services@open.ac.uk).

The Open University, Walton Hall, Milton Keynes, MK7 6AA.

First published 2014.

Edited, designed and typeset by The Open University, using the Open University TeX System.

Printed in the United Kingdom by Page Bros, Norwich.

ISBN 978 1 7800 7356 9

1.1

Contents

Contents

Trigonometry

Introduction

Trigonometry is about the properties of triangles. A typical problem in trigonometry requires you to calculate one of the side lengths or angles of a triangle from other information about the triangle. For instance, you might need to calculate the side length c of the triangle in Figure 1. Problems of this type arise in a wealth of scientific subjects, from astronomy to civil engineering, and also in everyday life. Suppose, for example, that you want to estimate the width of a river. Trigonometry provides you with mathematical tools to approach this task, as you will see later.

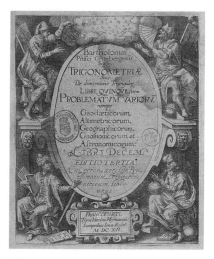

Figure 1 What is the length of the side c? You'll learn how to solve problems like this in Section 1

Figure 2 What is the width of the river?

Trigonometry goes far beyond triangles, though. All the angles of a triangle measure between 0° and 180°, but trigonometry also deals with larger angles, such as 300° or 500°, and even with negative angles, such as −100°. These deeper aspects of trigonometry have applications in electrical engineering and acoustics, among other scientific disciplines, as well as in more sophisticated branches of mathematics, such as *Fourier series*.

> The term 'trigonometry' is derived from the Greek words *trigonon* for triangle and *metron* for measure. It first appeared in the book *Trigonometriæ*, by Bartholomeo Pitiscus, published in 1595.

The frontispiece from Bartholomeo Pitiscus's Trigonometriæ (1612 edition)

Section 1 of this unit is about trigonometry in right-angled triangles (triangles with a right angle). You'll revise the trigonometric ratios sine, cosine and tangent, and use them to find angles and side lengths.

The angles of a right-angled triangle all measure between 0° and 90°. In Section 2, you'll learn the meanings of the sine, cosine and tangent of *any* angle (even negative angles). In this setting, sine, cosine and tangent are described as *trigonometric functions*: they are functions because each of them is a rule that takes an input number (the size of an angle) and produces an output number. In this section you'll also meet the graphs of the trigonometric functions, and learn about inverse trigonometric functions.

Section 3 returns to triangles, but considers those that don't necessarily have a right angle. You'll see how to use two important trigonometric rules, the sine rule and the cosine rule, to find angles and side lengths in such triangles.

Finally, in Section 4, you'll learn about many useful relationships between trigonometric functions, which are conveniently expressed as *trigonometric identities*. You'll need to use these identities when you study calculus, in Units 6 to 8, and complex numbers, in Unit 12.

Throughout the unit you'll practise working with angles measured in *radians*, rather than degrees, in preparation for topics that you'll study later in the module.

1 Right-angled triangles

In this section you'll revise the trigonometry of right-angled triangles. We begin with a reminder about *radians*.

1.1 Radians and degrees

Radians are units for measuring angles, which can be used as an alternative to degrees. They're used extensively in this module, and in many higher-level mathematics modules, as they're more convenient to work with in many contexts. For example, many mathematical formulas are simpler when angles are measured in radians rather than degrees. You'll see two such formulas in this subsection. When you study calculus and complex numbers later in the module, you'll use radians rather than degrees whenever you work with angles.

To understand what a radian is, consider any circle. An unbroken piece of its circumference is called an **arc**. For example, Figure 3 shows an arc of a circle. The centre of the circle is labelled O. The angle at the centre is said to be **subtended** by the arc.

Suppose that the circle has radius r, and you draw an arc also of length r on its circumference, as shown in Figure 4. Then the angle subtended by the arc is 1 radian. If the arc were of length $2r$ then the angle would be 2 radians, and so on. The definition of a radian is summarised in the following box.

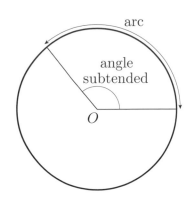

Figure 3 The angle subtended by an arc

Radians

One **radian** is the angle subtended at the centre of a circle by an arc that has the same length as the radius.

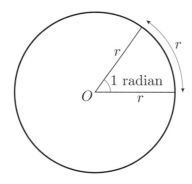

Figure 4   An angle of one radian

From this definition, you can find the number of radians in a full turn – that is, a turn of $360°$ (the symbol $°$ means degrees). The circumference of a circle of radius r is $2\pi r$, and each arc of length r subtends an angle of 1 radian. So the number of radians in a full turn is

$$\frac{2\pi r}{r} = 2\pi.$$

In other words, $360°$ is the same angle as 2π radians (about 6.28 radians).

$$2\pi \text{ radians} = 360°$$

This gives

$$1 \text{ radian} = \frac{360°}{2\pi} = \frac{180°}{\pi}.$$

Since

$$\frac{180}{\pi} = 57.295\ldots,$$

one radian is approximately $57°$.

In historical terms, the term 'radian' – a contraction of 'radial angle' – is relatively new. It appeared in print for the first time in 1873, in examination papers set by Professor James Thomson (brother of Lord Kelvin) at Queen's College, Belfast. Who actually coined the term radian is a matter of some debate. As a unit of measurement, but without the name, it was in use much earlier, appearing in the work of Roger Cotes (1682–1716), a close colleague of Isaac Newton.

Because a full turn is 2π radians, the number of radians in a simple fraction of a full turn can be conveniently expressed in terms of π. For instance, a quarter turn (90°) is $\pi/2$ radians, and a third of a full turn (120°) is $2\pi/3$ radians. Similarly, a twelfth of a full turn (30°) is $2\pi/12 = \pi/6$ radians. It is usual to leave these numbers of radians in this form, rather than finding decimal approximations. Reasoning in this way, we can assemble Table 1.

Table 1   A conversion table for common angles

Angle in degrees	Angle in radians
0°	0
30°	$\pi/6$
45°	$\pi/4$
60°	$\pi/3$
90°	$\pi/2$
180°	π
360°	2π

As with all fractions, you should usually write fractions of π in 'vertical' fraction notation, rather than using a slash symbol. For example, it is better to write $\dfrac{\pi}{2}$ rather than $\pi/2$ when you are doing an algebraic manipulation with this expression, in order to distinguish the numerator and the denominator clearly. However, we often use the slash symbol notation where a fraction is part of a line of typed text.

The fraction $\pi/2$ is usually read as 'pi by two', though you can also say 'pi over two'. Other fractions of π are read in a similar way.

Since

$$1 \text{ radian} = \frac{180°}{\pi},$$

the factor $180/\pi$ can be used to convert an angle measured in radians into degrees, and vice versa, as detailed below.

Converting between degrees and radians

$$\text{number of radians} = \frac{\pi}{180} \times \text{number of degrees}$$

$$\text{number of degrees} = \frac{180}{\pi} \times \text{number of radians}$$

Here are some examples of these types of conversions.

Example 1   *Converting between degrees and radians*

(a) Convert $120°$ to radians.

(b) Convert $5\pi/3$ radians to degrees.

Solution

(a) 🔍 Apply the degrees-to-radians conversion formula. 💬

$$120° = \left(\frac{\pi}{180} \times 120 \right) \text{ radians} = \frac{2\pi}{3} \text{ radians}$$

(b) 🔍 Apply the radians-to-degrees conversion formula. 💬

$$\frac{5\pi}{3} \text{ radians} = \left(\frac{180}{\pi} \times \frac{5\pi}{3} \right)^{\circ} = 300°$$

Here are some similar questions for you to try.

Activity 1   *Converting between degrees and radians*

(a) Convert the following angles from degrees to radians.

   (i) $1°$ (ii) $345°$

(b) Convert the following angles from radians to degrees.

   (i) $\dfrac{3\pi}{5}$ radians   (ii) $\dfrac{7\pi}{4}$ radians

As mentioned at the beginning of the subsection, some mathematical formulas are simpler when angles are measured in radians rather than degrees. An example is the formula for the length of an arc on the circumference of a circle of radius r, in terms of the subtended angle of size θ (in radians). (The symbol θ is the lower-case form of the Greek letter theta, which is pronounced 'thee-ta'. It is often used to represent angles.)

You know that

    an arc that subtends an angle of 1 radian has length r.

Hence

    an arc that subtends an angle of θ radians has length $r\theta$.

Such an arc is shown in Figure 5.

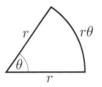

Figure 5   The arc length is $r\theta$

> **Length of an arc of a circle**
>
>   arc length $= r\theta,$
>
> where r is the radius of the circle and θ is the angle subtended by the arc, measured in radians.

For example, the formula tells you that an arc on a circle of radius 21 cm that subtends an angle of $\pi/7$ radians has the following length (in cm):

$$21 \times \frac{\pi}{7} = 3\pi = 9.42 \text{ (to 3 s.f.)}.$$

If the angle θ is measured in degrees rather than radians, then the formula for the length of an arc becomes

$$\text{arc length} = \frac{\pi}{180} \times r\theta = \frac{\pi r\theta}{180}.$$

This is a more cumbersome formula, which illustrates why radians are favoured over degrees in mathematical formulas.

Another formula that's simpler when radians are used rather than degrees is the formula for the area of a sector. A **sector** of a circle is the 'slice' of the circle lying between two radii, as shown in Figure 5. (Strictly speaking, a circle is just a curve, and a sector is really a slice of the *inside* of the circle. However, it is convenient to allow the word 'circle' to mean either a circle or its inside. With this convention, you can refer to the 'area of a circle', rather than the 'area enclosed by a circle'.)

Let's now obtain a formula for the area of a sector. Consider a circle of radius r. Its full area is πr^2. Half of the circle is a sector of angle π radians (a half turn), which has area $\frac{1}{2}\pi r^2$. That is,

    an angle of π radians gives a sector of area $\frac{1}{2}\pi r^2$.

Hence

    an angle of 1 radian gives a sector of area $\frac{1}{2}r^2$,

so

    an angle of θ radians gives a sector of area $\frac{1}{2}r^2\theta$.

Area of a sector of a circle

$$\text{area of sector} = \tfrac{1}{2}r^2\theta,$$

where r is the radius of the circle and θ is the angle of the sector, measured in radians.

In the next activity, you can practise using the formulas for the length of an arc and the area of a sector.

Activity 2 *Using the arc length and sector area formulas*

The classic computer game character shown in Figure 6 is constructed by removing a sector of angle $\pi/3$ radians from a circle of radius 1 cm.

(a) The shape is itself a sector – of what angle?

(b) What is the total perimeter of the shape? Give your answer in cm, to one decimal place.

(c) What is the area of the shape? Give your answer in cm^2, to one decimal place.

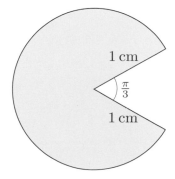

Figure 6 A circle with a sector of angle $\pi/3$ removed

Although radians usually give simpler mathematical formulas than degrees, there are many circumstances where degrees are the more appropriate choice of unit. This is because it can be more convenient to work with the large whole number 360 (for the number of degrees in a full turn) rather than the irrational number 2π (the number of radians in a full turn). Degrees tend to be used in practical situations – for example, by carpenters who want to measure the angles at the corners of pieces of wood.

In this module you will use both radians and degrees, and it is crucial that you always know what the current choice of unit is, especially when entering angle values into your calculator. Most calculators have an angle mode option for switching between degrees and radians. If your calculator is set to the wrong mode, then you will obtain incorrect results.

As you have seen, you must include the symbol $^\circ$ after the size of an angle measured in degrees. So far, we have indicated that the size of an angle is measured in radians by using the word 'radians'. For example, you have seen angles written as $\pi/2$ radians and $2\pi/3$ radians. In fact, it is usual to omit the word 'radians', and write these angles simply as $\pi/2$ and $2\pi/3$.

From now on, if the size of an angle is stated without the symbol $^\circ$, then the angle is measured in radians.

To help you be aware of the choice of unit, you should remember that angles in degrees are usually written as whole numbers or decimals, such as 37° and 156.4°, whereas angles in radians are usually written as fractions of π.

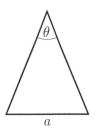

Figure 7 A triangle

Some useful conventions

Before you go on to Subsection 1.2, in which you'll start your revision of trigonometry, here are some standard conventions that we'll use in this subsection and throughout the rest of the unit.

First, we often use the same letter to denote either a line segment or its length. For example, we might say that the side a of the triangle in Figure 7 is horizontal, or we might write that a is 4 cm. We treat angles in a similar way. For example, we might say that the angle θ in Figure 7 is opposite the side a, or we might write that $\theta = \pi/4$.

Second, we often state the lengths of line segments, such as the sides of triangles, with no units. For example, we might say that one side of a triangle has length 5. When this is done, you should assume that the units are 'abstract' units, in the sense that they could represent any units that are used consistently. If you need to refer to them, then you can call them simply 'units'.

Finally, if you are asked to solve an abstract trigonometric problem, where no units of length are given, then (unless the question specifies otherwise) you should express your answers as exact values, rather than decimal approximations, whenever it is possible to do this reasonably concisely. For example, you might express an answer as a fraction or a surd, or in terms of π. If you are asked to solve a practical trigonometric problem, then you should normally give your answers as decimal approximations.

1.2 Sine, cosine and tangent

In this section you'll begin your revision of trigonometry by considering the relationships between angles and side lengths in *right-angled triangles*. A **right-angled triangle** is simply one that contains a right angle, that is, an angle of $\pi/2$ (90°), as illustrated in Figure 8.

Figure 8 A right-angled triangle

Each of the other two angles in a right-angled triangle is an **acute** angle, that is, an angle greater than 0 (0°) but less than $\pi/2$ (90°). This is because the three angles of a triangle add up to π (180°).

You already know a relationship between the three side lengths of a right-angled triangle, namely Pythagoras' theorem, which is repeated below. Remember that the side opposite the right angle in a right-angled triangle is called the **hypotenuse**, and it is always the longest side.

> **Pythagoras' theorem**
>
> For a right-angled triangle, the square of the hypotenuse is equal to the sum of the squares of the other two sides.

So if you know the lengths of two sides of a right-angled triangle, then you can use Pythagoras' theorem to work out the length of the third side. You saw some examples of this in Section 6 of Unit 1.

Sometimes, however, you may want to solve a problem that involves angles as well as side lengths in right-angled triangles. For example, you might have a triangle like the one in Figure 9(a), and you want to know the length of the side a. Or you might have a triangle like the one in Figure 9(b), and you want to know the size of the angle θ.

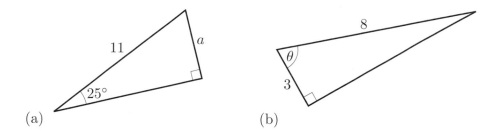

(a)   (b)

Figure 9   An unknown side a and an unknown angle θ

Problems like these can be solved by using the *sine*, *cosine* and *tangent* of an angle. These are numbers associated with the angle. All angles have a sine, cosine and tangent (except that some exceptional angles have no tangent), but in this section you'll consider the sine, cosine and tangent only of *acute* angles, as that's all you need to solve problems involving right-angled triangles. You'll learn about the sine, cosine and tangent of other angles later in the unit.

Here's how the sine, cosine and tangent of an acute angle θ are defined. Consider any right-angled triangle with θ as one of its acute angles, and label the sides of the triangle as follows: hyp for the *hypotenuse*, opp for the side *opposite* the angle θ, and adj for the side (other than the hypotenuse) *adjacent* to the angle θ. This is illustrated in Figure 10.

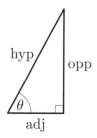

Figure 10   The opposite side, adjacent side and hypotenuse for an angle θ

The sine, cosine and tangent of θ are defined as follows.

Sine, cosine and tangent

The **sine** of the angle θ is

$$\sin\theta = \frac{\text{opp}}{\text{hyp}}.$$

The **cosine** of the angle θ is

$$\cos\theta = \frac{\text{adj}}{\text{hyp}}.$$

The **tangent** of the angle θ is

$$\tan\theta = \frac{\text{opp}}{\text{adj}}.$$

Sine, cosine and tangent are often referred to as sin, cos and tan, pronounced 'sine', 'coz' and 'tan', respectively.

A popular method for remembering the definitions above is to take the initial letters from

Sine = Opp/Hyp,   Cosine = Adj/Hyp,   Tangent = Opp/Adj,

to make the acronym SOH CAH TOA. This acronym is read to rhyme with *Krakatoa* (a famous volcano in Indonesia).

SOH CAH TOA

Another mnemonic used for these letters is 'Silly Old Harry, Chased A Horse, Through Our Attic'.

Let's try out the definitions of sine, cosine and tangent with the angle θ of the triangle shown in Figure 11. We obtain

$$\sin\theta = \frac{4}{5}, \quad \cos\theta = \frac{3}{5} \quad \text{and} \quad \tan\theta = \frac{4}{3}.$$

The other acute angle in the triangle in Figure 11 (the smallest angle) does not have the same values of sine, cosine and tangent as the angle θ. This is because the side opposite this other angle is not the side opposite the angle θ, and similarly the side adjacent to this angle is not the side adjacent to the angle θ.

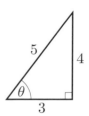

Figure 11   A right-angled triangle with side lengths 3, 4 and 5

You always get the same answers for the sine, cosine and tangent of a particular angle θ, no matter which right-angled triangle with θ as one of its acute angles you consider. To see why, first notice that all the different right-angled triangles with θ as one of their acute angles have the same three angles. This is because the sum of the three angles in a triangle is π (180°), so the angle other than θ and the right angle is given by

$$\pi - \frac{\pi}{2} - \theta = \frac{\pi}{2} - \theta.$$

It follows that all the right-angled triangles with θ as one of their angles are scaled-up or scaled-down (and possibly flipped over) versions of each other – in other words, they are all **similar**. For example, Figure 12 shows three different right-angled triangles with a particular acute angle θ. You can see that they are all essentially the same shape.

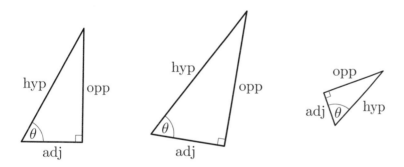

Figure 12   Similar triangles

Since all the right-angled triangles with a particular angle θ are scaled-up or scaled-down (and possibly flipped over) versions of each other, they all have their sides in the same proportions, and hence they all give the same values for $\sin\theta$, $\cos\theta$ and $\tan\theta$.

To help you see this, consider scaling the triangle shown in Figure 11 by a factor a, so that the new side lengths are $3a$, $4a$ and $5a$, as shown in Figure 13. Then

$$\sin\theta = \frac{4a}{5a} = \frac{4}{5}, \quad \cos\theta = \frac{3a}{5a} = \frac{3}{5} \quad \text{and} \quad \tan\theta = \frac{4a}{3a} = \frac{4}{3}.$$

These values of $\sin\theta$, $\cos\theta$ and $\tan\theta$ are the same as those obtained from the original triangle in Figure 11.

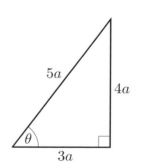

Figure 13   A right-angled triangle with side lengths $3a$, $4a$, and $5a$

The sine, cosine and tangent of an angle are known as **trigonometric ratios**, because each of them is defined as the ratio of one side of a right-angled triangle to another. (Remember that if a and b are two quantities, such as the lengths of sides of a triangle, then the **ratio** of a to b is a/b.)

You can write $\sin \theta$ as $\sin(\theta)$ if you prefer, and a similar comment applies to cos and tan.

Activity 3   *Finding trigonometric ratios*

Consider the angle θ in the triangle below.

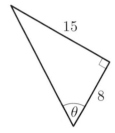

(a) Use Pythagoras' theorem to find the length of the hypotenuse.

(b) Find $\sin \theta$, $\cos \theta$ and $\tan \theta$.

If you know the sine, cosine or tangent of a particular acute angle, then you can find the other two trigonometric ratios for the angle by sketching a suitable right-angled triangle.

Activity 4   *Finding trigonometric ratios from another trigonometric ratio*

Suppose that θ is an acute angle and $\sin \theta = \frac{5}{13}$. Sketch a right-angled triangle with θ as one of its acute angles, and, by using Pythagoras' theorem, determine $\cos \theta$ and $\tan \theta$.

You can obtain the values of the sine, cosine and tangent of an angle using your calculator. You have to make sure that it is set to radians or degrees, as appropriate, or you will obtain incorrect answers.

Activity 5   *Using a calculator to find trigonometric ratios*

Use your calculator to find the values of $\sin 62°$, $\cos 62°$ and $\tan 62°$, to three significant figures.

In fact the angle θ in Activity 3 is about 62°, so the answers that you obtained in Activity 5 should be close to those that you obtained in Activity 3. (They won't be exactly the same, as the angle isn't exactly 62°.)

The Greek astronomer and mathematician Hipparchus of Rhodes (*c.* 190–120 BC) is widely recognised as the founder of trigonometry. He created the first table of trigonometric ratios, to enable him to calculate astronomical data. His work was used by another astronomer and mathematician, Ptolemy (*c.* AD 90–168), whose texts had considerable impact on the development of trigonometry and astronomy.

An image from the frontispiece of William Cunningham's *Cosmographical Glass* (1559). The same frontispiece was used for Henry Billingsley's *Euclid* (1570), the first edition of Euclid's *Elements* in English

1.3 Finding unknown side lengths in right-angled triangles

If you know one of the acute angles and one of the side lengths in a right-angled triangle, then you can use trigonometric ratios to find either of the other two side lengths. The next example illustrates this.

Example 2 *Finding an unknown side length*

Find the side length a in the triangle below, to two significant figures.

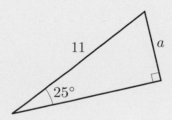

Solution

🔍 Label the sides of the triangle in relation to the given angle. 💭

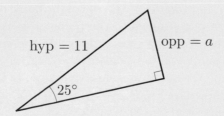

💬 The two labelled sides are opp and hyp, so use the equation $\sin 25° = \text{opp}/\text{hyp}$. 💬

$$\sin 25° = \frac{\text{opp}}{\text{hyp}} = \frac{a}{11}$$

💬 Rearrange this equation to find a. 💬

$$a = 11 \sin 25°$$

💬 Find $11 \sin 25°$ using your calculator. 💬

$$a = 4.648\ldots = 4.6 \quad \text{(to 2 s.f.)}.$$

You can practise calculating side lengths using sine, cosine and tangent in the next activity. The angle in part (a) is given in degrees, whereas the angles in parts (b) and (c) are given in radians, so make sure that your calculator is set to the appropriate unit each time.

Activity 6 *Finding unknown side lengths*

Calculate the side lengths p, q and r in the triangles below, to two significant figures.

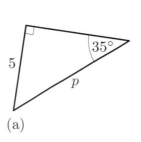

(a)

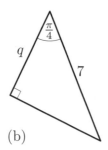

(b)

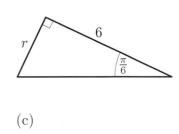

(c)

Let's now use trigonometry to solve the problem of how to estimate the width of a river, which was mentioned in the introduction to the unit. First you find a landmark on the opposite bank of the river. Let's suppose you choose a tree. You move to the point on your side of the river directly opposite the tree. You then walk alongside the river to a point further along. At this point you look back towards your starting position, and then towards the tree, and measure the angle between these two lines of sight. This is shown in Figure 14: the width of the river is w, the distance that you walk is d and the angle is θ.

Figure 14 A right-angled triangle can be used to estimate the width of the river

From the diagram,

$$\tan \theta = \frac{\text{opp}}{\text{adj}} = \frac{w}{d},$$

so

$$w = d \tan \theta.$$

You can now calculate w from d and θ; the better your measurements of d and θ are, the better your estimate of w is.

Activity 7 *Estimating the width of a river*

Suppose that you carry out the procedure described above, and the distance that you walk is 50 m. If the angle between your two lines of sight is 57°, how wide is the river? Give your answer to the nearest metre.

When you use the method described above, it's best to walk a reasonable distance – perhaps roughly as far as the river is wide. If you walk only a short distance, then you're likely to obtain an inaccurate estimate, because then the angle θ will be close to 90°, and small errors in the measurement of an angle close to 90° result in large errors in the value of its tangent. You can see this from the graph of tangent, which is given in Subsection 2.3.

The next activity involves a similar application of trigonometry.

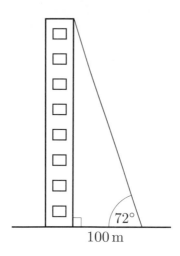

Figure 15   A tall building

Suppose that you stand 100 m from a tall building and measure the angle between the horizontal and the top of the building as 72°, as in Figure 15. How high is the building? Give your answer to the nearest metre.

1.4   Finding unknown angles in right-angled triangles

Let's now turn to the problem of finding an angle in a right-angled triangle when you know two side lengths. Take, for example, the triangle in Figure 16.

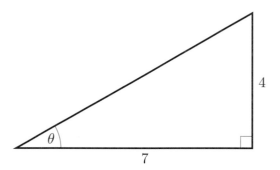

Figure 16   A right-angled triangle with two known side lengths

The side opposite the angle θ has length 4, and the side adjacent to the angle θ has length 7. Therefore

$$\tan \theta = \frac{\text{opp}}{\text{adj}} = \frac{4}{7}.$$

If you know the tangent of an acute angle (or the sine or cosine of the angle), then you can use your calculator to find the angle. The notation used for the acute angle whose tangent is the number x is

$$\tan^{-1} x.$$

Similarly, the notations used for the acute angle whose sine is x and the acute angle whose cosine is x are

$$\sin^{-1} x \quad \text{and} \quad \cos^{-1} x,$$

respectively.

Note that you may choose to write either $\tan^{-1} x$ or $\tan^{-1}(x)$, whichever seems clearer, just as you may choose to write either $\tan \theta$ or $\tan(\theta)$. A similar comment applies to sine and cosine.

The angles $\sin^{-1} x$, $\cos^{-1} x$ and $\tan^{-1} x$ are called the **inverse sine**, **inverse cosine** and **inverse tangent** of the number x, respectively. You can use your calculator to find them. For the triangle in Figure 16, $\tan \theta = 4/7$, so you can work out using your calculator that

$$\theta = \tan^{-1}\left(\tfrac{4}{7}\right) = 29.74\ldots^{\circ} = 29.7^{\circ} \quad \text{(to 3 s.f.)}.$$

The notation used for inverse sine, inverse cosine and inverse tangent is essentially the notation for inverse functions that you met in Unit 3. This is because inverse sine, inverse cosine and inverse tangent are types of inverse functions. You'll learn more about this in Subsection 2.4.

A common error when working with inverse sine, inverse cosine or inverse tangent is to confuse $\tan^{-1} x$ with $(\tan x)^{-1}$, for example. Remember that

$$(\tan x)^{-1} = \frac{1}{\tan x},$$

and this is very different from $\tan^{-1} x$. A similar warning applies to $\sin^{-1} x$ and $\cos^{-1} x$.

The inverse sine, inverse cosine and inverse tangent of a number x are also called the **arcsine**, **arccosine** and **arctangent** of x, with the following alternative notations:

$$\arcsin(x) = \sin^{-1} x, \quad \arccos(x) = \cos^{-1} x, \quad \arctan(x) = \tan^{-1} x.$$

Here's another example of finding an unknown angle in a right-angled triangle.

Example 3   *Finding an unknown angle*

Find the angle θ in the triangle below, to the nearest degree.

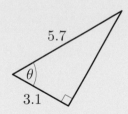

5.7

3.1

θ

Solution

🗨 Label the sides of the triangle in relation to the given angle. 🗨

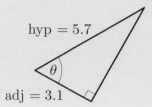

🗨 The two labelled sides are adj and hyp, so use the equation $\cos\theta = \text{adj}/\text{hyp}$. 🗨

$$\cos\theta = \frac{\text{adj}}{\text{hyp}} = \frac{3.1}{5.7}$$

🗨 Use inverse cosine on your calculator to find θ. 🗨

$$\theta = \cos^{-1}\left(\frac{3.1}{5.7}\right) = 57.053\ldots° = 57° \quad \text{(to the nearest degree)}$$

In the next activity, you can practise finding unknown angles in right-angled triangles. Notice that two of the angles in this activity are labelled α and β: these are the lower-case forms of the Greek letters alpha and beta, which are pronounced 'al-fa' and 'bee-ta'. Angles are often represented by Greek letters. The full Greek alphabet is given in the *Handbook*.

Activity 9   *Finding unknown angles*

Find the angles θ, α and β in the triangles below, to the nearest degree.

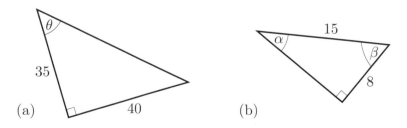

It is important to remember that the strategies that you've met so far for finding unknown side lengths and angles are valid only in *right-angled* triangles. In Section 3 you'll learn how to find unknown side lengths and angles in other triangles.

The Great Trigonometric Survey

The Great Trigonometric Survey was a survey of the geography of India, carried out in the nineteenth century. Trigonometry was fundamental to the survey, and was used to calculate measurements such as the heights of mountains in the Himalayas, including Mount Everest and K2. The superintendent of the latter parts of the survey was Colonel Sir George Everest, after whom Mount Everest is named.

George Everest (1790–1866)

1.5   Trigonometric ratios of special angles

You can work out the trigonometric ratios for the special angles $\pi/6$, $\pi/4$ and $\pi/3$ (that is, 30°, 45° and 60°, respectively) without using a calculator. These values are useful to know. Later in the unit you'll learn how to calculate sine, cosine and tangent for other special angles.

Let's begin with the angle $\pi/3$ (60°). This angle is one of the angles of an *equilateral triangle*, that is, a triangle in which all angles are equal. This is because $\pi/3$ (60°) is a third of the total angle sum π (180°) of a triangle.

Figure 17 shows an equilateral triangle that is split into two right-angled triangles by a vertical line. The equilateral triangle has sides of length 2, and the vertical line divides the base of the triangle into two equal parts, each of length 1. (Choosing the equilateral triangle to have sides of length 2 makes the calculations easier.)

By Pythagoras' theorem, the length of the vertical line is

$$\sqrt{2^2 - 1^2} = \sqrt{3},$$

as marked in the diagram. You can now apply the formulas

$$\sin\frac{\pi}{3} = \frac{\text{opp}}{\text{hyp}}, \quad \cos\frac{\pi}{3} = \frac{\text{adj}}{\text{hyp}} \quad \text{and} \quad \tan\frac{\pi}{3} = \frac{\text{opp}}{\text{adj}}$$

to the right-angled triangle on the left-hand side of the equilateral triangle in Figure 17. This gives

$$\sin\frac{\pi}{3} = \frac{\sqrt{3}}{2}, \quad \cos\frac{\pi}{3} = \frac{1}{2} \quad \text{and} \quad \tan\frac{\pi}{3} = \frac{\sqrt{3}}{1} = \sqrt{3}.$$

Remember that you can write $\sin\dfrac{\pi}{3}$ as $\sin\left(\dfrac{\pi}{3}\right)$ or $\sin(\pi/3)$ if you prefer, and a similar comment applies for cos and tan.

You can find the trigonometric ratios for the angle $\pi/6$ (30°) by using the same diagram, Figure 17. This is because the other acute angle in the left-hand triangle in Figure 17 is $\pi/6$, as marked in Figure 18, since it is half of the top angle $\pi/3$ of the equilateral triangle. This gives

$$\sin\frac{\pi}{6} = \frac{1}{2}, \quad \cos\frac{\pi}{6} = \frac{\sqrt{3}}{2} \quad \text{and} \quad \tan\frac{\pi}{6} = \frac{1}{\sqrt{3}}.$$

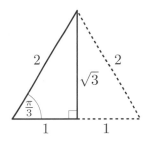

Figure 17   An equilateral triangle split into two right-angled triangles

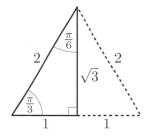

Figure 18   The right-angled triangle on the left has acute angles $\pi/3$ and $\pi/6$

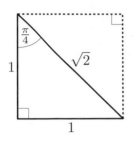

Figure 19 A right-angled triangle with two acute angles of size $\pi/4$

Let's now consider the angle $\pi/4$ (45°). To find the trigonometric ratios for this angle, you can use the right-angled triangle shown in Figure 19.

It is created by splitting a square down one of its diagonals. Because each angle of a square is a right angle, $\pi/2$, each of the acute angles of the triangle is half of a right angle, $\pi/4$. By Pythagoras' theorem, the length of the diagonal line is

$$\sqrt{1^2 + 1^2} = \sqrt{2},$$

as marked in the diagram. You can now apply the formulas

$$\sin\frac{\pi}{4} = \frac{\text{opp}}{\text{hyp}}, \quad \cos\frac{\pi}{4} = \frac{\text{adj}}{\text{hyp}} \quad \text{and} \quad \tan\frac{\pi}{4} = \frac{\text{opp}}{\text{adj}}$$

to obtain

$$\sin\frac{\pi}{4} = \frac{1}{\sqrt{2}}, \quad \cos\frac{\pi}{4} = \frac{1}{\sqrt{2}} \quad \text{and} \quad \tan\frac{\pi}{4} = 1.$$

The trigonometric ratios for the angles $\pi/6$, $\pi/4$ and $\pi/3$ are listed in Table 2, which will be referred to as the *special angles table*. This table is also given in the *Handbook*. It's useful to learn these trigonometric ratios, or to learn how to work them out quickly by sketching the triangles in Figures 18 and 19, as they come up frequently.

Table 2   Sine, cosine and tangent of special angles

θ in radians	θ in degrees	$\sin\theta$	$\cos\theta$	$\tan\theta$
$\dfrac{\pi}{6}$	30°	$\dfrac{1}{2}$	$\dfrac{\sqrt{3}}{2}$	$\dfrac{1}{\sqrt{3}}$
$\dfrac{\pi}{4}$	45°	$\dfrac{1}{\sqrt{2}}$	$\dfrac{1}{\sqrt{2}}$	1
$\dfrac{\pi}{3}$	60°	$\dfrac{\sqrt{3}}{2}$	$\dfrac{1}{2}$	$\sqrt{3}$

Note that the surd $1/\sqrt{2}$, which appears in Table 2, can also be written as $\sqrt{2}/2$. Your calculator may display it like this. This alternative form is obtained by multiplying both the numerator and the denominator of the original fraction by $\sqrt{2}$, to rationalise the denominator. Similarly the surd $1/\sqrt{3}$ can be written as $\sqrt{3}/3$.

You can also use Table 2 to find some values of inverse sine, inverse cosine and inverse tangent. For example, from the first row you can see that

$$\cos^{-1}\left(\frac{\sqrt{3}}{2}\right) = \frac{\pi}{6}.$$

Notice that the values of sine and cosine in Table 2 are all less than 1. This is because the longest side of any right-angled triangle is the hypotenuse, so opp and adj are both smaller than hyp. It follows that, for any acute angle θ, the values of

$$\sin\theta = \frac{\text{opp}}{\text{hyp}} \quad \text{and} \quad \cos\theta = \frac{\text{adj}}{\text{hyp}}$$

are both less than 1. However, as you can see from Table 2, the tangent of an acute angle can be less than 1, equal to 1, or greater than 1.

> **Spherical geometry**
>
> The angles of a triangle always add up to π (180°) ... or do they? In *plane* geometry (which is the only geometry that you'll meet in this module) they certainly do, but in *spherical* geometry the sum of the angles of a triangle is always greater than π! The Earth, which is approximately spherical, provides a useful model for thinking about spherical geometry. The triangle shown in Figure 20, with one vertex at the North Pole and the other two vertices on the equator – one in Ecuador and the other in Gabon – has three right angles!

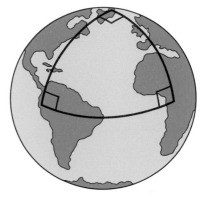

Figure 20   A spherical triangle with three right angles

1.6   Trigonometric identities

In Unit 1 you learned that an identity is an equation that is satisfied by all possible values of its variables. A **trigonometric identity** is an identity that involves one or more trigonometric ratios. In this subsection you'll meet several important trigonometric identities.

For our first trigonometric identity, consider any acute angle θ, and choose a right-angled triangle that has θ as one of its acute angles, and whose hypotenuse has length 1, as shown in Figure 21. You can always obtain such a triangle by scaling up or down any right-angled triangle that has θ as one of its acute angles. (The hypotenuse is chosen to have length 1 to simplify the algebra later on.)

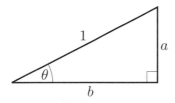

Figure 21   A right-angled triangle with hypotenuse of length 1 and other sides of lengths a and b

For this triangle,

$$\sin\theta = \frac{a}{1} = a, \quad \cos\theta = \frac{b}{1} = b \quad \text{and} \quad \tan\theta = \frac{a}{b}.$$

It follows that

$$\frac{\sin\theta}{\cos\theta} = \frac{a}{b} = \tan\theta,$$

which is our first trigonometric identity.

$$\tan\theta = \frac{\sin\theta}{\cos\theta}$$

This equation is an identity because it is true for *any* acute angle θ.

To obtain our second identity, let's apply Pythagoras's theorem to the right-angled triangle in Figure 21. This gives

$$a^2 + b^2 = 1^2 = 1.$$

Since $\sin\theta = a$ and $\cos\theta = b$, it follows that

$$(\sin\theta)^2 + (\cos\theta)^2 = 1.$$

It is conventional to write $(\sin\theta)^2$ and $(\cos\theta)^2$ as $\sin^2\theta$ and $\cos^2\theta$, respectively, so the identity above is usually written as follows.

$$\sin^2\theta + \cos^2\theta = 1$$

The notation $\sin^2\theta$ for $(\sin\theta)^2$ is convenient as it avoids some brackets. Similarly we usually write $\sin^3\theta$ for $(\sin\theta)^3$, and so on. However, remember that $\sin^{-1}x$ does *not* mean $(\sin x)^{-1}$, which is a way of writing $1/\sin x$. Instead $\sin^{-1}x$ is the inverse sine of x. This is an awkward clash of notation that you just need to become used to.

You can use the two trigonometric identities above to deduce the values of all the trigonometric ratios for a particular acute angle if you know the value of one of these ratios. This is an alternative to sketching a suitable right-angled triangle, as you were asked to do in Activity 4, and you're asked to try it in the following activity.

Activity 10 *Finding trigonometric ratios from another trigonometric ratio by using trigonometric identities*

Suppose that the acute angle θ is such that $\cos\theta = \frac{3}{7}$. Use the identities above to find the exact values of $\sin\theta$ and $\tan\theta$.

The next two trigonometric identities involve both the acute angles in a right-angled triangle. The sum of these two angles is $\pi/2$, so if one acute angle is θ, then the other is $(\pi/2) - \theta$, as shown in Figure 22.

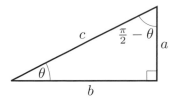

Figure 22 A right-angled triangle with acute angles θ and $(\pi/2) - \theta$

You can see from Figure 22 that

$$\sin \theta = \frac{a}{c} \quad \text{and} \quad \cos \theta = \frac{b}{c},$$

and also

$$\sin \left(\frac{\pi}{2} - \theta \right) = \frac{b}{c} \quad \text{and} \quad \cos \left(\frac{\pi}{2} - \theta \right) = \frac{a}{c}.$$

This gives us two more identities.

$$\sin \left(\frac{\pi}{2} - \theta \right) = \cos \theta$$
$$\cos \left(\frac{\pi}{2} - \theta \right) = \sin \theta$$

These identities tell you that if you have two acute angles that add up to $\pi/2$ (90°), then the sine of one is the cosine of the other, and vice versa. This explains the repeated values that you can see in the sine and cosine columns of the special angles table (Table 2 on page 22). For example, if $\theta = \pi/6$ then $(\pi/2) - \theta = \pi/3$, so the first of the two identities gives

$$\sin \frac{\pi}{3} = \cos \frac{\pi}{6},$$

which is confirmed by Table 2.

You're asked to prove an identity involving $\tan ((\pi/2) - \theta)$ in the next activity.

Activity 11 *Proving a trigonometric identity*

Using Figure 22, show that, for every acute angle θ,

$$\tan \left(\frac{\pi}{2} - \theta \right) = \frac{1}{\tan \theta}.$$

2 Trigonometric functions

In this section you'll learn what's meant by the sine, cosine and tangent of angles of any size, and you'll see that sine, cosine and tangent are functions.

2.1 Angles of any size

In Section 1 you worked with acute angles and right angles. However, you can also have:

- **obtuse** angles (those between 90° and 180°, that is, between $\pi/2$ and π)

- **straight** angles (those of 180°, that is, π)

- **reflex** angles (those between 180° and 360°, that is, between π and 2π).

These five types of angle are illustrated in Figure 23.

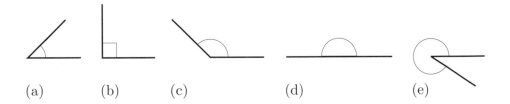

(a)   (b)   (c)   (d)   (e)

Figure 23   (a) Acute angle (b) right angle (c) obtuse angle (d) straight angle (e) reflex angle

You can also have angles larger than 360° (2π). For example, if a wheel rotates through a full turn followed by another half turn, then altogether it has rotated through an angle of 540° (3π). You can even have negative angles. For example, if a wheel rotates through a half turn followed by another half turn in the opposite direction, then you can say that it has rotated through 180° (π) followed by $-180°$ $(-\pi)$.

In this section you'll learn about the sine, cosine and tangent of every angle, even negative angles. The first step is to learn to associate with each angle θ a particular point P on the **unit circle**, which is the circle with radius 1 centred on the origin. The position of the point P is determined by the angle θ: it is obtained by a rotation around the origin through the angle θ, starting from the point on the x-axis with x-coordinate 1. If the angle θ is positive, then the rotation is anticlockwise; if θ is negative, then the rotation is clockwise.

Figure 24 shows some examples of how angles give rise to points on the unit circle.

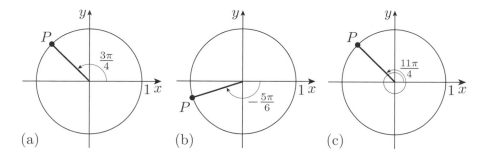

(a)   (b)   (c)

Figure 24   Angles and their associated points on the unit circle

The point P lies in the same position in Figures 24(a) and (c), despite having rotated through different angles, $3\pi/4$ and $11\pi/4$. This is because $11\pi/4$ is exactly one full turn more than $3\pi/4$, since

$$\frac{11\pi}{4} = \frac{3\pi}{4} + 2\pi.$$

In general, whenever two angles differ by an even multiple of π (such as 4π, -6π or 100π), they are both associated with the same point P on the unit circle. For instance, because

$$\frac{3\pi}{4} = -\frac{13\pi}{4} + 4\pi,$$

the point P associated with the angle $-13\pi/4$ is the same as the point P associated with the angle $3\pi/4$.

Skateboard tricks

Skateboarders sometimes perform tricks in which they launch themselves and their board into the air and rotate as much as they can before landing. The name of the trick depends on the amount that they rotate in degrees. For example, a one-full-turn trick is called a 360, a two-full-turn trick is called a 720, and a one-and-a-half-full-turn trick is called a 540. The landing positions of some of these tricks are the same: following a 180, a 540 or a 900, a skateboarder lands in the opposite direction from which he started, because these three angles differ by multiples of 360.

Skateboarders seem unaware of radians!

To help us describe the approximate location of the point P associated with an angle, it is useful to introduce the idea of a *quadrant*. A **quadrant** is one of the four regions separated off by the x-axis and y-axis. The names of the quadrants are shown in Figure 25.

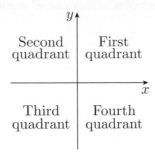

Figure 25   The four quadrants

So, for example, in Figures 24(a) and (c) the point P lies in the second quadrant, whereas in Figure 24(b) it lies in the third quadrant.

Activity 12   *Plotting points on the unit circle associated with angles*

For each of the following angles, draw a diagram similar to those in Figure 24 that shows the location of the point P on the unit circle, and state the quadrant in which P lies.

(a) $-\pi/3$ (b) $6\pi/5$ (c) $11\pi/3$ (d) $-16\pi/5$

2.2 Sine, cosine and tangent of any angle

In this subsection you'll learn how the sine, cosine and tangent of any angle are defined. Before seeing the definition, consider any *acute* angle θ and its associated point P on the unit circle, as illustrated in Figure 26(a). A line has been drawn from P to the x-axis, to complete a right-angled triangle. A close-up of this triangle is shown in Figure 26(b).

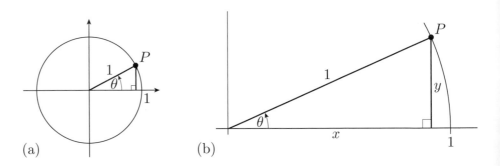

(a)   (b)

Figure 26   (a) The point P on the unit circle associated with an acute angle θ (b) a close-up of the right-angled triangle

Suppose that the coordinates of the point P are (x, y). Then you can see from Figure 26 that

$$\sin \theta = \frac{\text{opp}}{\text{hyp}} = \frac{y}{1} = y,$$

$$\cos \theta = \frac{\text{adj}}{\text{hyp}} = \frac{x}{1} = x,$$

$$\tan \theta = \frac{\text{opp}}{\text{adj}} = \frac{y}{x}.$$

These equations are used to define the sine, cosine and tangent of *any* angle θ, as follows.

> ### Sine, cosine and tangent
>
> Suppose that θ is any angle and (x, y) are the coordinates of its associated point P on the unit circle. Then
>
> $$\sin \theta = y, \quad \cos \theta = x,$$
>
> and, provided that $x \neq 0$,
>
> $$\tan \theta = \frac{y}{x}.$$
>
> (If $x = 0$, then $\tan \theta$ is undefined.)

In other words, the sine and cosine of an angle θ are just the y- and x-coordinates, in that order, of the point P on the unit circle associated with θ. The tangent of θ is the y-coordinate of P divided by the x-coordinate, provided that the x-coordinate isn't zero. You can see a demonstration of these definitions in the *Sine, cosine and tangent of any angle* applet.

For example, Figure 27(a) shows the point P associated with the angle $\theta = 0$. It has coordinates $(1, 0)$, which tells you that

$$\sin 0 = 0, \quad \cos 0 = 1 \quad \text{and} \quad \tan 0 = \frac{0}{1} = 0.$$

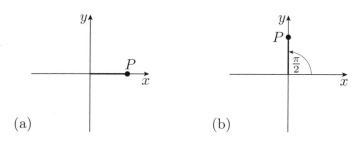

(a)   (b)

Figure 27   The points on the unit circle associated with the angles (a) 0 (b) $\pi/2$

Similarly, Figure 27(b) shows the point P associated with the angle $\theta = \pi/2$. It has coordinates $(0, 1)$, which tells you that

$$\sin\frac{\pi}{2} = 1, \quad \cos\frac{\pi}{2} = 0 \quad \text{and} \quad \tan\frac{\pi}{2} \text{ is undefined.}$$

Activity 13 *Finding sines, cosines and tangents*

Find the following values, where they are defined, without using a calculator.

(a) $\sin\pi$, $\cos\pi$ and $\tan\pi$

(b) $\sin(-\pi/2)$, $\cos(-\pi/2)$ and $\tan(-\pi/2)$

You can see that it's straightforward to write down the sine, cosine and tangent (if it's defined) of any angle whose associated point P lies on one of the coordinate axes – that is, any angle that's an integer multiple of $\pi/2$.

Notice also that if the point P associated with an angle θ lies on the y-axis, then the tangent of θ is undefined (because at such points the value of x is zero). So every angle of the form

$$\frac{\pi}{2} + n\pi, \quad \text{where } n \text{ is an integer,}$$

has no tangent.

The next example shows you a method for finding the sine, cosine and tangent of any angle θ whose associated point P doesn't lie on one of the coordinate axes. The method is based on first finding the sine, cosine and tangent of a particular *acute* angle that's related to θ.

Example 4 *Finding the sine, cosine and tangent of an angle that's not an integer multiple of $\pi/2$*

Find the sine, cosine and tangent of $3\pi/4$.

Solution

🔍 Draw a sketch showing the approximate position of the associated point P (the important thing is to draw it in the correct quadrant). Work out and mark the size of the acute angle between the line OP and the x-axis. Draw a line from P to the x-axis, at right angles to the x-axis. 💬

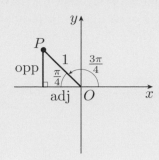

🔍 Use basic trigonometry to find the lengths of the adjacent and opposite sides of the resulting right-angled triangle. Hence find the coordinates of P, and write down the sine, cosine and tangent of the original angle. 💬

For the triangle in the diagram,

$$\cos\frac{\pi}{4} = \frac{\text{adj}}{1} = \text{adj}, \quad \text{so} \quad \text{adj} = \cos\frac{\pi}{4} = \frac{1}{\sqrt{2}},$$

$$\sin\frac{\pi}{4} = \frac{\text{opp}}{1} = \text{opp}, \quad \text{so} \quad \text{opp} = \sin\frac{\pi}{4} = \frac{1}{\sqrt{2}}.$$

Hence the coordinates of P are $\left(-\dfrac{1}{\sqrt{2}}, \dfrac{1}{\sqrt{2}}\right)$. Therefore

$$\sin\left(\frac{3\pi}{4}\right) = \frac{1}{\sqrt{2}},$$

$$\cos\left(\frac{3\pi}{4}\right) = -\frac{1}{\sqrt{2}},$$

$$\tan\left(\frac{3\pi}{4}\right) = \left(\frac{1}{\sqrt{2}}\right) \Big/ \left(-\frac{1}{\sqrt{2}}\right) = -1.$$

In the next activity, you can practise using the method demonstrated in Example 4. When you use this method, you should always find the size of the acute angle between OP and the x-axis (never the y-axis).

Activity 14   *Finding the sine, cosine and tangent of an angle that's not an integer multiple of $\pi/2$*

Find the sine, cosine and tangent of the following angles.

(a) $5\pi/6$ (b) $-\pi/4$

You can use the special angles table on page 22 (it is also in the *Handbook*) to find the sines, cosines and tangents of acute angles that you'll need.

Second quadrant	First quadrant
S	**A**
T	**C**
Third quadrant	Fourth quadrant

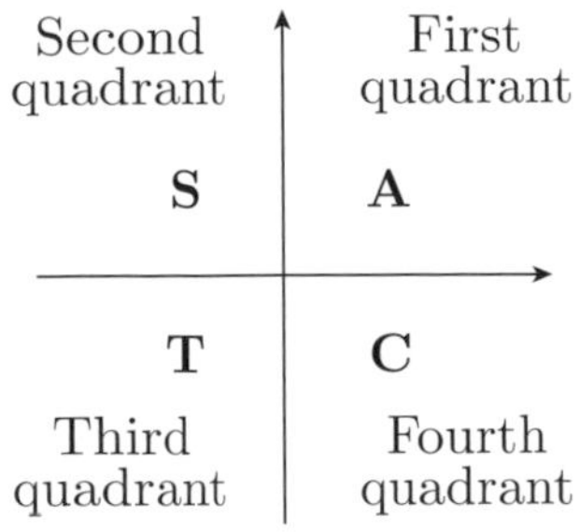

Figure 28   The ASTC diagram

There's a convenient way to shorten the working when you use the method demonstrated in Example 4. It's based on the diagram in Figure 28. In this diagram the letter in each quadrant indicates which of $\sin\theta$, $\cos\theta$ and $\tan\theta$ are positive when the point P associated with the angle θ lies in that quadrant:

- A stands for all
- S stands for sin
- T stands for tan
- C stands for cos.

This diagram, which we'll call the *ASTC diagram*, is often useful, so it's a good idea to memorise it, if you can. You might find it helpful to use a mnemonic, such as 'All Silly Tom Cats'. In some texts it's called the CAST, rather than ASTC, diagram, which is easier to remember, but has the disadvantage that the first letter of the acronym doesn't correspond to the first quadrant. To use the ASTC diagram, you combine it with the following useful fact, which is illustrated by the working in Example 4 and Activity 14. (Here the symbol ϕ is the lower-case form of the Greek letter phi, which is pronounced 'fie'.)

Suppose that θ is an angle whose associated point P does not lie on either the x- or y-axis, and ϕ is the acute angle between OP and the x-axis. Then

$$\sin\theta = \pm\sin\phi$$
$$\cos\theta = \pm\cos\phi$$
$$\tan\theta = \pm\tan\phi.$$

The ASTC diagram tells you which sign applies in each case.

(The values $\sin\phi$, $\cos\phi$ and $\tan\phi$ are all positive, because ϕ is acute.)

The next example repeats Example 4 above, but uses the ASTC diagram to shorten the working.

Example 5   *Finding values of sine, cosine and tangent using the ASTC diagram*

Find the sine, cosine and tangent of $3\pi/4$.

Solution

🔍 Draw a sketch showing the approximate position of the associated point P (the important thing is to draw it in the correct quadrant). Use it to work out the size of the acute angle between OP and the x-axis. 💬

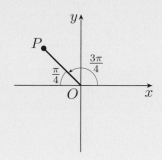

🗨 Use the ASTC diagram to express the sine, cosine and tangent of the original angle in terms of the sine, cosine and tangent of the acute angle. Then obtain the final answers by finding the sine, cosine and tangent of the acute angle. Here you can use the special angles table. 🗨

Since $3\pi/4$ is a second quadrant angle, its sine is positive and its cosine and tangent are negative. Hence

$$\sin\left(\frac{3\pi}{4}\right) = \sin\frac{\pi}{4} = \frac{1}{\sqrt{2}},$$

$$\cos\left(\frac{3\pi}{4}\right) = -\cos\frac{\pi}{4} = -\frac{1}{\sqrt{2}},$$

$$\tan\left(\frac{3\pi}{4}\right) = -\tan\frac{\pi}{4} = -1.$$

Activity 15 *Finding trigonometric ratios using the ASTC diagram*

Use the ASTC diagram and the special angles table (page 22) to find the sine, cosine and tangent of each of the following angles.

(a) $2\pi/3$ (b) $7\pi/6$ (c) $-7\pi/3$

Another way to find the sine, cosine or tangent of any angle is simply to use your calculator, in the same way that you do for acute angles. You might like to use your calculator to check your answers to Activity 15.

However, it's still important that you understand the method demonstrated in Examples 4 and 5. One reason for this is that you can sometimes use this method to obtain exact values of sine, cosine and tangent where a calculator will give you only approximate values. Another reason is that you can use the ideas of the method to solve trigonometric equations, as you'll see later in this section.

2.3 Graphs of sine, cosine and tangent

You have seen that sine, cosine and tangent are rules whose inputs are the sizes of angles and whose outputs are numbers. In other words, sine, cosine and tangent are *functions*. They are known as **trigonometric functions**.

You may think at first that the trigonometric functions aren't quite the same as the functions that you met in Unit 3. For a start, functions in Unit 3 were usually written as a single letter, such as f, whereas the sine, cosine and tangent functions are written as three letters, namely sin, cos and tan.

Another difference is that you wrote $f(x)$ in Unit 3 for the image of an element under a function, whereas here we have been writing $\sin\theta$, $\cos\theta$ and $\tan\theta$. This is a convention in trigonometry: angles are usually represented by θ in preference to x, and brackets are usually omitted from expressions such as $\sin\theta$. It is also perfectly correct to write $\sin(\theta)$, or to represent an angle by x and write $\sin x$ or $\sin(x)$.

Another apparent difference is that the input values of the trigonometric functions are angles, rather than real numbers. In fact, you can think of the input values of trigonometric functions as real numbers, and it's often convenient to do so. The notation that we've been using for angle sizes helps us to do this. For example, when we write $\sin(\pi/2)$, the input value $\pi/2$ is a real number that is the size of an angle measured in radians. In general, the input values of the trigonometric functions are real numbers that are the sizes of angles measured in radians. (However, it still makes sense to write $\sin(90°)$, for example, because $90° = \pi/2$.)

As you saw in Unit 3, a useful way to understand the properties of a function is to draw its graph. In this subsection you'll see the graphs of the trigonometric functions, and use these graphs as an alternative to the ASTC diagram to work out values of sine, cosine and tangent.

In the next activity, you can see the graphs of the sine and cosine functions generated directly from their definitions in terms of the coordinates of a point on the unit circle.

Activity 16   *Understanding graphs of trigonometric functions*

Open the *Graphs of sine and cosine* applet. Explore the graphs of the sine and cosine functions as directed.

Let's now look at some of the properties of the graphs of the sine, cosine and tangent functions in more detail.

The graph of the sine function

The graph of sine is shown in Figure 29.

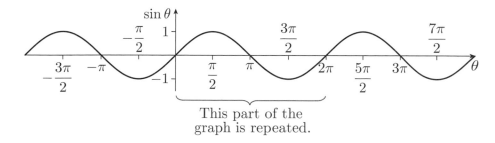

Figure 29   The graph of the sine function

First look at the part of the graph for values of θ between 0 and 2π. As the angle θ increases from 0 to 2π, the value of $\sin\theta$ oscillates from 0 to 1 to 0 to -1 and back to 0. To see why this is, remember that $\sin\theta$ is the y-coordinate of the point P on the unit circle (see Figure 30). As the angle θ increases from 0 to 2π, the point P starts on the positive x-axis and rotates once anticlockwise around the unit circle, back to where it started. As P rotates, its y-coordinate oscillates from 0 to 1 to 0 to -1 and back to 0. Nowhere is $\sin\theta$ greater than 1 or less than -1, because P is constrained to lie on the unit circle.

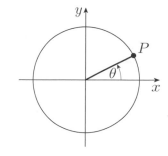

Since P returns to its original position after a complete rotation through 2π, you can see that $\sin(\theta + 2\pi) = \sin\theta$ for any angle θ. This implies that the graph of sine oscillates endlessly to the right and to the left, repeating its shape after every interval of 2π. This fact is expressed by saying that the graph is **periodic**, with **period** 2π.

Figure 30   The point P has coordinates $(\cos\theta, \sin\theta)$

The graph of sine has other symmetry features. For instance, if you rotate the whole graph through a half-turn about the origin, then it remains unchanged. Also, any vertical line through the centre of a peak or trough of the graph is a line of mirror symmetry.

The graph of the cosine function

The graph of cosine is shown in Figure 31.

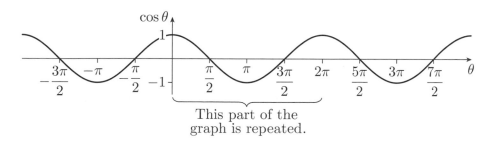

Figure 31   The graph of the cosine function

To understand why the graph of cosine has the shape that it does, you can think about it in a similar way to the graph of sine, remembering that

$\cos \theta$ is the x-coordinate of the point P on the unit circle, rather than the y-coordinate. Like the graph of sine, the graph of cosine is periodic with period 2π, and any vertical line through the centre of a peak or trough is a line of mirror symmetry. In fact, you can obtain the graph of cosine by translating the graph of sine to the left by $\pi/2$.

The graph of the tangent function

The graph of the tangent function, shown in Figure 32, differs from the other two graphs in that it is broken up into separate pieces, and it takes arbitrarily large positive values and arbitrarily large negative values.

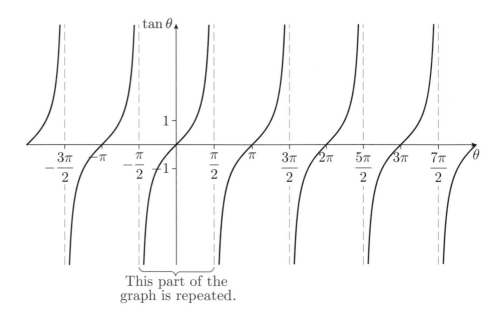

This part of the graph is repeated.

Figure 32   The graph of the tangent function

Like the graphs of sine and cosine, the graph of tangent is periodic, but its period is π rather than 2π. The breaks in the graph occur when $\theta = \pi/2 + n\pi$, for some integer n. These are the values of θ for which $\tan \theta$ is undefined, because the y-coordinate of the point P is zero, as you saw on page 30. The vertical dashed lines drawn on the graph are asymptotes: the graph approaches but never reaches them. (You met the idea of an asymptote in Unit 3.)

Using the graphs to find values of trigonometric functions

You can use the graphs that you've met in this subsection to work out the sine, cosine or tangent of an angle from the sine, cosine or tangent of an acute angle, as an alternative to using the ASTC diagram. The method is demonstrated in the following example.

Example 6   *Finding sines, cosines and tangents by using graphs*

Use the graphs of sine and tangent, and the special angles table, to find the following values.

(a) $\sin\left(\dfrac{5\pi}{6}\right)$ (b) $\tan\left(-\dfrac{\pi}{3}\right)$

Solution

(a) 🔍 Find the approximate location of $5\pi/6$ on the θ-axis of the graph of sine (the important thing is to locate it between $\pi/2$ and π). Mark the corresponding point on the graph. 💬

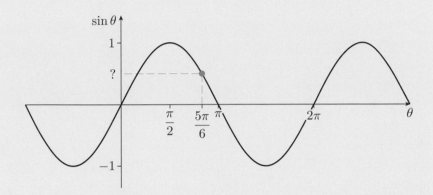

🔍 Use the symmetry of the graph to relate $\sin(5\pi/6)$ to the sine of an acute angle. You can use the vertical line of symmetry through $\theta = \pi/2$. 💬

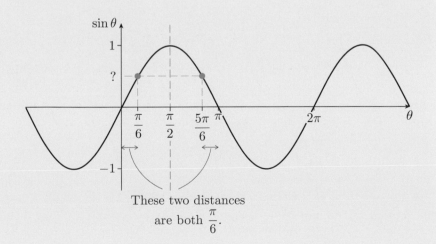

These two distances
are both $\dfrac{\pi}{6}$.

From the graph,

$$\sin\left(\frac{5\pi}{6}\right) = \sin\frac{\pi}{6}.$$

Since $\sin(\pi/6) = \frac{1}{2}$, it follows that

$$\sin\left(\frac{5\pi}{6}\right) = \frac{1}{2}.$$

(b) 🔍 Find the approximate location of $-\pi/3$ on the θ-axis of the graph of tangent (the important thing is to locate it between $-\pi/2$ and 0). Mark the corresponding point on the graph. 💬

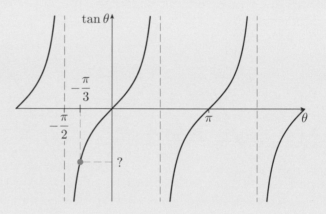

🔍 Use the symmetry of the graph to relate $\tan(-\pi/3)$ to the tangent of an acute angle. 💬

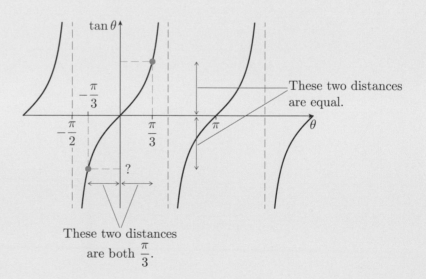

These two distances are equal.

These two distances are both $\dfrac{\pi}{3}$.

From the graph,
$$\tan\left(-\frac{\pi}{3}\right) = -\tan\frac{\pi}{3}.$$
Since $\tan(\pi/3) = \sqrt{3}$, it follows that
$$\tan\left(-\frac{\pi}{3}\right) = -\sqrt{3}.$$

In the next activity, you can practise finding values of sine, cosine and tangent using the graph method demonstrated in Example 6. The graphs that you sketch don't need to be accurate: they just need to illustrate the symmetry properties of the trigonometric functions.

Activity 17   *Finding sines, cosines and tangents by using graphs*

Use the graphs of sine, cosine and tangent to find the following values.

(a) $\sin\left(-\dfrac{\pi}{4}\right)$ (b) $\cos\left(-\dfrac{\pi}{3}\right)$ (c) $\tan\left(\dfrac{5\pi}{4}\right)$

Using the variables x and y for trigonometric functions

Sometimes it's convenient to use a letter other than θ to denote the input variable of a trigonometric function. For example, it's often convenient to use the letter x to denote the input variable and the letter y to denote the output variable. These are the standard letters for the input and output variables of functions, as you saw in Unit 3. You'll use this notation in the next subsection, and also in the calculus units later in the module. Figure 33 shows the graphs of the trigonometric functions with this notation used.

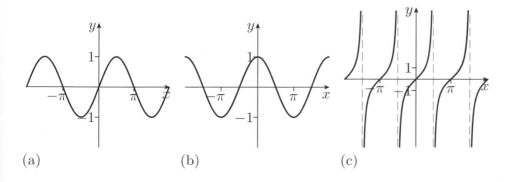

(a)   (b)   (c)

Figure 33   The graphs of (a) $y = \sin x$ (b) $y = \cos x$ (c) $y = \tan x$

You need to be careful with this change of notation. Earlier in this unit, the letters x and y denoted the coordinates of the point P on the unit circle. With the changed notation, we're using the same letters for completely different quantities. In particular, remember that x denotes the quantity that was previously denoted by θ.

Modelling waves

In physics, a *wave* is an oscillation that transfers energy from one place to another. There are waves that you can see, such as water waves and waves on a guitar string, and waves that are invisible to the human eye, such as sound waves and microwaves. When waves are invisible, imaging devices can be used to represent them graphically.

Simple periodic waves can be modelled by translating and scaling the sine or cosine function. However, periodic waves may have a more complicated form, as illustrated in Figure 34.

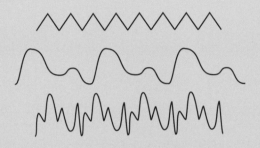

Figure 34   A selection of waves

You can model complicated periodic waves by scaling sine and cosine functions and adding them together. For example, Figure 35 shows the graph of the function

$$f(t) = 1.4\sin(t) + 0.3\cos(2t) + \sin(5t).$$

In this case, the letter t is used for the input variable of the function, rather than θ. This is because a function that models a wave often has an input variable that represents time.

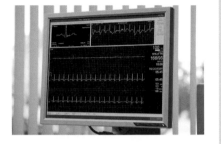

An electrocardiogram displays the heart's electrical activity, which varies periodically with every heartbeat

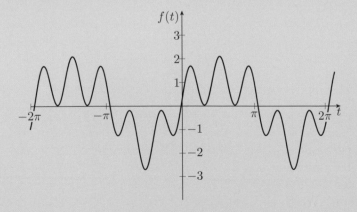

Figure 35   The graph of $f(t) = 1.4\sin(t) + 0.3\cos(2t) + \sin(5t)$

If you add together many scaled sine and cosine functions, then you obtain a type of function called a *Fourier series*. Such functions can be used to model *any* periodic wave. They were developed by the French mathematician Joseph Fourier (1768–1830), in order to model variations in temperatures.

2.4 Inverse trigonometric functions

In this subsection you'll learn more about the *inverse trigonometric functions* $\sin^{-1}$, $\cos^{-1}$ and $\tan^{-1}$, which you used in Subsection 1.4 to find acute angles in right-angled triangles.

In Unit 3 you saw that if a function f is one-to-one, then it has an *inverse function* f^{-1}, whose rule is given by

$$f^{-1}(y) = x, \quad \text{where} \quad f(x) = y.$$

The sine, cosine and tangent functions are not one-to-one. Take the sine function, for example, whose graph is shown in Figure 36. You can see that there are many input numbers that have the output number $\frac{1}{2}$, such as $\pi/6$, $5\pi/6$ and $-7\pi/6$. In fact, because the sine function is periodic, there are infinitely many input numbers with the output number $\frac{1}{2}$.

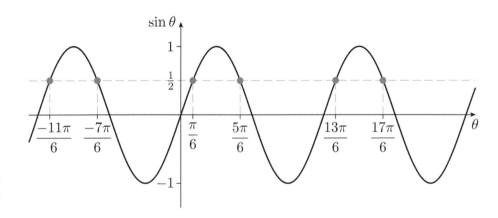

Figure 36   The graph of the sine function, with solutions of $\sin x = \frac{1}{2}$ labelled

As you saw in Unit 3, to obtain 'some sort of inverse function' for a function that isn't one-to-one, we need to start by specifying a new function that has the same rule as the original function, but a smaller domain. (Remember that such a function is called a *restriction* of the original function.) We choose the smaller domain to ensure that the new function is one-to-one and has the same image set as the original function.

For the sine function, the most convenient smaller domain is the interval $[-\pi/2, \pi/2]$, which includes all the acute angles. The graph of the sine function with this restricted domain is shown in Figure 37.

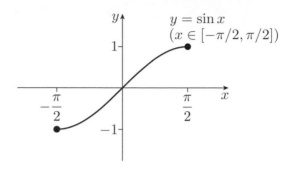

Figure 37   The graph of $y = \sin x$ $(x \in [-\pi/2, \pi/2])$

The function in Figure 37 has the same image set as the sine function, namely the interval $[-1, 1]$. It is increasing on the whole of its domain, so it is one-to-one, and therefore has an inverse function. Its inverse function is called the **inverse sine function** and is denoted by $\sin^{-1}$. (It is convenient to use this terminology and notation, even though $\sin^{-1}$ is actually the inverse function of a restricted version of the sine function.)

Inverse sine function

The **inverse sine function** $\sin^{-1}$ is the function with domain $[-1, 1]$ and rule

$$\sin^{-1} x = y,$$

where y is the number in the interval $[-\pi/2, \pi/2]$ such that $\sin y = x$.

As before, you may choose to write either $\sin^{-1} x$ or $\sin^{-1}(x)$, whichever seems clearer.

You can find the inverse sines of some numbers by using the sines of angles that you know already. For example,

$$\sin 0 = 0, \quad \text{so} \quad \sin^{-1} 0 = 0,$$

$$\sin \frac{\pi}{2} = 1, \quad \text{so} \quad \sin^{-1} 1 = \frac{\pi}{2},$$

and

$$\sin \frac{\pi}{6} = \frac{1}{2}, \quad \text{so} \quad \sin^{-1} \frac{1}{2} = \frac{\pi}{6}.$$

However, you have to be careful. For example, $\sin(5\pi/6) = \frac{1}{2}$, but it doesn't follow that $\sin^{-1} \frac{1}{2} = 5\pi/6$, because $5\pi/6$ isn't in the interval $[-\pi/2, \pi/2]$. In fact, $\sin^{-1} \frac{1}{2} = \pi/6$, as stated above. There's more about finding the inverse sines of numbers (and inverse cosines and inverse tangents) later in this subsection, and in Subsection 2.5.

You saw in Unit 3 that the graphs of a one-to-one function and its inverse function are the reflections of each other in the line $y = x$ (when the coordinate axes have equal scales). So the graph of the inverse sine function is as shown in Figure 38(b).

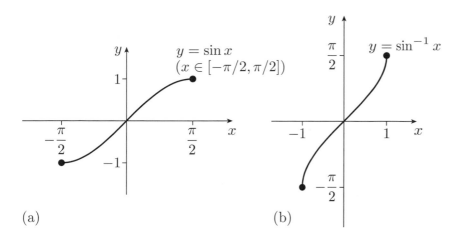

(a)   (b)

Figure 38   The graphs of (a) $y = \sin x$ $(x \in [-\pi/2, \pi/2])$ (b) $y = \sin^{-1} x$

Like the sine function, the cosine function is not one-to-one, so to obtain an inverse function we must restrict its domain. The most convenient smaller domain for the cosine function is the interval $[0, \pi]$, which again includes all the acute angles. The graph of the function obtained by restricting the domain of the cosine function to this interval is shown in Figure 39(a). It is decreasing on the whole of its domain, so it has an inverse function, called the **inverse cosine function** and denoted by $\cos^{-1}$.

Inverse cosine

The **inverse cosine function** $\cos^{-1}$ is the function with domain $[-1, 1]$ and rule

$$\cos^{-1} x = y,$$

where y is the number in the interval $[0, \pi]$ such that $\cos y = x$.

The graph of the inverse cosine function is obtained by reflecting the graph in Figure 39(a) in the line $y = x$, and is shown in Figure 39(b).

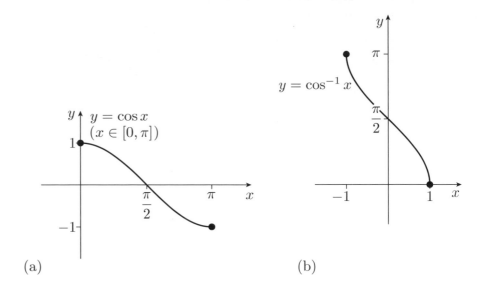

(a)   (b)

Figure 39   The graphs of (a) $y = \cos x$ $(x \in [0, \pi])$ (b) $y = \cos^{-1} x$

We can carry out a similar process for the tangent function. The most convenient smaller domain for this function is the interval $(-\pi/2, \pi/2)$. The function obtained by restricting the tangent function to this domain is shown in Figure 40(a). Its inverse function is called the **inverse tangent function**, denoted by $\tan^{-1}$, and its graph is shown in Figure 40(b).

Inverse tangent

The **inverse tangent function** $\tan^{-1}$ is the function with domain $\mathbb{R}$ and rule

$$\tan^{-1} x = y,$$

where y is the number in the interval $(-\pi/2, \pi/2)$ such that $\tan y = x$.

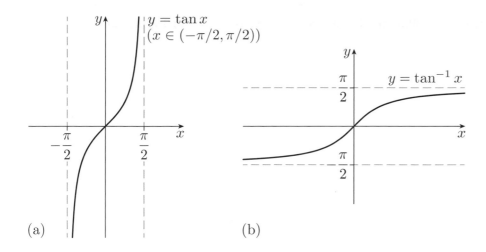

(a)   (b)

Figure 40   The graphs of (a) $y = \tan x$ $(x \in (-\pi/2, \pi/2))$ (b) $y = \tan^{-1} x$

The graph in Figure 40(a) has two vertical asymptotes, with equations $x = -\pi/2$ and $x = \pi/2$. Accordingly, the graph of the inverse tangent function, in Figure 40(b), has two horizontal asymptotes, with equations $y = -\pi/2$ and $y = \pi/2$.

The inverse sine, inverse cosine and inverse tangent functions are known as **inverse trigonometric functions**. As you saw earlier, alternative names for these three functions are arcsin, arccos and arctan, respectively. Calculators and computers may also use the names INV SIN, INV COS, INV TAN or asin, acos, atan.

One way to find the inverse sine, inverse cosine or inverse tangent of a number is to use your calculator. You did this for positive numbers in Subsection 1.4, and you can find the inverse sine, inverse cosine or inverse tangent of any suitable number in the same way. For example, a calculator gives $\cos^{-1}(-0.6) = 2.214\,297\,43\ldots$.

However, a calculator may give a decimal approximation where it is possible to find an exact value. As you saw earlier, you can find the exact values of the inverse sine, inverse cosine or inverse tangent of some special numbers by using values of sine, cosine and tangent that you know already.

For example, you know from the special angles table on page 22 that $\tan(\pi/6) = 1/\sqrt{3}$. So, since the angle $\pi/6$ lies in the interval to which we restricted the domain of the tangent function earlier, namely $(-\pi/2, \pi/2)$, it follows that $\tan^{-1}(1/\sqrt{3}) = \pi/6$.

Activity 18 *Finding exact values of inverse sines, inverse cosines and inverse tangents*

Find the following angles without using your calculator.

(a) $\sin^{-1}(\sqrt{3}/2)$ (b) $\cos^{-1}\frac{1}{2}$ (c) $\cos^{-1}0$ (d) $\cos^{-1}1$

(e) $\cos^{-1}(\sqrt{3}/2)$ (f) $\tan^{-1}0$ (g) $\tan^{-1}1$

All the values of sine, cosine and tangent in the special angles table are positive, so you can't use this table directly to find the exact values of the inverse sine, inverse cosine or inverse tangent of any negative numbers. However, you can find these values by using symmetry properties of the inverse trigonometric functions that follow from the symmetry properties of the trigonometric functions.

For example, as you can see from the graph of $y = \sin^{-1} x$ in Figure 38 on page 43, the following identity holds:

$$\sin^{-1}(-x) = -\sin^{-1} x.$$

So, for instance, since $\sin^{-1}\frac{1}{2} = \pi/6$, you can deduce that

$$\sin^{-1}\left(-\frac{1}{2}\right) = -\sin^{-1}\frac{1}{2} = -\frac{\pi}{6}.$$

The graphs of $y = \cos^{-1} x$ and $y = \tan^{-1} x$, in Figures 39 and 40, also have symmetry properties that give rise to similar identities. These identities are listed below.

$$\sin^{-1}(-x) = -\sin^{-1} x$$
$$\cos^{-1}(-x) = \pi - \cos^{-1} x$$
$$\tan^{-1}(-x) = -\tan^{-1} x$$

These identities enable you to find inverse sines, inverse cosines and inverse tangents of negative numbers. The following activity gives you a chance to try this.

Activity 19 *Finding further exact values of inverse sines, inverse cosines and inverse tangents*

Use the identities above and your answers to Activity 18 to find the following angles without using your calculator.

(a) $\sin^{-1}(-\sqrt{3}/2)$ (b) $\cos^{-1}(-\frac{1}{2})$ (c) $\cos^{-1}(-1)$

(d) $\cos^{-1}(-\sqrt{3}/2)$ (e) $\tan^{-1}(-1)$

2.5 Solving simple trigonometric equations

Equations that contain trigonometric functions of the unknown(s) are called **trigonometric equations**. Simple trigonometric equations such as

$$\sin\theta = \frac{1}{2}, \quad \cos\theta = 0.3 \quad \text{and} \quad \tan\theta = -1$$

occur frequently when you're working with trigonometric functions.

One solution of such a simple trigonometric equation can be obtained by using an inverse trigonometric function described in the previous subsection. For instance, one solution of the equation $\sin\theta = \frac{1}{2}$ is

$$\theta = \sin^{-1}\frac{1}{2} = \frac{\pi}{6}.$$

As you saw earlier, however, there are other solutions, such as $5\pi/6$ and $-7\pi/6$, as illustrated in Figure 41. In fact there are infinitely many solutions of the equation $\sin\theta = \frac{1}{2}$, since the sine function is periodic.

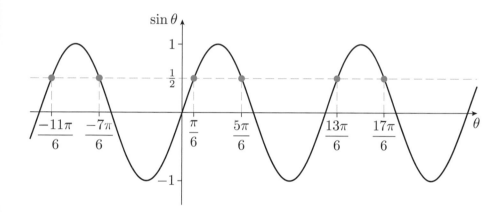

Figure 41   The graph of the sine function, with solutions of $\sin x = \frac{1}{2}$ labelled

Usually when you want to solve a simple trigonometric equation, it's best to begin by finding all the solutions that lie in an interval of length 2π ($360°$), such as $[0, 2\pi]$ or $[-\pi, \pi]$. There are usually two such solutions. Then you can obtain any other solutions that you want by adding integer multiples of 2π to the first solutions that you found.

In this subsection you'll be shown two methods for finding all the solutions of a simple trigonometric equation that lie in a particular interval of length 2π.

In the first method, you use the ASTC diagram, in Figure 42, and the facts in the box below, which are repeated from page 32.

Second quadrant	First quadrant
S	**A**
T	**C**
Third quadrant	Fourth quadrant

Figure 42 The ASTC diagram

Suppose that θ is any angle whose associated point P does not lie on either the x- or y-axis, and ϕ is the acute angle between OP and the x-axis. Then

$$\sin\theta = \pm\sin\phi$$
$$\cos\theta = \pm\cos\phi$$
$$\tan\theta = \pm\tan\phi.$$

The ASTC diagram tells you which sign applies in each case.

(The values $\sin\phi$, $\cos\phi$ and $\tan\phi$ are all positive, because ϕ is acute.)

The method is illustrated in the next example.

Example 7 *Solving simple trigonometric equations using the ASTC diagram*

(a) Find all solutions between $-\pi$ and π of the equation $\tan\theta = -1$. Give exact answers.

(b) Find all solutions between $0°$ and $360°$ of the equation $\cos\theta = 0.3$. Give your answers to the nearest degree.

Solution

(a) 🔍 Use the ASTC diagram to find the quadrants of the solutions. 💬

The tangent of θ is negative, so θ is a second- or fourth-quadrant angle.

🔍 Sketch each of the possible quadrants with a line OP in each. On each sketch mark the associated angle θ that lies in the interval $[-\pi, \pi]$, and the acute angle ϕ between OP and the x-axis. 💬

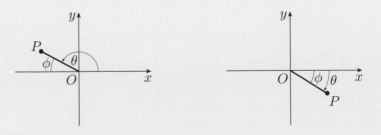

💬 Use the given equation and the facts in the box above to write down the value of $\tan \phi$. Hence use the special angles table or your calculator to find ϕ. 💬

Here
$$\tan \theta = -1,$$
so
$$\tan \phi = 1,$$
and hence
$$\phi = \tan^{-1} 1 = \frac{\pi}{4}.$$

💬 Now use your sketches to find the possible values of θ. 💬

The solutions are
$$\theta = \pi - \phi = \pi - \frac{\pi}{4} = \frac{3\pi}{4}$$
and
$$\theta = -\phi = -\frac{\pi}{4}.$$

(b) 💬 Use the ASTC diagram to find the quadrants of the solutions. 💬

The cosine of θ is positive, so θ is a first- or fourth-quadrant angle.

💬 Sketch each of the possible quadrants with a line OP in each. On each sketch mark the associated angle θ that lies in the interval $[0°, 360°]$, and the acute angle ϕ between OP and the x-axis. 💬

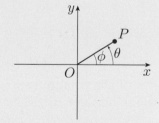
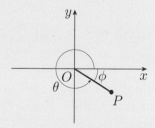

💬 Use the given equation and the facts in the box above to write down the value of $\cos \phi$. Hence use your calculator to find ϕ. 💬

Here

$$\cos \theta = 0.3,$$

so

$$\cos \phi = 0.3,$$

and hence

$$\phi = \cos^{-1} 0.3 = 72.542\ldots^{\circ}.$$

💬 Use your sketches to find the possible values of θ. 💬

The solutions are

$$\theta = \phi = 72.542\ldots^{\circ}$$

and

$$\begin{aligned} \theta &= 360^{\circ} - \phi \\ &= 360^{\circ} - 72.542\ldots^{\circ} \\ &= 287.457\ldots^{\circ}. \end{aligned}$$

So the solutions are 73° and 287°, to the nearest degree.

When you use the method demonstrated in Example 7, it is helpful to check your answers. For example, in Example 7(b), you can use your calculator to check that $\cos 73^{\circ}$ and $\cos 287^{\circ}$ are both approximately 0.3.

In the next activity, remember to set your calculator to degrees or radians, as appropriate, and to check your answers.

Activity 20 *Solving simple trigonometric equations using the ASTC diagram*

(a) Find all solutions between $-\pi$ and π of the equation $\sin \theta = -\frac{1}{2}$. Give exact answers. Hence find all solutions between π and 3π of this equation.

(b) Find all solutions between -180° and 180° of the equation $\tan \theta = -5$. Give your answers to the nearest degree.

The next example demonstrates an alternative strategy for solving simple trigonometric equations. It involves using the graphs of the trigonometric functions. Usually it doesn't matter which of the two methods you use to solve a simple trigonometric equation: you should choose the one that you prefer.

Example 8   *Solving simple trigonometric equations using the graphs of the trigonometric functions*

(a) Find all solutions between 0 and 2π of the equation $\sin\theta = \sqrt{3}/2$.

(b) Find all solutions between $-180°$ and $180°$ of the equation $\cos\theta = -0.6$.

Solution

(a) 🔍 Sketch the graph of sine in the interval 0 to 2π. Sketch the horizontal line at height $\sqrt{3}/2$, and mark the crossing points. The θ-coordinates of these points are the required solutions of $\sin\theta = \sqrt{3}/2$. 💭

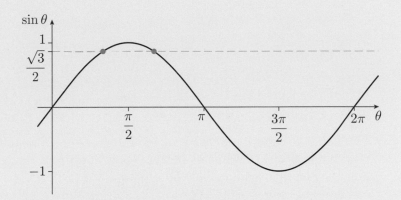

🔍 Find one solution using inverse sine. 💭

One solution is

$$\theta = \sin^{-1}\left(\frac{\sqrt{3}}{2}\right) = \frac{\pi}{3}.$$

🔍 Use the symmetry of the graph to find the other solution. 💭

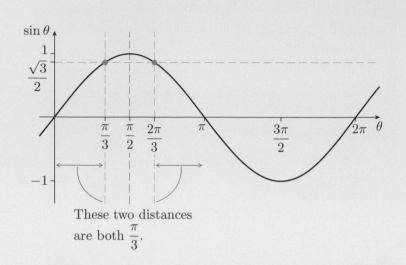

These two distances
are both $\dfrac{\pi}{3}$.

From the graph, the other solution is

$$\theta = \pi - \frac{\pi}{3} = \frac{2\pi}{3}.$$

So the solutions are $\pi/3$ and $2\pi/3$.

(b) 🔍 Sketch the graph of cosine in the interval $-180°$ to $180°$.
Sketch the horizontal line at height -0.6, and mark the crossing
points. The θ-coordinates of these points are the required
solutions of $\cos\theta = -0.6$. 💬

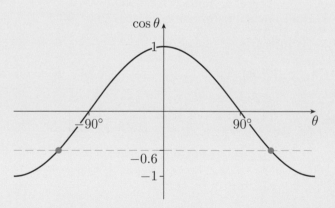

🔍 Find one solution using inverse cosine on a calculator. 💬

One solution is

$$\theta = \cos^{-1}(-0.6) = 126.869\ldots°.$$

🔍 Use the symmetry of the graph to find the other solution. 💬

From the graph, the other solution is

$$\theta = -126.869\ldots^\circ.$$

So the solutions are -127° and 127°, to the nearest degree.

In the next activity, you can practise using the graph method demonstrated in Example 8 to solve simple trigonometric equations. As before, the graphs that you sketch don't need to be accurate: they just need to illustrate the symmetry properties of the trigonometric functions.

Activity 21 *Solving simple trigonometric equations using the graphs of the trigonometric functions*

(a) Find all solutions between -180° and 180° of the equation $\tan\theta = 10$. Give your answers to the nearest degree.

(b) Find all solutions between $-\pi$ and π of the equation $\sin\theta = -1/\sqrt{2}$.

Although it doesn't usually matter which of the two methods you use to solve a simple trigonometric equation, you can't use the ASTC method if the solutions of the equation are multiples of $\pi/2$. That is, you can't use it to solve any of the following seven 'special' trigonometric equations:

$$\sin\theta = 1, \quad \cos\theta = 1,$$
$$\sin\theta = -1, \quad \cos\theta = -1,$$
$$\sin\theta = 0, \quad \cos\theta = 0, \quad \tan\theta = 0.$$

You can solve these equations by using the graph method, or just by thinking about the definitions of sine, cosine and tangent. For example, suppose that you want to solve the equation $\sin\theta = 1$. This equation tells you that the point P associated with the angle θ has y-coordinate 1. So the solutions are $\theta = \pi/2$ and all angles obtained from $\pi/2$ by adding or subtracting integer multiples of 2π.

Activity 22 *Solving simple trigonometric equations whose solutions are multiples of $\pi/2$*

(a) Find all solutions in the interval $[-\pi, \pi]$ of the equation $\sin\theta = 0$.

(b) Find all solutions in the interval $[0, 4\pi]$ of the equation $\cos\theta = -1$.

3 Sine and cosine rules

In this section you'll see how to use trigonometry to find side lengths and angles in triangles that don't have a right angle. You'll also meet a useful trigonometric formula for the area of a triangle, and another formula that expresses the relationship between the gradient of a straight line and the angle that it makes with the x-axis.

3.1 The sine rule

Suppose that you want to work out the length of the side labelled b in the triangle in Figure 43. You have learned how to find side lengths of *right-angled* triangles, but the triangle here does not have a right angle, so the methods from Section 1 do not apply. Instead you must use a different method. The most convenient method is the *sine rule*, which is the subject of this subsection.

The sine rule is most easily stated using the notation shown in Figure 44. Here the vertices of a triangle are labelled as A, B and C, and the sides are labelled as a, b and c. The labels are chosen in such a way that vertex A is opposite side a, vertex B is opposite side b, and vertex C is opposite side c. This is common notation for a triangle, which makes formulas easier to remember. It will be used throughout the rest of this unit.

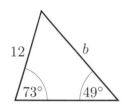

Figure 43   A triangle with an unknown side length b

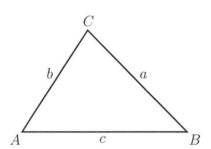

Figure 44   A triangle with vertices A, B and C and sides a, b and c

Note that the letters A, B and C will be used to represent both the vertices of the triangle *and* the angles at those vertices. For instance, we will write the sine of the angle at vertex A as $\sin A$.

Let's move on to discuss the sine rule. Figure 45 shows a triangle in which a dashed line of length h has been drawn from the vertex C, perpendicular to the opposite side c. Remember that two lines are **perpendicular** if they are at right angles to each other.

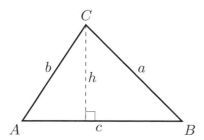

Figure 45 A triangle split into two right-angled triangles

The dashed line divides the triangle into two right-angled triangles. Because sine equals opposite over hypotenuse, you can see from the left-hand triangle that

$$\sin A = \frac{h}{b}, \quad \text{so} \quad h = b \sin A.$$

In the same way, using the right-hand triangle, you can see that

$$\sin B = \frac{h}{a}, \quad \text{so} \quad h = a \sin B.$$

Therefore

$$b \sin A = h = a \sin B.$$

This equation can be rearranged to give

$$\frac{a}{\sin A} = \frac{b}{\sin B}.$$

In a similar way, using a dashed line drawn from the vertex A perpendicular to the opposite side a, you can show that

$$\frac{b}{\sin B} = \frac{c}{\sin C}.$$

Combining this equation with the one above gives the following rule.

Sine rule

$$\frac{a}{\sin A} = \frac{b}{\sin B} = \frac{c}{\sin C}$$

The angles of the triangle in Figure 45 are all acute. However the sine rule holds for any triangle, even if it has an obtuse angle (an angle that is greater than 90° but less than 180°). The justification of the sine rule for such a triangle is similar to the justification above, but the dashed line of length h may lie outside the triangle, as illustrated in Figure 46.

You can use the sine rule to find either unknown side lengths or unknown angles in triangles. Let's focus on unknown side lengths first. The following box describes when you can use the sine rule to find a side length of a triangle.

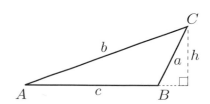

Figure 46 A triangle with an obtuse angle: the dashed line lies outside the triangle

Using the sine rule to find a side length

You can use the sine rule to find an unknown side length of a triangle if you know

- the opposite angle
- another side length and its opposite angle.

Example 9   *Using the sine rule to find unknown side lengths*

Find the side length b of the triangle below, giving your answer to one decimal place.

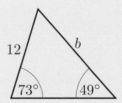

Solution

🔍 Label the vertices and the unknown side of the triangle. 💭

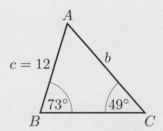

🔍 The unknown side is b, and the known sides and angles are c, B and C. So use the sine rule in the form $\dfrac{b}{\sin B} = \dfrac{c}{\sin C}$. 💭

By the sine rule,
$$\frac{b}{\sin B} = \frac{c}{\sin C},$$
so
$$b = \frac{c \sin B}{\sin C} = \frac{12 \sin 73°}{\sin 49°} = 15.205\ldots = 15.2 \quad \text{(to 1 d.p.)}.$$

Notice that in Example 9 the sine rule in the form

$$\frac{b}{\sin B} = \frac{c}{\sin C}$$

was rearranged to give

$$b = \frac{c \sin B}{\sin C},$$

before the values for B, C and c were substituted in. It's usually simpler to rearrange a trigonometric formula, like the sine rule, into the form that you want before you substitute in.

In the next activity, remember to set your calculator to degrees, rather than radians.

Activity 23   *Using the sine rule to find an unknown side length*

Find the side lengths b and c of the triangle below. Give your answers in centimetres to one decimal place.

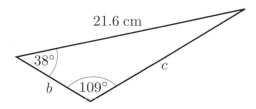

Activity 24   *Using the sine rule to find a distant height*

The diagram below shows a building of unknown height x, in metres, and the values of two angles between the horizontal and a line to a point C on the top of the building, measured from points A and B that are 100 m apart. Use the sine rule to find the distance BC, and hence deduce the height of the building, both to the nearest metre.

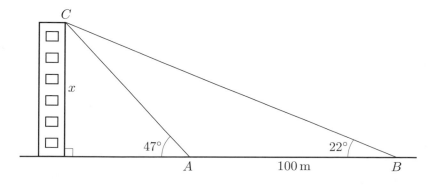

Now let's look at how you can use the sine rule to find unknown *angles*.

Suppose that you know that two of the side lengths of a triangle are $a = 51$ and $b = 22$, and that one of the angles is $B = 23°$, and you want to find the angle A. (Here we're using the usual notation for triangles, so side a is opposite angle A, and side b is opposite angle B.)

You can rearrange the sine rule in the form

$$\frac{b}{\sin B} = \frac{a}{\sin A}$$

to make $\sin A$ the subject:

$$\sin A = \frac{a \sin B}{b}.$$

You can then substitute in the values of a, b and B, to obtain

$$\sin A = \frac{a \sin B}{b} = \frac{51 \sin 23°}{22} = 0.905 \ldots$$

Because A is an angle of a triangle, it lies between $0°$ and $180°$. However the equation $\sin A = 0.905 \ldots$ has *two* solutions between $0°$ and $180°$, namely $65°$ (to the nearest degree) and $180° - 65° = 115°$ (to the nearest degree), as shown in Figure 47.

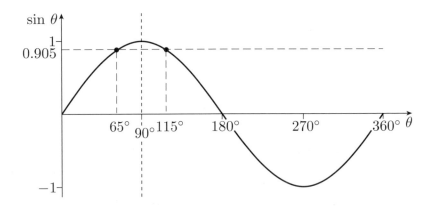

Figure 47   Two solutions to $\sin A = 0.905 \ldots$

So the sine rule has provided two possible values for the angle A. Both of these possibilities can occur. You can draw a triangle with $a = 51$, $b = 22$, $B = 23°$ and $A \approx 65°$, and you can draw another triangle with $a = 51$, $b = 22$, $B = 23°$ and $A \approx 115°$, as shown in Figure 48.

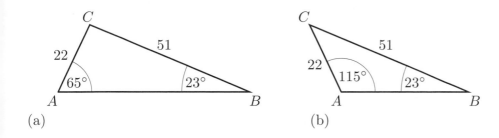

Figure 48   Two triangles that have $a = 51$, $b = 22$ and $B = 23°$

So if you use the sine rule to find an unknown angle, then you may only be able to narrow down the answer to two possibilities: an acute angle, and an obtuse angle that is equal to $180°$ minus the acute angle. You can find the correct answer only if you have other information that tells you whether the unknown angle is acute or obtuse.

Activity 25   *Using the sine rule to find an unknown acute angle*

Suppose that a triangle has $A = 19.9°$, $a = 7.6$ and $c = 16.4$. Suppose also that C is acute. Find the angle C, in degrees to one decimal place.

You have seen that when you use the sine rule to find an unknown angle you actually find two angles, one acute and one obtuse. The acute angle is always a valid solution, in the sense that you can always find a triangle with that acute angle and the other known sides and angles. In contrast, the obtuse angle is sometimes a valid solution, and sometimes it is not. For example, if adding the obtuse angle to the angle that you already know gives a total greater than $180°$, then the obtuse angle is not a valid solution, because the sum of all three angles of a triangle is $180°$.

You have seen an example where both the acute angle and the obtuse angle are valid solutions. Let's now look at an example in which the obtuse angle is not a valid solution.

Example 10   *Using the sine rule to find an unknown angle*

Suppose that one angle in a triangle is $A = 37.0°$, and two of its side lengths are $a = 4.6$ and $c = 2.1$. Find the angle C, in degrees to one decimal place.

Solution

🔍 Sketch the triangle (the sides and angles need not be accurately drawn), and label the known sides and angles. 💬

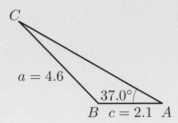

🔍 The unknown angle is C, and the known sides and angles are a, c and A. So use the sine rule in the form $c/\sin C = a/\sin A$. 💬

By the sine rule,

$$\frac{c}{\sin C} = \frac{a}{\sin A}.$$

Rearranging gives

$$\sin C = \frac{c\sin A}{a} = \frac{2.1\sin 37.0°}{4.6} = 0.274\ldots.$$

🔍 Find the acute and obtuse angles that satisfy $\sin C = 0.274\ldots$ 💬

The two possible solutions are

$$C = \sin^{-1}(0.274\ldots) = 15.946\ldots°$$

and

$$C = 180° - 15.946\ldots° = 164.053\ldots°.$$

🔍 Check whether the obtuse angle is possible. 💬

If $C = 164.053\ldots°$, then

$$A + C = 37.0° + 164.053\ldots° = 201.053\ldots°.$$

This is impossible, because the sum of the angles $A + B + C$ must be 180°. Therefore $C = 15.9°$, to one decimal place.

You may find it helpful to remember that, in a triangle, *larger angles are found opposite longer sides, and vice versa.* In Example 10, side a is longer than side c, so angle A must be larger than angle C. This gives you another way to check that angle C cannot be 164.1°, since angle C must be smaller than 37.0°, the value of angle A.

The following box summarises when you can use the sine rule to find an unknown angle.

Using the sine rule to find an angle

You can use the sine rule to find an unknown angle in a triangle if you know:

- the opposite side length
- another side length and its opposite angle.

Sometimes you also need to know whether the unknown angle is acute or obtuse.

Activity 26   *Using the sine rule to find an unknown angle*

One angle in a triangle is $B = 23.4°$, and two side lengths are $b = 9.3$ and $c = 8.1$. Find the angle C, in degrees to one decimal place.

3.2   The cosine rule

There is another rule, known as the *cosine rule*, that you can use to find unknown side lengths and angles in triangles that are not necessarily right-angled triangles.

This rule can be used in some circumstances where the sine rule cannot be used. Take Figure 49, for example, in which the side length a is unknown. You cannot use the sine rule, because neither of the two known side lengths 13 and 15 is opposite the known angle 33°. Instead you can apply the cosine rule, as you'll see shortly.

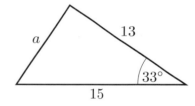

Figure 49   A triangle with an unknown side length a

Here's how the cosine rule is obtained. Once again, divide a triangle into two right-angled triangles by a dashed line of length h, as shown in Figure 50. The side of length c has been split into two parts: one part has length y, so the other part has length $c - y$.

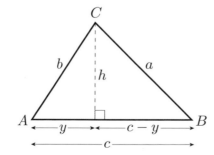

Figure 50   The dashed line divides the triangle into two right-angled triangles

Applying Pythagoras' theorem to each of the right-angled triangles gives

$$b^2 = y^2 + h^2,$$
$$a^2 = (c - y)^2 + h^2.$$

Expanding the brackets in the second of these equations gives

$$a^2 = c^2 - 2cy + y^2 + h^2.$$

Since $y^2 + h^2 = b^2$ it follows that

$$a^2 = c^2 - 2cy + b^2$$
$$= b^2 + c^2 - 2cy.$$

Next, using the right-angled triangle on the left in Figure 50 you find that

$$\cos A = \frac{y}{b}, \quad \text{so} \quad y = b \cos A.$$

Substituting this expression for y into $a^2 = b^2 + c^2 - 2cy$ gives

$$a^2 = b^2 + c^2 - 2bc \cos A.$$

This equation is one form of the cosine rule.

> **Cosine rule**
>
> $$a^2 = b^2 + c^2 - 2bc \cos A$$

There are two other equivalent forms of the cosine rule, that use other sides and angles:

$$b^2 = c^2 + a^2 - 2ca \cos B$$
$$c^2 = a^2 + b^2 - 2ab \cos C.$$

The triangle in Figure 50 has only acute angles. However, like the sine rule, the cosine rule holds for any triangle, even if it has an obtuse angle. The justification of the cosine rule for such a triangle is similar to the justification above, but the dashed line of length h may lie outside the triangle, as illustrated in Figure 51.

Notice that if C is a right angle ($\pi/2$ or $90°$), then $\cos C = 0$, and the last equation above becomes $a^2 + b^2 = c^2$, which is Pythagoras' theorem for a right-angled triangle. In this way you can see that the cosine rule is a more general version of Pythagoras' theorem. It applies to any triangle, whereas Pythagoras' theorem applies only to right-angled triangles.

The following box describes when you can use the cosine rule to find an unknown side length.

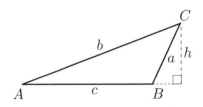

Figure 51   A triangle with an obtuse angle: the dashed line lies outside the triangle

Using the cosine rule to find a side length

You can use the cosine rule to find an unknown side length of a triangle if you know the other two side lengths and the angle between them.

Example 11   *Using the cosine rule to find an unknown side length*

Find the length of the side a in the triangle below, to one decimal place.

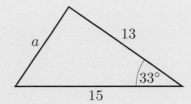

Solution

💬 Label the angles and sides of the triangle. 💬

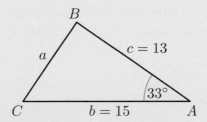

💬 The known angle is A. So use the cosine rule in the form $a^2 = b^2 + c^2 - 2bc \cos A$. 💬

By the cosine rule,
$$a^2 = b^2 + c^2 - 2bc \cos A.$$

This gives
$$a = \sqrt{b^2 + c^2 - 2bc \cos A}$$
$$= \sqrt{15^2 + 13^2 - 2 \times 15 \times 13 \times \cos 33°}$$
$$= 8.180\ldots = 8.2 \quad \text{(to 1 d.p.)}.$$

In a calculation like the one at the end of the example above, it's best to type the whole numerical expression, including the square root, into your calculator in order to avoid rounding errors. If instead you evaluate the expression under the square root sign first, then don't round it before taking the square root.

Activity 27   *Using the cosine rule to find an unknown side length*

Find the length of the side b in the triangle below, in millimetres to two decimal places.

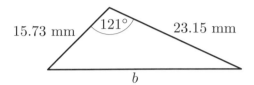

You've seen that you can use the cosine rule to find an unknown side length of a triangle if you know the other two side lengths and the angle between them. In fact, there's another situation in which you can sometimes use the cosine rule to find an unknown side length, namely if you know the other two side lengths and the angle opposite one of them. However, in such circumstances it's simpler to start by using the sine rule. Note that there may be two possible answers.

Let's now use the cosine rule to find unknown angles. This is simpler than using the sine rule to find unknown angles, because you never obtain two possible angles. The box below describes when you can use the cosine rule to find an unknown angle.

Using the cosine rule to find an angle

You can use the cosine rule to find an unknown angle if you know all three side lengths.

Example 12   *Using the cosine rule to find an unknown angle*

Use the cosine rule to find the angle C in the triangle below, in degrees to one decimal place.

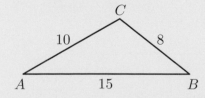

Solution

🗨 Label the sides a, b and c. 🗨

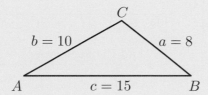

🗨 You want to find angle C, so use the cosine rule in the form $c^2 = a^2 + b^2 - 2ab\cos C$. Rearrange it to obtain an expression for $\cos C$. 🗨

Rearranging $c^2 = a^2 + b^2 - 2ab\cos C$ gives

$$\cos C = \frac{a^2 + b^2 - c^2}{2ab}.$$

🗨 Substitute in the values of a, b and c. 🗨

$$\cos C = \frac{8^2 + 10^2 - 15^2}{2 \times 8 \times 10}$$

🗨 Use inverse cosine to obtain a solution between $0°$ and $180°$. 🗨

$$C = \cos^{-1}\left(\frac{8^2 + 10^2 - 15^2}{2 \times 8 \times 10}\right) = 112.4° \quad \text{(to 1 d.p.)}.$$

Here's an example for you to try.

Activity 28   *Using the cosine rule to find an unknown angle*

Find the angle opposite the side of length $3.6\,\text{m}$ in a triangle with side lengths $1.5\,\text{m}$, $2.5\,\text{m}$ and $3.6\,\text{m}$. Give your answer to the nearest degree.

You have now seen four methods of finding unknown side lengths and angles in a triangle:

- Pythagoras' theorem
- the trigonometric ratios sine, cosine and tangent
- the sine rule
- the cosine rule.

The process of choosing which of these methods to use can be summarised in the form of a decision tree, as shown in Figure 52.

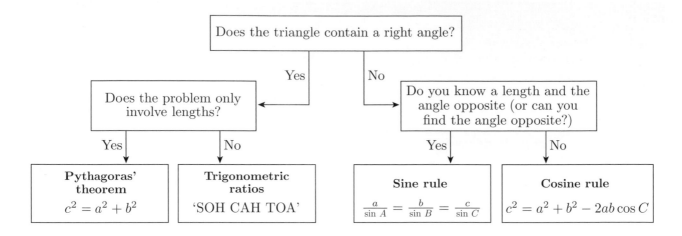

Figure 52 A decision tree showing methods of solving a triangle

All of these methods are used by surveyors when producing detailed plans for road and building construction, and they were used historically for creating maps, such as in the Great Trigonometric Survey (see page 21).

3.3 The area of a triangle

In this short subsection you'll meet a useful formula for the area of a triangle, which involves the sine of one of the angles of the triangle. Our starting point is the more familiar formula below.

> **Area of a triangle**
>
> For a triangle,
> $$\text{area} = \tfrac{1}{2} \times \text{base} \times \text{height}.$$

Remember that when you use this formula, the **base** of the triangle is one of its sides. Any side will do; different sides just lead to different calculations. The **height** of the triangle is the perpendicular distance from the base to the opposite vertex. Again, the height depends on the choice of base. Usually you draw the base horizontally and the height vertically, as shown in Figure 53.

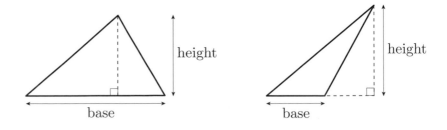

Figure 53 The bases and heights of two triangles

Let's use the formula above to obtain another formula for the area of a triangle, in terms of the lengths of two sides and the angle between these sides. Consider the triangle in Figure 54. The sides are labelled a and b, and the angle between them is labelled θ.

First draw a dashed line of length h perpendicular to the base b, as shown in Figure 55. Then the area of the triangle is $\frac{1}{2}bh$. From the right-angled triangle on the left of Figure 55,

$$\sin\theta = \frac{h}{a}, \quad \text{so} \quad h = a\sin\theta.$$

Substituting this expression for h into the formula $\frac{1}{2}bh$ gives

$$\text{area} = \tfrac{1}{2}bh = \tfrac{1}{2}b \times a\sin\theta = \tfrac{1}{2}ab\sin\theta.$$

This is the new formula for the area of a triangle.

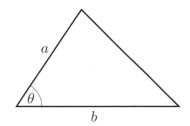

Figure 54 A triangle with an angle θ between two sides of lengths a and b

---

Area of a triangle

For a triangle with an angle θ between two sides of lengths a and b,

$$\text{area} = \tfrac{1}{2}ab\sin\theta.$$

In this derivation of the formula for the area of a triangle, the angle θ was acute. If the angle θ is obtuse, then the area formula still works, but its justification is slightly different because the dashed line lies outside the triangle; the details are omitted.

You can use this area formula in the following activity. The activity involves a *regular* pentagon, which is a pentagon with equal angles and equal side lengths.

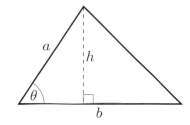

Figure 55 The triangle in Figure 54 with its height labelled as h

---

Activity 29   *Finding the area of a pentagon*

By dividing the regular pentagon below into triangles, find its area in m^2, to one decimal place.

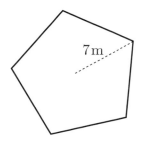

7 m

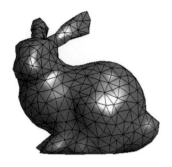

A triangulated rabbit

Triangulation

In mathematics, the word *triangulate* means to divide up into triangles. Any polygon can be triangulated, as illustrated in Figure 56. (A *polygon* is a flat shape whose boundary consists of line segments.)

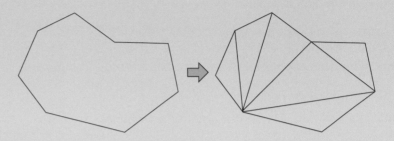

Figure 56   Triangulating a polygon

You can calculate the area of a polygon by triangulating it, calculating the areas of each of the individual triangles, and then adding these to give the total area.

You can also triangulate surfaces in three dimensions. This technique is particularly useful for computer programmers who work with graphics. After triangulating a surface, a programmer can use the triangulation to animate the object.

The next activity asks you to think about other formulas for the area of a triangle. In each part, you should try to think of a mathematical reason why there is or isn't a formula – you don't need to actually find any formulas (which would be difficult).

Activity 30   *Thinking about other formulas for the area of a triangle*

(a) Do you think that there is a formula for the area of a triangle in terms of only the angles A, B and C?

(b) Do you think that there is a formula for the area of a triangle in terms of only the side lengths a, b and c?

3.4 The angle of inclination of a line

In Unit 2 you saw that every straight line (that isn't vertical) has an equation of the form $y = mx + c$. The number m is the *gradient* of the line: if it is positive, then the line slopes up from left to right, and if it is negative, then the line slopes down from left to right. The number c is the y-intercept. In this subsection you'll learn how the trigonometric function tangent can be helpful in describing the gradient of a straight line.

The **angle of inclination** of a straight line is the angle that it makes with the x-axis, measured anticlockwise from the positive direction of the x-axis, when the line is drawn on axes *with equal scales*. A line with a positive gradient has an angle of inclination between 0 and $\pi/2$, as illustrated in Figure 57(a). A line with a negative gradient has an angle of inclination between $\pi/2$ and π, as illustrated in Figure 57(b).

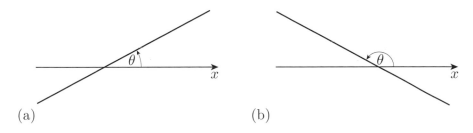

(a) (b)

Figure 57   The angle of inclination θ of (a) a line with a positive gradient (b) a line with a negative gradient

To understand the relationship between the gradient of a line and its angle of inclination, consider any angle θ between 0 and π (but not equal to $\pi/2$), and its associated point $P(x, y)$ on the unit circle, as illustrated in Figure 58. The angle θ is the angle of inclination of the line OP and, since $\theta \neq \pi/2$, the line OP is not vertical, and hence has a gradient.

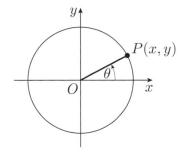

Figure 58   An angle θ and its associated point P on the unit circle

You saw earlier that

$$\tan\theta = \frac{y}{x}.$$

Also, by the usual formula for gradient,

$$\text{gradient of line } OP = \frac{y - 0}{x - 0} = \frac{y}{x}.$$

So we have the following useful fact.

Gradient and angle of inclination of a straight line

For any non-vertical straight line with angle of inclination θ,

$\text{gradient} = \tan\theta.$

Remember that the angle of inclination is measured when the line is drawn on axes *with equal scales*.

Example 13   *Finding the equation of a line with a given angle of inclination*

Without using a calculator, find the equation of the straight line shown below.

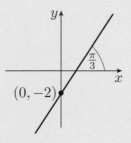

Solution

🔍 Write down the general equation of a line. 💬

The equation of the line is $y = mx + c$, where m is the gradient and c is the y-intercept.

🔍 Find the y-intercept. 💬

The y-intercept is -2, since the line passes through the point $(0, -2)$.

🔍 Use the formula for gradient in the box above. 💬

The gradient is $\tan(\pi/3) = \sqrt{3}$. So the equation of the line is

$y = \sqrt{3}\,x - 2.$

Activity 31 *Finding the equation of a line with a given angle of inclination*

Without using a calculator, find the equation of the straight line shown below.

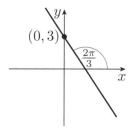

4 Further trigonometric identities

In this final section you'll see some of the many identities that involve the sines, cosines and tangents of angles. These identities are useful in many areas of mathematics. For example, you'll use some of them in the units on calculus and complex numbers later in the module.

There's no need to memorise all the trigonometric identities that you'll meet in this section: it's more important that you become familiar with using them, and you'll achieve this through practice in applying them. They're all listed in the *Handbook*. However, it's worth memorising the two simple identities in Subsection 4.1, as they're used very frequently.

4.1 Two simple trigonometric identities

You have met the two trigonometric identities in this subsection already: you saw in Subsection 1.6 that they're true for *acute angles*. Here you'll see that they're true for *all* angles for which the expressions in them are defined.

For the first identity, remember that $\cos\theta$ and $\sin\theta$ are the x- and y-coordinates of the point P on the unit circle associated with the angle θ, and $\tan\theta$ is the y-coordinate divided by the x-coordinate (when the x-coordinate is not zero). This gives the identity below.

$$\tan\theta = \frac{\sin\theta}{\cos\theta}$$

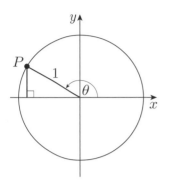

Figure 59 A point P on the unit circle

For the second identity, again consider an angle θ and its associated point P on the unit circle. If P doesn't lie on one of the axes, then you can draw a line from P perpendicular to the x-axis to form a right-angled triangle. Let's consider the case in which P lies in the second quadrant, as illustrated in Figure 59. The length of the vertical side of the triangle is the y-coordinate of P, which is $\sin\theta$. The length of the horizontal side is the negative of the x-coordinate of P (since the x-coordinate is negative), so it is $-\cos\theta$. Hence, by Pythagoras' theorem,

$$(\sin\theta)^2 + (-\cos\theta)^2 = 1^2,$$

which simplifies to

$$(\sin\theta)^2 + (\cos\theta)^2 = 1.$$

You can see that a similar argument holds if P is in any of the other three quadrants, so the equation above is true for all the corresponding values of θ. The equation is also true if P lies on one of the axes: for example, if $\theta = \pi/2$, then P is at the top of the circle, so $\sin\theta = 1$ and $\cos\theta = 0$. So the equation is an identity.

As mentioned earlier, the expressions $(\sin\theta)^2$ and $(\cos\theta)^2$ are usually written as $\sin^2\theta$ and $\cos^2\theta$, so the identity above is usually written as follows.

$$\sin^2\theta + \cos^2\theta = 1$$

Activity 32   *Writing sine in terms of cosine*

Show that

$$\sin\theta = \begin{cases} \sqrt{1 - \cos^2\theta} & \text{if } \sin\theta \text{ is positive,} \\ -\sqrt{1 - \cos^2\theta} & \text{if } \sin\theta \text{ is negative.} \end{cases}$$

Claudius Ptolemy
(*c.* AD 90–168)

Many of the trigonometric identities in this section were known, in somewhat different forms, to the ancient Egyptian mathematician, astronomer and geographer Claudius Ptolemy. Ptolemy, who was of Greek descent, authored the influential book on astronomy *Almagest* – the name derives from the Arabic word 'al-majisti', which in turn derives from the Greek word for 'greatest'. The book is a rich source of trigonometry, some of which was based on the work (now lost) of the ancient Greek mathematician Hipparchus (see page 15).

4.2 Trigonometric identities from the graphs of sine, cosine and tangent

In this subsection you'll see how to use the symmetry properties of the graphs of the sine, cosine and tangent functions (Figure 60) to deduce some trigonometric identities.

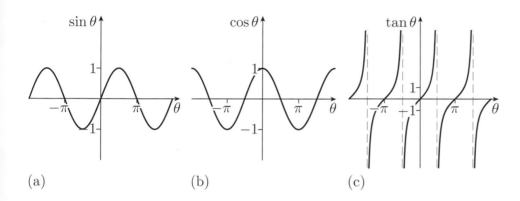

(a)   (b)   (c)

Figure 60   The graphs of the sine, cosine and tangent functions

As you learned earlier, the trigonometric functions are periodic: sine and cosine have period 2π, and tangent has period π. These facts give the identities below.

$$\sin(\theta + 2\pi) = \sin\theta$$
$$\cos(\theta + 2\pi) = \cos\theta$$
$$\tan(\theta + \pi) = \tan\theta$$

The next set of identities comes from other symmetry properties of the graphs of the trigonometric functions. The vertical axis is a line of mirror symmetry for the graph of cosine, which means that $\cos\theta$ and $\cos(-\theta)$ are equal, for every angle θ. This gives the identity $\cos(-\theta) = \cos\theta$. However, the sine of $-\theta$ is equal to the *negative* of the sine of θ, as you can see from Figure 60(a). That is, $\sin(-\theta) = -\sin\theta$, for every angle θ. There is a similar identity for tangent.

$$\sin(-\theta) = -\sin\theta$$
$$\cos(-\theta) = \cos\theta$$
$$\tan(-\theta) = -\tan\theta$$

For the final pair of identities in this subsection, notice from Figure 60 that if you translate the graph of cosine to the left by $\pi/2$ and then reflect it in the vertical axis, you obtain the graph of sine. In other words, from what you saw about translating and reflecting graphs in Unit 3, the graph of the function

$$g(\theta) = \cos\left(-\theta + \frac{\pi}{2}\right)$$

is the same as the graph of the sine function. This in turn tells you that the equation

$$\cos\left(-\theta + \frac{\pi}{2}\right) = \sin\theta$$

is an identity.

Notice also that if you translate the graph of sine to the left by $\pi/2$ and then reflect it in the vertical axis, you obtain the graph of cosine. This gives the identity

$$\sin\left(-\theta + \frac{\pi}{2}\right) = \cos\theta.$$

These two identities are stated in a slightly neater form below.

$$\sin\left(\frac{\pi}{2} - \theta\right) = \cos\theta$$
$$\cos\left(\frac{\pi}{2} - \theta\right) = \sin\theta$$

You met these identities for acute angles earlier in the unit.

You can use the symmetries of the graphs of the sine, cosine and tangent functions to obtain many more trigonometric identities.

4.3   Sine rule and cosine rule

In Section 1, the sine, cosine and tangent of an acute angle θ were defined as *ratios* of the sides of a right-angled triangle that has θ as one of its acute angles (Figure 61).   Specifically, they were defined by

$$\sin\theta = \frac{\text{opp}}{\text{hyp}}, \quad \cos\theta = \frac{\text{adj}}{\text{hyp}} \quad \text{and} \quad \tan\theta = \frac{\text{opp}}{\text{adj}}.$$

There are three further ratios of the sides of such a triangle. These ratios are known as the **cosecant**, **secant** and **cotangent** of θ (pronounced as 'co-see-cant', 'see-cant' and 'co-tan-gent'). They are written as $\operatorname{cosec}\theta$, $\sec\theta$ and $\cot\theta$, and defined as follows:

$$\operatorname{cosec}\theta = \frac{\text{hyp}}{\text{opp}}, \quad \sec\theta = \frac{\text{hyp}}{\text{adj}} \quad \text{and} \quad \cot\theta = \frac{\text{adj}}{\text{opp}}.$$

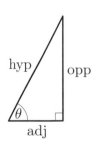

Figure 61   A right-angled triangle with acute angle θ

Cosec, sec and cot are pronounced as 'co-seck', 'seck' and 'cot'.

From these definitions you can see that the equations below hold. We use these equations as the definitions of cosecant, secant and cotangent for *any* angle θ – not just for acute angles.

Cosecant, secant and cotangent

$$\operatorname{cosec}\theta = \frac{1}{\sin\theta} \quad (\text{provided } \sin\theta \neq 0)$$

$$\sec\theta = \frac{1}{\cos\theta} \quad (\text{provided } \cos\theta \neq 0)$$

$$\cot\theta = \frac{\cos\theta}{\sin\theta} \quad (\text{provided } \sin\theta \neq 0)$$

Since you have already seen that

$$\tan\theta = \frac{\sin\theta}{\cos\theta} \quad (\text{provided } \cos\theta \neq 0),$$

the third equation above gives the following equation.

$$\cot\theta = \frac{1}{\tan\theta} \quad (\text{provided } \sin\theta \neq 0 \text{ and } \cos\theta \neq 0)$$

So, essentially, the cosecant, secant and cotangent functions are the reciprocals of the sine, cosine and tangent functions, respectively. Since the reciprocal of a periodic function has the same period as the original function, the cosecant and secant functions have period 2π and the cotangent function has period π.

Sine, cosine and tangent, together with cosecant, secant and cotangent, form the complete set of six trigonometric functions. The graphs of cosecant, secant and cotangent are shown in Figure 62.

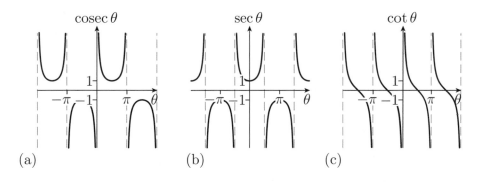

(a)   (b)   (c)

Figure 62   The graphs of the cosecant, secant and cotangent functions

You can work out values of cosecant, secant and cotangent for some special angles by using the values of sine, cosine and tangent for these angles, as illustrated in the next example.

Example 14   *Finding values of cosecant, secant and cotangent*

Find the exact values of cosec $(\pi/6)$, sec $(\pi/6)$ and cot $(\pi/6)$, without using a calculator.

Solution

🔍 Use the values of $\sin(\pi/6)$ and $\cos(\pi/6)$ from the special angles table. 💬

$$\operatorname{cosec}\frac{\pi}{6} = \frac{1}{\sin\dfrac{\pi}{6}} = \frac{1}{1/2} = 2$$

$$\sec\frac{\pi}{6} = \frac{1}{\cos\dfrac{\pi}{6}} = \frac{1}{\sqrt{3}/2} = \frac{2}{\sqrt{3}}$$

$$\cot\frac{\pi}{6} = \frac{\cos\dfrac{\pi}{6}}{\sin\dfrac{\pi}{6}} = \frac{\sqrt{3}/2}{1/2} = \sqrt{3}$$

Activity 33   *Finding values of cosecant, secant and cotangent*

Find the value of each of the following cosecants, secants and cotangents (or state that it is undefined), without using a calculator.

(a) cosec 0, sec 0 and cot 0

(b) cosec $\dfrac{\pi}{2}$, sec $\dfrac{\pi}{2}$ and cot $\dfrac{\pi}{2}$

(c) cosec $\dfrac{\pi}{4}$, sec $\dfrac{\pi}{4}$ and cot $\dfrac{\pi}{4}$

You can use the identity

$$\sin^2\theta + \cos^2\theta = 1$$

to obtain two new identities involving cosecant, secant and cotangent. Dividing both sides of the identity above by $\cos^2\theta$ gives

$$\frac{\sin^2\theta}{\cos^2\theta} + \frac{\cos^2\theta}{\cos^2\theta} = \frac{1}{\cos^2\theta}; \quad \text{that is,} \quad \tan^2\theta + 1 = \sec^2\theta.$$

Dividing both sides of the original identity by $\sin^2\theta$ instead of $\cos^2\theta$ gives another new identity. Both of these new identities are sometimes useful, and are stated in the following box.

$$\tan^2 \theta + 1 = \sec^2 \theta$$
$$1 + \cot^2 \theta = \operatorname{cosec}^2 \theta$$

4.4 Angle sum and angle difference identities

In this subsection and the next you'll meet some further trigonometric identities. These allow you to obtain the exact values of the sine, cosine and tangent of many more angles than the few special angles that you've seen so far, and they're also useful in other contexts, such as calculus.

Let's begin with an identity that expresses $\sin(A + B)$ in terms of $\sin A$, $\sin B$, $\cos A$ and $\cos B$. This identity is known as the *angle sum identity for sine*. The letters A and B represent any angles (they don't have to be two angles from a triangle).

Here's how the identity can be obtained in the case where A and B are acute angles. Suppose that you have a right-angled triangle with an acute angle A, an adjacent side of length 1, and hypotenuse of length p, as shown on the left of Figure 63. You also have another right-angled triangle with an acute angle B, an adjacent side of length 1, and hypotenuse of length q, as shown on the right of Figure 63.

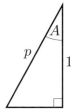 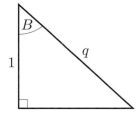

Figure 63   Two right-angled triangles

If you stick these two triangles together along their sides of length 1, then you obtain the larger triangle shown in Figure 64.

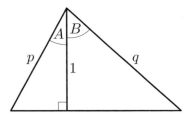 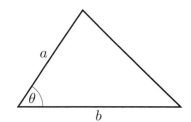

Figure 64   A triangle divided into two right-angled triangles

Let's now apply the formula for the area of a triangle that you met earlier. Remember that it tells you that the area of a triangle with an angle θ between sides of lengths a and b (as shown in Figure 65) is $\frac{1}{2}ab \sin \theta$. We'll

Figure 65   A triangle with an angle θ between two sides of lengths a and b

apply this formula three times to the triangle in Figure 64, as follows. The area of the right-angled triangle on the left is $\frac{1}{2}p\sin A$, the area of the right-angled triangle on the right is $\frac{1}{2}q\sin B$, and the area of the large triangle is $\frac{1}{2}pq\sin(A+B)$. But the area of the large triangle is also equal to the sum of the areas of the two right-angled triangles. That is,

$$\tfrac{1}{2}pq\sin(A+B) = \tfrac{1}{2}p\sin A + \tfrac{1}{2}q\sin B.$$

You can multiply both sides of this equation by 2 and then divide both sides by pq to obtain

$$\sin(A+B) = \frac{1}{q}\sin A + \frac{1}{p}\sin B.$$

The right-angled triangle on the left of Figure 64 gives

$$\cos A = \frac{\text{adj}}{\text{hyp}} = \frac{1}{p},$$

and the right-angled triangle on the right of Figure 64 gives

$$\cos B = \frac{\text{adj}}{\text{hyp}} = \frac{1}{q}.$$

Together the last three equations give

$$\sin(A+B) = \sin A \cos B + \cos A \sin B.$$

This is the angle sum identity for sine. Although the justification above applies only when the angles A and B are acute, the identity holds for *all* angles A and B. This can be proved by considering various types of angles A and B, and using symmetry properties of sine and cosine to deduce the identity for each of these types from the case of acute angles.

You can obtain a similar identity for cosine. Since the angle sum identity for sine is true for any angles A and B, it remains true if you replace A by $\pi/2 - A$, and B by $-B$, where again A and B are any angles. This gives

$$\sin\left(\frac{\pi}{2} - A - B\right) = \sin\left(\frac{\pi}{2} - A\right)\cos(-B) + \cos\left(\frac{\pi}{2} - A\right)\sin(-B).$$

Note that $\sin(\pi/2 - A - B) = \sin(\pi/2 - (A+B))$. Earlier on, in Subsection 4.2, you met the identities

$$\sin\left(\frac{\pi}{2} - \theta\right) = \cos\theta, \quad \cos\left(\frac{\pi}{2} - \theta\right) = \sin\theta,$$
$$\sin(-\theta) = -\sin\theta, \quad \cos(-\theta) = \cos\theta.$$

You can apply these identities as follows:

$$\underbrace{\sin\left(\frac{\pi}{2} - (A+B)\right)}_{\cos(A+B)} = \underbrace{\sin\left(\frac{\pi}{2} - A\right)}_{\cos A}\underbrace{\cos(-B)}_{\cos B} + \underbrace{\cos\left(\frac{\pi}{2} - A\right)}_{\sin A}\underbrace{\sin(-B)}_{-\sin B}.$$

This gives the angle sum identity for cosine:

$$\cos(A+B) = \cos A \cos B - \sin A \sin B.$$

The angle sum identities for sine and cosine are stated again in the following box, for convenience.

Angle sum identities for sine and cosine

$$\sin(A + B) = \sin A \cos B + \cos A \sin B$$
$$\cos(A + B) = \cos A \cos B - \sin A \sin B$$

If you divide the angle sum identity for sine by the angle sum identity for cosine, then you obtain

$$\tan(A + B) = \frac{\sin A \cos B + \cos A \sin B}{\cos A \cos B - \sin A \sin B}.$$

Dividing both the numerator and denominator of the fraction on the right-hand side by $\cos A \cos B$ gives

$$\tan(A + B) = \frac{\dfrac{\sin A}{\cos A} + \dfrac{\sin B}{\cos B}}{1 - \dfrac{\sin A \sin B}{\cos A \cos B}} = \frac{\tan A + \tan B}{1 - \tan A \tan B}.$$

This is the angle sum identity for tangent.

Angle sum identity for tangent

$$\tan(A + B) = \frac{\tan A + \tan B}{1 - \tan A \tan B}$$

You have now seen all three angle sum identities. If you replace B by $-B$ in each of the three angle sum identities, and use the identities

$$\sin(-B) = -\sin B, \quad \cos(-B) = \cos B \quad \text{and} \quad \tan(-B) = -\tan B,$$

then you obtain the following three *angle difference identities*.

Angle difference identities

$$\sin(A - B) = \sin A \cos B - \cos A \sin B$$
$$\cos(A - B) = \cos A \cos B + \sin A \sin B$$
$$\tan(A - B) = \frac{\tan A - \tan B}{1 + \tan A \tan B}$$

Let's now look at how you can use the angle sum and angle difference identities to find the exact values of the sine, cosine and tangent of some more angles. If you know the exact values of the sine, cosine and tangent of two particular angles A and B (for example, from the special angles table), then you can apply the angle sum and angle difference identities to find the exact values of the sine, cosine and tangent of the angles $A + B$ and $A - B$. Here's an example.

Example 15   *Finding an exact value of cosine*

Find the exact value of $\cos(7\pi/12)$, without using a calculator.

Solution

🔍 Find angles A and B such that you know the exact values of $\sin A$, $\sin B$, $\cos A$ and $\cos B$, and one of the equations $A + B = 7\pi/12$ or $A - B = 7\pi/12$ holds. 💬

Let $A = \pi/3$ and $B = \pi/4$. Then

$$A + B = \frac{\pi}{3} + \frac{\pi}{4} = \frac{4\pi}{12} + \frac{3\pi}{12} = \frac{7\pi}{12}.$$

🔍 Use the angle sum identity for cosine. 💬

The identity $\cos(A + B) = \cos A \cos B - \sin A \sin B$ gives

$$\cos\left(\frac{7\pi}{12}\right) = \cos\left(\frac{\pi}{3} + \frac{\pi}{4}\right)$$

$$= \cos\frac{\pi}{3}\cos\frac{\pi}{4} - \sin\frac{\pi}{3}\sin\frac{\pi}{4}$$

🔍 Use the special angles table. 💬

$$= \frac{1}{2} \times \frac{1}{\sqrt{2}} - \frac{\sqrt{3}}{2} \times \frac{1}{\sqrt{2}}$$

$$= \frac{1}{2\sqrt{2}} - \frac{\sqrt{3}}{2\sqrt{2}}$$

$$= \frac{1 - \sqrt{3}}{2\sqrt{2}}$$

🔍 For a neater answer, rationalise the denominator. You saw how to do this in Unit 1. Here you multiply both the numerator and denominator by $\sqrt{2}$. 💬

$$= \frac{\sqrt{2}(1 - \sqrt{3})}{2\sqrt{2}\sqrt{2}}$$

$$= \frac{\sqrt{2} - \sqrt{6}}{2 \times 2}$$

$$= \frac{1}{4}\left(\sqrt{2} - \sqrt{6}\right).$$

Activity 34 *Finding exact values of sine, cosine and tangent*

Find the exact values of the following, without using a calculator.

(a) $\sin\left(\dfrac{7\pi}{12}\right)$ (b) $\tan\left(\dfrac{\pi}{12}\right)$

Richard of Wallingford

Richard of Wallingford (1292–1336) was a priest and a scholar at Oxford University. He wrote a book on trigonometry and its applications to astronomy, called *Quadripartitum de sinibus demonstratis* (Demonstrations of sines, in four parts). The first part of the book is on trigonometric identities, which he used to calculate values of sine and cosine.

Richard of Wallingford, working in cramped conditions

4.5 Double-angle and half-angle identities

This subsection is about two more sets of trigonometric identities, the *double-angle identities* and the *half-angle identities*. The double-angle identities are obtained from the angle sum identities for sine, cosine and tangent by choosing A and B to be the same angle, say θ.

The angle sum identity for sine is

$$\sin(A + B) = \sin A \cos B + \cos A \sin B.$$

Taking $A = \theta$ and $B = \theta$ gives

$$\sin(\theta + \theta) = \sin\theta\cos\theta + \cos\theta\sin\theta;$$

that is,

$$\sin(2\theta) = 2\sin\theta\cos\theta.$$

Next, the angle sum identity for cosine is

$$\cos(A + B) = \cos A \cos B - \sin A \sin B.$$

Taking $A = \theta$ and $B = \theta$ gives

$$\cos(\theta + \theta) = \cos\theta\cos\theta - \sin\theta\sin\theta;$$

that is,

$$\cos(2\theta) = \cos^2\theta - \sin^2\theta.$$

Finally, the angle sum identity for tangent is

$$\tan(A + B) = \frac{\tan A + \tan B}{1 - \tan A \tan B}.$$

Taking $A = \theta$ and $B = \theta$ gives

$$\tan(\theta + \theta) = \frac{\tan\theta + \tan\theta}{1 - \tan\theta\tan\theta};$$

that is,

$$\tan(2\theta) = \frac{2\tan\theta}{1 - \tan^2\theta}.$$

These three identities are stated again below, for convenience.

Double-angle identities

$$\sin(2\theta) = 2\sin\theta\cos\theta$$
$$\cos(2\theta) = \cos^2\theta - \sin^2\theta$$
$$\tan(2\theta) = \frac{2\tan\theta}{1 - \tan^2\theta}$$

There are two alternative forms of the cosine double-angle identity. To obtain these, recall that $\sin^2\theta + \cos^2\theta = 1$, from which it follows that $\sin^2\theta = 1 - \cos^2\theta$ and $\cos^2\theta = 1 - \sin^2\theta$. Therefore

$$\begin{aligned}
\cos(2\theta) &= \cos^2\theta - \sin^2\theta \\
&= (1 - \sin^2\theta) - \sin^2\theta \\
&= 1 - 2\sin^2\theta,
\end{aligned}$$

and

$$\begin{aligned}
\cos(2\theta) &= \cos^2\theta - \sin^2\theta \\
&= \cos^2\theta - (1 - \cos^2\theta) \\
&= 2\cos^2\theta - 1.
\end{aligned}$$

Alternative double-angle identities for cosine

$$\cos(2\theta) = 1 - 2\sin^2\theta$$
$$\cos(2\theta) = 2\cos^2\theta - 1$$

These alternative double-angle identities for cosine can be rearranged into the forms below. In these forms they are known as the *half-angle identities*.

Half-angle identities

$$\sin^2\theta = \tfrac{1}{2}(1 - \cos(2\theta))$$
$$\cos^2\theta = \tfrac{1}{2}(1 + \cos(2\theta))$$

The description 'half-angle' refers to the fact that these identities are sometimes stated with θ and 2θ replaced by $\frac{1}{2}\theta$ and θ, respectively, as follows:

$$\sin^2\left(\tfrac{1}{2}\theta\right) = \tfrac{1}{2}(1 - \cos\theta)$$
$$\cos^2\left(\tfrac{1}{2}\theta\right) = \tfrac{1}{2}(1 + \cos\theta).$$

Like the angle sum and angle difference identities in the last subsection, the half-angle identities can be used to provide the exact values of the sines, cosines and tangents of some further angles. Specifically, if you know the exact value of the cosine of a particular angle, then you can use the half-angle identities to find the exact values of the sine and cosine (and hence tangent) of half of that angle. The exact values that you obtain can be quite complicated, however, as they often contain square roots within square roots. Here's an example.

Example 16   *Using a half-angle identity to find an exact value of sine*

Find the exact value of $\sin(\pi/8)$, without using a calculator.

Solution

🔍 The angle $\pi/8$ is half of $\pi/4$, which is one of the angles in the special angles table. So use a half-angle identity. 💬

The half-angle identity for sine is

$$\sin^2\theta = \tfrac{1}{2}(1 - \cos(2\theta)).$$

🔍 Substitute in $\theta = \pi/8$. 💬

So

$$\sin^2\frac{\pi}{8} = \frac{1}{2}\left(1 - \cos\frac{\pi}{4}\right)$$

🔍 Use the fact that $\cos\dfrac{\pi}{4} = \dfrac{1}{\sqrt{2}}$. 💬

$$= \frac{1}{2}\left(1 - \frac{1}{\sqrt{2}}\right)$$

$$= \frac{1}{2}\left(\frac{\sqrt{2}}{\sqrt{2}} - \frac{1}{\sqrt{2}}\right)$$

$$= \frac{\sqrt{2} - 1}{2\sqrt{2}}$$

🔍 Rationalise the denominator. 💬

$$= \frac{\sqrt{2}(\sqrt{2}-1)}{2\sqrt{2}\sqrt{2}}$$

$$= \frac{2-\sqrt{2}}{4}.$$

🔍 To obtain the required answer, take square roots of both sides. 💬

The angle $\pi/8$ is acute, so $\sin(\pi/8)$ is positive, and hence

$$\sin\frac{\pi}{8} = \sqrt{\frac{2-\sqrt{2}}{4}} = \frac{\sqrt{2-\sqrt{2}}}{2}.$$

Here is a similar example for you to try.

Activity 35   *Using a half-angle identity to find an exact value of cosine*

Use a half-angle identity to find the exact value of $\cos(\pi/8)$, without using a calculator.

As pointed out in Section 1, once you've found the exact value of the sine, cosine or tangent of a particular acute angle, you can find the exact values of the other two trigonometric ratios for the angle by sketching a suitable right-angled triangle, and using Pythagoras' theorem and the definitions of sine, cosine and tangent. (Alternatively you can find them without sketching a triangle by using the identities $\sin^2\theta + \cos^2\theta = 1$ and $\tan\theta = \sin\theta/\cos\theta$.) So you can use the answer to Example 16 to obtain the answer to Activity 35, instead of using a half-angle identity. You can also use it to obtain the exact value of $\tan(\pi/8)$. However, the answer you obtain this way is

$$\tan\frac{\pi}{8} = \sqrt{\frac{2-\sqrt{2}}{2+\sqrt{2}}},$$

which is quite complicated. You can obtain a simpler form of the answer by finding it in a different way, using a trigonometric identity, as you'll see in the next activity. This illustrates that there are often various ways of working with trigonometric ratios.

Activity 36   *Using a half-angle identity to find an exact value of tangent*

Use the double-angle formula for tangent with $2\theta = \pi/4$ to calculate an exact value for $\tan(\pi/8)$.

Hint: if you write $t = \tan(\pi/8)$, then you can use the double-angle formula for tangent to give you a quadratic equation for t.

At the end of the solution to Activity 36 there is an explanation of why the simpler form of the exact value of $\tan(\pi/8)$ is equal to the more complicated form given above.

4.6 Yet more trigonometric identities

The angle sum and angle difference identities, and the double-angle identities, can be used to deduce many new trigonometric identities, some of which are useful in other subjects such as calculus.

For example, consider the angle sum and angle difference identities for sine:

$$\sin(A + B) = \sin A \cos B + \cos A \sin B$$
$$\sin(A - B) = \sin A \cos B - \cos A \sin B.$$

Adding these gives

$$\sin(A + B) + \sin(A - B) = 2 \sin A \cos B.$$

This identity enables you to convert a product of a sine and a cosine on the right-hand side into the sum of two sines on the left-hand side, which is sometimes useful. There are similar identities, which can be obtained in a similar way, that convert products of two cosines and products of two sines into sums or differences of cosines.

The new identity above can be rearranged to give a slightly different identity that has some useful applications. Suppose that you let

$$C = A + B \quad \text{and} \quad D = A - B.$$

Solving these equations for A and B, by first adding them and then subtracting them, gives

$$A = \frac{C + D}{2} \quad \text{and} \quad B = \frac{C - D}{2}.$$

Substituting into the identity above gives

$$\sin C + \sin D = 2 \sin\left(\frac{C + D}{2}\right) \cos\left(\frac{C - D}{2}\right).$$

This identity relates a sum of two sines on the left-hand side to a product of a sine and a cosine on the right-hand side. There are similar identities, which can be obtained in a similar way, for a difference of two sines, and for a sum and difference of two cosines. These are listed in the following box, with the variables C and D replaced by the usual variables A and B.

$$\sin A + \sin B = 2\sin\left(\frac{A+B}{2}\right)\cos\left(\frac{A-B}{2}\right)$$

$$\sin A - \sin B = 2\sin\left(\frac{A-B}{2}\right)\cos\left(\frac{A+B}{2}\right)$$

$$\cos A + \cos B = 2\cos\left(\frac{A+B}{2}\right)\cos\left(\frac{A-B}{2}\right)$$

$$\cos A - \cos B = -2\sin\left(\frac{A+B}{2}\right)\sin\left(\frac{A-B}{2}\right)$$

These identities can be used whenever you find it useful to change a sum or difference of sines or cosines into a product of trigonometric functions, or vice versa. As with other trigonometric identities, there is no need for you to memorise them.

You can use trigonometric identities to explain an interesting effect that's obtained when two musical notes with similar frequencies are played at the same time.

Consider the graphs of the functions $f(t) = \sin(20t)$ and $g(t) = \sin(22t)$, which are shown in Figure 66. They represent waves, such as sound waves, that are almost the same but have slightly different periods.

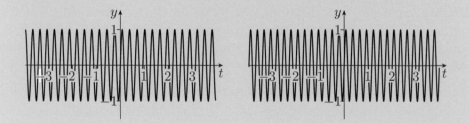

Figure 66   The graphs of (a) $f(t) = \sin(20t)$ (b) $g(t) = \sin(22t)$

Now consider what happens when you add these two functions. You obtain the function

$$h(t) = \sin(20t) + \sin(22t),$$

whose graph is shown in Figure 67.

Figure 67   The graph of $h(t) = \sin(20t) + \sin(22t)$

So 'adding' these two similar waves produces a wave with an interesting shape, consisting of fast oscillations with a slow variation in the magnitude of these oscillations. This shape can be explained by applying the 'sum of sines' identity above to give

$$h(t) = \sin(20t) + \sin(22t) = 2\sin(21t)\cos t.$$

So the graph of the function h can be thought of as the rapidly oscillating graph of $\sin(21t)$ scaled by the factor $2\cos t$, which produces a slow variation in magnitude, known as *beating*.

You can observe this phenomenon when two musical notes with similar frequencies are played simultaneously, and the resulting slow variation in magnitude is heard as 'beats'.

5   Using the computer for trigonometry

Activity 37   *Working with trigonometric functions on the computer*

To complete your study of Unit 4, work through Section 6 of the *Computer algebra guide*, where you will learn how to use the computer to work with trigonometric functions.

Learning outcomes

After studying this unit, you should be able to:

- use radians as a measure of angle, and convert between radians and degrees
- use sine, cosine and tangent to find unknown side lengths and angles of right-angled triangles
- define the sine, cosine and tangent of any angle
- sketch the graphs of sine, cosine and tangent
- use the ASTC diagram or graphs to find values of sine, cosine and tangent
- define inverse sine, inverse cosine and inverse tangent for any angle
- solve trigonometric equations using the ASTC diagram or graphs
- find unknown side lengths and angles in triangles using the sine rule and cosine rule
- calculate the area of a triangle from two side lengths and the angle between them
- define the cosecant, secant and cotangent of any angle
- understand and use trigonometric identities.

Solutions to activities

Solution to Activity 1

(a) (i) Applying the degrees-to-radians conversion formula gives
$$1° = \left(\frac{\pi}{180} \times 1\right) \text{ radians} = \frac{\pi}{180} \text{ radians}.$$

(ii) Applying the degrees-to-radians conversion formula gives
$$345° = \left(\frac{\pi}{180} \times 345\right) \text{ radians} = \frac{23\pi}{12} \text{ radians}.$$

(b) (i) Applying the radians-to-degrees conversion formula gives
$$\frac{3\pi}{5} \text{ radians} = \left(\frac{180}{\pi} \times \frac{3\pi}{5}\right)° = 108°.$$

(ii) Applying the radians-to-degrees conversion formula gives
$$\frac{7\pi}{4} \text{ radians} = \left(\frac{180}{\pi} \times \frac{7\pi}{4}\right)° = 315°.$$

Solution to Activity 2

(a) There are 2π radians in a full turn. A sector of $\pi/3$ radians has been removed, and $2\pi - \pi/3 = 5\pi/3$, so the shape is a sector of angle $5\pi/3$ radians.

(b) The perimeter of the shape consists of two straight lines of length $1\,\text{cm}$, and an arc that subtends an angle of $5\pi/3$ radians. Using the arc length formula gives $5\pi/3 \times 1 = 5\pi/3$, so the arc length is $5\pi/3\,\text{cm}$. Then
$$1 + 1 + \frac{5\pi}{3} = 2 + \frac{5\pi}{3} = 7.235\ldots,$$
so the total perimeter of the shape is $7.2\,\text{cm}$ (to 1 d.p.).

(c) The area of a sector formula gives
$$\frac{1}{2} \times 1^2 \times \frac{5\pi}{3} = \frac{5\pi}{6} = 2.617\ldots,$$
so the shape has area $2.6\,\text{cm}^2$ (to 1 d.p.).

Solution to Activity 3

(a) Pythagoras' theorem says that the square of the hypotenuse is the sum of the squares of the other two sides. The sum of the squares of the other two sides is
$$8^2 + 15^2 = 289.$$

Therefore the length of the hypotenuse is $\sqrt{289} = 17$.

(b) For this angle θ, opp $= 15$, adj $= 8$ and hyp $= 17$. Therefore
$$\sin\theta = \frac{\text{opp}}{\text{hyp}} = \frac{15}{17},$$
$$\cos\theta = \frac{\text{adj}}{\text{hyp}} = \frac{8}{17},$$
$$\tan\theta = \frac{\text{opp}}{\text{adj}} = \frac{15}{8}.$$

Solution to Activity 4

Since $\sin\theta = \frac{5}{13}$, you can draw a right-angled triangle with one acute angle θ, such that opp $= 5$ and hyp $= 13$.

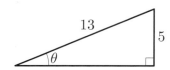

Then, by Pythagoras' theorem,
$$13^2 = 5^2 + \text{adj}^2,$$
so
$$\text{adj} = \sqrt{169 - 25} = 12.$$
Hence
$$\cos\theta = \frac{\text{adj}}{\text{hyp}} = \frac{12}{13},$$
$$\tan\theta = \frac{\text{opp}}{\text{adj}} = \frac{5}{12}.$$

Solution to Activity 5

$$\sin 62° = 0.883 \quad \text{(to 3 s.f.)}$$
$$\cos 62° = 0.469 \quad \text{(to 3 s.f.)}$$
$$\tan 62° = 1.88 \quad \text{(to 3 s.f.)}$$

Solution to Activity 6

(a) The labelled side lengths are opp $= 5$ and hyp $= p$, so
$$\sin 35° = \frac{\text{opp}}{\text{hyp}} = \frac{5}{p}.$$
Rearranging this in terms of p gives
$$p = \frac{5}{\sin 35°} = 8.717\ldots = 8.7 \text{ (to 2 s.f.)}.$$

(b) The labelled side lengths are adj $= q$ and hyp $= 7$, so
$$\cos\frac{\pi}{4} = \frac{\text{adj}}{\text{hyp}} = \frac{q}{7}.$$
Rearranging this in terms of q gives
$$q = 7\cos\frac{\pi}{4} = 4.949\ldots = 4.9 \text{ (to 2 s.f.)}.$$

(c) The labelled side lengths are opp $= r$ and adj $= 6$, so
$$\tan\frac{\pi}{6} = \frac{\text{opp}}{\text{adj}} = \frac{r}{6}.$$
Rearranging this in terms of r gives
$$r = 6\tan\frac{\pi}{6} = 3.464\ldots = 3.5 \text{ (to 2 s.f.)}.$$

Solution to Activity 7

By the equation stated before the activity, the width of the river in metres is given by
$$50 \times \tan 57° = 76.993\ldots.$$
So the width of the river is 77 m, to the nearest metre.

Solution to Activity 8

Let h be the height of the building in metres. Then
$$\frac{h}{100} = \tan 72°.$$
Therefore
$$h = 100\tan 72° = 307.768\ldots.$$
So the height of the building is 308 m, to the nearest metre.

Solution to Activity 9

(a) For the angle θ, the side lengths are opp $= 40$ and adj $= 35$. Therefore
$$\tan\theta = \frac{\text{opp}}{\text{adj}} = \frac{40}{35}.$$
Hence
$$\theta = \tan^{-1}\left(\frac{40}{35}\right) = 48.814\ldots° = 49°,$$
to the nearest degree.

(b) For the angle α, the side lengths are opp $= 8$ and hyp $= 15$. Therefore
$$\sin\alpha = \frac{\text{opp}}{\text{hyp}} = \frac{8}{15}.$$
Hence
$$\alpha = \sin^{-1}\left(\frac{8}{15}\right) = 32.230\ldots° = 32°,$$

to the nearest degree.

For the angle β, the side lengths are adj $= 8$ and hyp $= 15$. Therefore
$$\cos\beta = \frac{\text{adj}}{\text{hyp}} = \frac{8}{15}.$$
Hence
$$\beta = \cos^{-1}\left(\frac{8}{15}\right) = 57.769\ldots° = 58°,$$
to the nearest degree.

Alternatively, because the sum of the two acute angles in a right-angled triangle is $90°$,
$$\beta = 90° - \alpha = 57.769\ldots° = 58°,$$
to the nearest degree.

Solution to Activity 10

The identity $\sin^2\theta + \cos^2\theta = 1$ gives
$$\sin^2\theta = 1 - \cos^2\theta,$$
$$\sin\theta = \sqrt{1 - \cos^2\theta}.$$
Here the positive square root has been taken because $\sin\theta$ is positive. So
$$\sin\theta = \sqrt{1 - \left(\frac{3}{7}\right)^2}$$
$$= \frac{\sqrt{40}}{7}$$
$$= \frac{2\sqrt{10}}{7}.$$
Then
$$\tan\theta = \frac{\sin\theta}{\cos\theta}$$
$$= \frac{2\sqrt{10}/7}{3/7}$$
$$= \frac{2\sqrt{10}}{3}.$$

Solution to Activity 11

Consider the right-angled triangle below (which is the same as the right-angled triangle in Figure 22).

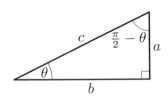

You can see that
$$\tan\theta = \frac{a}{b}, \quad \text{so} \quad \frac{1}{\tan\theta} = \frac{b}{a}.$$
Also,
$$\tan\left(\frac{\pi}{2} - \theta\right) = \frac{b}{a}.$$
Therefore
$$\tan\left(\frac{\pi}{2} - \theta\right) = \frac{1}{\tan\theta}.$$

Solution to Activity 12

(a)

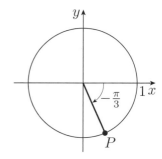

The point P lies in the fourth quadrant.

(b)

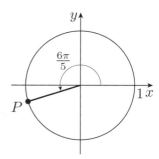

The point P lies in the third quadrant.

(c)

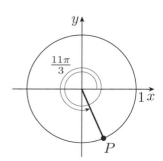

The point P lies in the fourth quadrant.

(d)

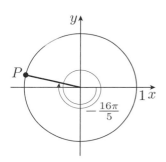

The point P lies in the second quadrant.

Solution to Activity 13

(a)

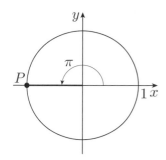

The point P has coordinates $(-1, 0)$. Therefore
$$\sin\pi = 0, \quad \cos\pi = -1 \quad \text{and} \quad \tan\pi = 0.$$

(b)

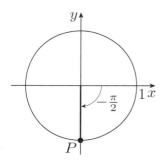

The point P has coordinates $(0, -1)$. Therefore
$$\sin\left(-\frac{\pi}{2}\right) = -1, \quad \cos\left(-\frac{\pi}{2}\right) = 0$$
and $\tan(-\pi/2)$ is undefined.

Solution to Activity 14

(a)

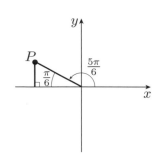

For the right-angled triangle in the diagram,

$$\sin \frac{\pi}{6} = \frac{\text{opp}}{1} = \text{opp} \quad \text{and} \quad \cos \frac{\pi}{6} = \frac{\text{adj}}{1} = \text{adj}.$$

Since

$$\sin \frac{\pi}{6} = \frac{1}{2} \quad \text{and} \quad \cos \frac{\pi}{6} = \frac{\sqrt{3}}{2},$$

the coordinates of P are $\left(-\sqrt{3}/2, 1/2\right)$.

Therefore

$$\sin \left(\frac{5\pi}{6}\right) = \frac{1}{2},$$

$$\cos \left(\frac{5\pi}{6}\right) = -\frac{\sqrt{3}}{2},$$

$$\tan \left(\frac{5\pi}{6}\right) = \left(\frac{1}{2}\right) \Big/ \left(-\frac{\sqrt{3}}{2}\right) = -\frac{1}{\sqrt{3}}.$$

(b)

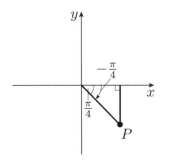

For the right-angled triangle in the diagram,

$$\sin \frac{\pi}{4} = \frac{\text{opp}}{1} = \text{opp} \quad \text{and} \quad \cos \frac{\pi}{4} = \frac{\text{adj}}{1} = \text{adj}.$$

Since

$$\sin \frac{\pi}{4} = \cos \frac{\pi}{4} = \frac{1}{\sqrt{2}},$$

the coordinates of P are $\left(1/\sqrt{2}, -1/\sqrt{2}\right)$.

Therefore

$$\sin \left(-\frac{\pi}{4}\right) = -\frac{1}{\sqrt{2}},$$

$$\cos \left(-\frac{\pi}{4}\right) = \frac{1}{\sqrt{2}},$$

$$\tan \left(-\frac{\pi}{4}\right) = \left(-\frac{1}{\sqrt{2}}\right) \Big/ \left(\frac{1}{\sqrt{2}}\right) = -1.$$

Solution to Activity 15

(a)

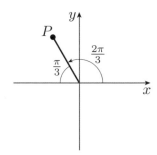

Since $2\pi/3$ is a second quadrant angle, its sine is positive and its cosine and tangent are negative. Hence

$$\sin \left(\frac{2\pi}{3}\right) = \sin \frac{\pi}{3} = \frac{\sqrt{3}}{2},$$

$$\cos \left(\frac{2\pi}{3}\right) = -\cos \frac{\pi}{3} = -\frac{1}{2},$$

$$\tan \left(\frac{2\pi}{3}\right) = -\tan \frac{\pi}{3} = -\sqrt{3}.$$

(b)

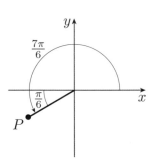

Since $7\pi/6$ is a third quadrant angle, its tangent is positive and its sine and cosine are negative.

Hence
$$\sin\left(\frac{7\pi}{6}\right) = -\sin\frac{\pi}{6} = -\frac{1}{2},$$
$$\cos\left(\frac{7\pi}{6}\right) = -\cos\frac{\pi}{6} = -\frac{\sqrt{3}}{2},$$
$$\tan\left(\frac{7\pi}{6}\right) = \tan\frac{\pi}{6} = \frac{1}{\sqrt{3}}.$$

(c)

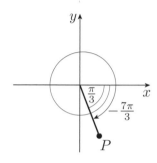

Since $-7\pi/3$ is a fourth quadrant angle, its cosine is positive and its sine and tangent are negative. Hence
$$\sin\left(-\frac{7\pi}{3}\right) = -\sin\frac{\pi}{3} = -\frac{\sqrt{3}}{2},$$
$$\cos\left(-\frac{7\pi}{3}\right) = \cos\frac{\pi}{3} = \frac{1}{2},$$
$$\tan\left(-\frac{7\pi}{3}\right) = -\tan\frac{\pi}{3} = -\sqrt{3}.$$

Solution to Activity 17

(a)

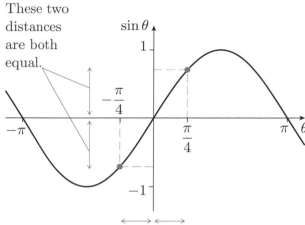

These two distances are both equal.

These two distances are both $\frac{\pi}{4}$.

From the graph,
$$\sin\left(-\frac{\pi}{4}\right) = -\sin\frac{\pi}{4}.$$
Since $\sin(\pi/4) = 1/\sqrt{2}$, it follows that
$$\sin\left(-\frac{\pi}{4}\right) = -\frac{1}{\sqrt{2}}.$$

(b)

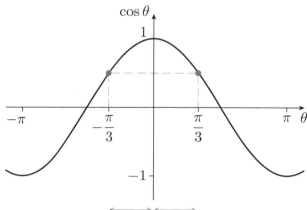

These two distances are both $\frac{\pi}{3}$.

From the graph,
$$\cos\left(-\frac{\pi}{3}\right) = \cos\frac{\pi}{3}.$$

Since $\cos(\pi/3) = \frac{1}{2}$, it follows that
$$\cos\left(-\frac{\pi}{3}\right) = \frac{1}{2}.$$

(c)

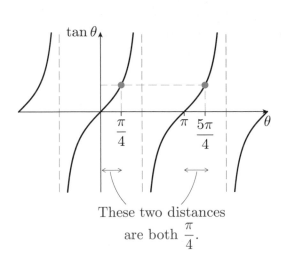

These two distances
are both $\dfrac{\pi}{4}$.

From the graph,
$$\tan\left(\frac{5\pi}{4}\right) = \tan\frac{\pi}{4}.$$
Since $\tan(\pi/4) = 1$, it follows that
$$\tan\left(\frac{5\pi}{4}\right) = 1.$$

Solution to Activity 18

(a) $\sin^{-1}(\sqrt{3}/2) = \pi/3$

(b) $\cos^{-1}\frac{1}{2} = \pi/3$

(c) $\cos^{-1} 0 = \pi/2$

(d) $\cos^{-1} 1 = 0$

(e) $\cos^{-1}(\sqrt{3}/2) = \pi/6$

(f) $\tan^{-1} 0 = 0$

(g) $\tan^{-1} 1 = \pi/4$

Solution to Activity 19

(a) $\sin^{-1}(-\sqrt{3}/2) = -\sin^{-1}(\sqrt{3}/2) = -\pi/3$

(b) $\cos^{-1}(-\frac{1}{2}) = \pi - \cos^{-1}\frac{1}{2} = \pi - \pi/3 = 2\pi/3$

(c) $\cos^{-1}(-1) = \pi - \cos^{-1} 1 = \pi - 0 = \pi$

(d) $\cos^{-1}(-\sqrt{3}/2) = \pi - \cos^{-1}(\sqrt{3}/2)$
$$= \pi - \pi/6 = 5\pi/6$$

(e) $\tan^{-1}(-1) = -\tan^{-1} 1 = -\pi/4$

Solution to Activity 20

(a) The sine of θ is negative, so θ is a third- or fourth-quadrant angle.

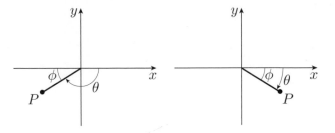

Here
$$\sin\theta = -\frac{1}{2}, \quad \text{so} \quad \sin\phi = \frac{1}{2}.$$
Therefore, from the special angles table,
$$\phi = \pi/6.$$
Hence the solutions of this equation between $-\pi$ and π are
$$\theta = -\pi + \phi = -\pi + \frac{\pi}{6} = -\frac{5\pi}{6}$$
and
$$\theta = -\phi = -\pi/6.$$
Since the sine function has period 2π, the solutions of this equation between π and 3π are
$$-\frac{5\pi}{6} + 2\pi = \frac{7\pi}{6} \quad \text{and} \quad -\frac{\pi}{6} + 2\pi = \frac{11\pi}{6}.$$

(b) The tangent of θ is negative, so θ is a second- or fourth-quadrant angle.

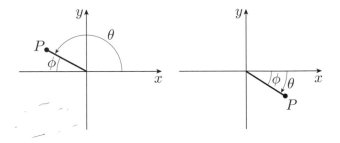

Here
$$\tan\theta = -5, \quad \text{so} \quad \tan\phi = 5.$$
Therefore, using a calculator,
$$\phi = \tan^{-1} 5 = 78.690\ldots°.$$
Hence
$$\theta = 180° - \phi = 180° - 78.690\ldots° = 101.309\ldots°$$
and
$$\theta = -\phi = -78.690\ldots°.$$

So the solutions are $-79°$ and $101°$, to the nearest degree.

Solution to Activity 21

(a)

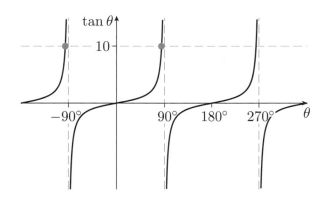

The solution between $0°$ and $90°$ is

$$\theta = \tan^{-1} 10 = 84.289\ldots°.$$

From the graph, the other solution is

$$\theta = 84.289\ldots° - 180° = -95.710\ldots°.$$

So the solutions are $84°$ and $-96°$, to the nearest degree.

(b)

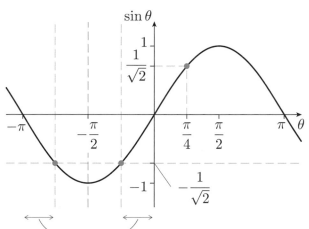

These two distances are both $\dfrac{\pi}{4}$.

From the graph, one solution is $-\pi/4$.
Symmetry of the graph about the line $x = -\pi/2$ shows that the other solution is

$$\theta = -\pi + \frac{\pi}{4} = -\frac{3\pi}{4}.$$

It follows that the solutions are $-\pi/4$ and $-3\pi/4$.

Solution to Activity 22

(a) The equation $\sin\theta = 0$ tells you that the associated point P on the unit circle with angle θ has y-coordinate 0. That is, P lies on the x-axis, so the solutions in $[-\pi, \pi]$ are $-\pi$, 0 and π.

(b) The equation $\cos\theta = -1$ tells you that the associated point P on the unit circle with angle θ has x-coordinate -1. That is, P lies on the negative x-axis, so the solutions in $[0, 4\pi]$ are π and 3π.

Solution to Activity 23

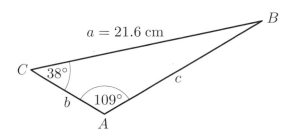

Rearranging the sine rule

$$\frac{c}{\sin C} = \frac{a}{\sin A}$$

gives

$$c = \frac{a\sin C}{\sin A} = \frac{21.6 \times \sin 38°}{\sin 109°} = 14.064\ldots.$$

Therefore $c = 14.1\,\text{cm}$, to one decimal place.

Next, the angle B satisfies

$$B + 38° + 109° = 180°, \quad \text{so} \quad B = 33°.$$

Rearranging the sine rule

$$\frac{b}{\sin B} = \frac{a}{\sin A}$$

gives

$$b = \frac{a\sin B}{\sin A} = \frac{21.6 \times \sin 33°}{\sin 109°} = 12.442\ldots.$$

Therefore $b = 12.4\,\text{cm}$, to one decimal place.

Solution to Activity 24

In triangle ABC the angle A is $180° - 47° = 133°$, so angle C is $180° - 133° - 22° = 25°$. In this triangle, the side length opposite the angle C is known, so to find the distance BC, use the sine rule in the form

$$\frac{a}{\sin A} = \frac{c}{\sin C}.$$

Rearranging this gives

$$a = \frac{c \sin A}{\sin C} = \frac{100 \sin 133°}{\sin 25°} = 173.053\ldots .$$

So the distance BC is 173 m, to the nearest metre.

Finally the height x satisfies the equation $x/BC = \sin B$, so

$$x = BC \sin B = 173.053\ldots \times \sin 22 = 64.82\ldots .$$

Hence the height of the building is 65 m to the nearest metre.

Solution to Activity 25

Rearranging the sine rule

$$\frac{c}{\sin C} = \frac{a}{\sin A}$$

gives

$$\sin C = \frac{c \sin A}{a} = \frac{16.4 \times \sin 19.9°}{7.6} = 0.734\ldots .$$

Therefore either

$$C = \sin^{-1}(0.734\ldots) = 47.265\ldots°,$$

or

$$C = 180° - 47.265\ldots° = 132.734\ldots°.$$

But C is acute, so it is less than $90°$. Therefore

$$C = 47.265\ldots° = 47.3°\quad\text{(to 1 d.p.).}$$

Solution to Activity 26

Rearranging the sine rule

$$\frac{c}{\sin C} = \frac{b}{\sin B}$$

gives

$$\sin C = \frac{c \sin B}{b} = \frac{8.1 \sin 23.4°}{9.3} = 0.345\ldots .$$

Therefore

$$C = \sin^{-1}(0.345\ldots) = 20.2°$$

or

$$C = 180° - 20.2° = 159.8°,$$

to one decimal place. The obtuse angle $C = 159.8°$ is impossible, because

$$159.8° + 23.4° > 180°.$$

Therefore $C = 20.2°$ to one decimal place.

Solution to Activity 27

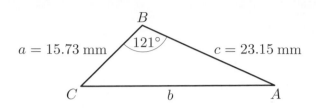

Applying the cosine rule in the form

$$b^2 = c^2 + a^2 - 2ca \cos B$$

gives

$$b = \sqrt{23.15^2 + 15.73^2 - 2 \times 23.15 \times 15.73 \cos 121°}$$
$$= 34.036\ldots .$$

Therefore $b = 34.04$ mm, to two decimal places.

Solution to Activity 28

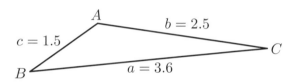

Rearrange the cosine rule $a^2 = b^2 + c^2 - 2bc \cos A$ to give

$$\cos A = \frac{b^2 + c^2 - a^2}{2bc}.$$

So

$$\cos A = \frac{2.5^2 + 1.5^2 - 3.6^2}{2 \times 2.5 \times 1.5}.$$

Therefore

$$A = \cos^{-1}\left(\frac{2.5^2 + 1.5^2 - 3.6^2}{2 \times 2.5 \times 1.5}\right) = 126.4\ldots° = 126°,$$

to the nearest degree.

Solution to Activity 29

By drawing lines from the centre of the pentagon to each of the vertices, divide the pentagon into five triangles.

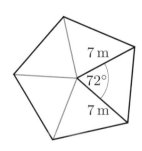

The central angle of each of these triangles is
$$\frac{360°}{5} = 72°.$$
The area of each triangle is
$$\tfrac{1}{2} \times 7 \times 7 \times \sin 72° = \frac{49}{2} \sin 72°,$$
by the formula for the area of a triangle. Then
$$5 \times \frac{49}{2} \sin 72° = 116.504\ldots,$$
so the area of the pentagon is $116.5\,\text{m}^2$ (to 1 d.p.).

Solution to Activity 30

(a) No, there is not a formula for area in terms of only A, B and C. This is because similar triangles, which can vary in area, have the same angles. For instance, the three triangles shown below have the same angles but different areas.

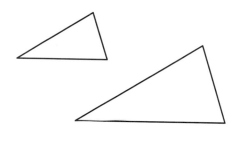

(b) Yes, there is a formula for area in terms of a, b and c. You should expect this, because any two different triangles with side lengths a, b and c are *congruent*, which means that one is a rotated, and possibly flipped over, version of the other. Two congruent triangles (one flipped over) are shown below.

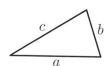 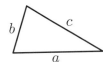

The formula for the area of a triangle in terms of a, b and c is known as *Heron's formula*. It is given by
$$\text{area} = \sqrt{s(s-a)(s-b)(s-c)},$$
where $s = \tfrac{1}{2}(a + b + c)$.

Solution to Activity 31

The gradient of the line is $\tan(2\pi/3) = -\sqrt{3}$. The y-intercept is 3. Therefore the equation of the line is $y = -\sqrt{3}x + 3$.

Solution to Activity 32

Rearrange the identity $\sin^2\theta + \cos^2\theta = 1$ to give
$$\sin^2\theta = 1 - \cos^2\theta.$$
Therefore
$$\sin\theta = \pm\sqrt{1 - \cos^2\theta},$$
and you take the positive square root if $\sin\theta$ is positive, and the negative square root if $\sin\theta$ is negative.

Solution to Activity 33

(a) Since $\sin 0 = 0$, it follows that $\operatorname{cosec} 0$ and $\cot 0$ are not defined, whereas
$$\sec 0 = \frac{1}{\cos 0} = \frac{1}{1} = 1.$$

(b) Since $\cos(\pi/2) = 0$, it follows that $\sec(\pi/2)$ is not defined, whereas
$$\operatorname{cosec} \frac{\pi}{2} = \frac{1}{\sin\dfrac{\pi}{2}} = \frac{1}{1} = 1,$$
and
$$\cot \frac{\pi}{2} = \frac{\cos\dfrac{\pi}{2}}{\sin\dfrac{\pi}{2}} = \frac{0}{1} = 0.$$

(c) In this case
$$\operatorname{cosec} \frac{\pi}{4} = \frac{1}{\sin\dfrac{\pi}{4}} = \frac{1}{1/\sqrt{2}} = \sqrt{2},$$
$$\sec \frac{\pi}{4} = \frac{1}{\cos\dfrac{\pi}{4}} = \frac{1}{1/\sqrt{2}} = \sqrt{2},$$
$$\cot \frac{\pi}{4} = \frac{\cos\dfrac{\pi}{4}}{\sin\dfrac{\pi}{4}} = \frac{1/\sqrt{2}}{1/\sqrt{2}} = 1.$$

Solution to Activity 34

(a) Let $A = \pi/3$ and $B = \pi/4$, so $A + B = 7\pi/12$.

The identity
$$\sin(A + B) = \sin A \cos B + \cos A \sin B$$
gives
$$\sin\left(\frac{7\pi}{12}\right) = \sin\left(\frac{\pi}{3} + \frac{\pi}{4}\right)$$
$$= \sin\frac{\pi}{3}\cos\frac{\pi}{4} + \cos\frac{\pi}{3}\sin\frac{\pi}{4}$$
$$= \frac{\sqrt{3}}{2} \times \frac{\sqrt{2}}{2} + \frac{1}{2} \times \frac{\sqrt{2}}{2}$$
$$= \frac{1}{4}\left(\sqrt{6} + \sqrt{2}\right).$$

(b) Let $A = \pi/3$ and $B = \pi/4$, so $A - B = \pi/12$.

The identity
$$\tan(A - B) = \frac{\tan A - \tan B}{1 + \tan A \tan B}$$
gives
$$\tan\frac{\pi}{12} = \tan\left(\frac{\pi}{3} - \frac{\pi}{4}\right)$$
$$= \frac{\tan\frac{\pi}{3} - \tan\frac{\pi}{4}}{1 + \tan\frac{\pi}{3}\tan\frac{\pi}{4}}$$
$$= \frac{\sqrt{3} - 1}{1 + \sqrt{3}}$$
$$= \frac{\sqrt{3} - 1}{\sqrt{3} + 1} \times \frac{\sqrt{3} - 1}{\sqrt{3} - 1}$$
$$= \frac{4 - 2\sqrt{3}}{2}$$
$$= 2 - \sqrt{3}.$$

Solution to Activity 35

The half-angle identity for cosine is
$$\cos^2\theta = \tfrac{1}{2}\left(1 + \cos(2\theta)\right).$$
So
$$\cos^2\frac{\pi}{8} = \frac{1}{2}\left(1 + \cos\frac{\pi}{4}\right)$$
$$= \frac{1}{2}\left(\frac{\sqrt{2}}{\sqrt{2}} + \frac{1}{\sqrt{2}}\right)$$
$$= \frac{\sqrt{2} + 1}{2\sqrt{2}}$$
$$= \frac{\sqrt{2}(\sqrt{2} + 1)}{2\sqrt{2}\sqrt{2}}$$
$$= \frac{2 + \sqrt{2}}{4}.$$
Because $\pi/8$ is acute, $\cos(\pi/8)$ is positive. Therefore
$$\cos\frac{\pi}{8} = \sqrt{\frac{2 + \sqrt{2}}{4}} = \frac{\sqrt{2 + \sqrt{2}}}{2}.$$

Solution to Activity 36

The double-angle formula for tangent is
$$\tan 2\theta = \frac{2\tan\theta}{1 - \tan^2\theta}.$$
So, with $2\theta = \pi/4$,
$$\tan\frac{\pi}{4} = \frac{2\tan(\pi/8)}{1 - \tan^2(\pi/8)}.$$
Following the hint, put $t = \tan(\pi/8)$. Then, since $\tan(\pi/4) = 1$,
$$1 = \frac{2t}{1 - t^2}$$
$$1 - t^2 = 2t \quad (\text{since } t^2 \neq 1)$$
$$t^2 + 2t - 1 = 0.$$
By the quadratic formula,
$$t = \frac{-2 \pm \sqrt{2^2 - 4 \times 1 \times (-1)}}{2}$$
$$= \frac{-2 \pm \sqrt{8}}{2}$$
$$= -1 \pm \sqrt{2}.$$
Since $t = \tan(\pi/8)$ is positive, the only possibility is
$$\tan\frac{\pi}{8} = \sqrt{2} - 1.$$
(You can check that this answer is the same as the more complicated answer given before the activity, by showing that the squares of both expressions are

equal. Since

$$\left(\sqrt{\frac{2-\sqrt{2}}{2+\sqrt{2}}}\right)^2 = \frac{2-\sqrt{2}}{2+\sqrt{2}}$$

and

$$\left(\sqrt{2}-1\right)^2 = 2 - 2\sqrt{2} + 1 = 3 - 2\sqrt{2},$$

you need to check only that

$$\frac{2-\sqrt{2}}{2+\sqrt{2}} = 3 - 2\sqrt{2}.$$

This equation follows by multiplying both sides by $2 + \sqrt{2}$, since

$$(3 - 2\sqrt{2})(2 + \sqrt{2}) = 6 - \sqrt{2} + 4 = 2 - \sqrt{2}.)$$

Coordinate geometry and vectors

Introduction

In Unit 2 you saw how lines and parabolas can be represented using equations. The use of equations and the coordinates of points to investigate geometric problems is an area of mathematics known as *coordinate geometry*. In the first part of this unit you will study more of this topic.

A fundamental concept in geometry is that of distance. In Section 1, you will learn how to calculate the distance between two points from their coordinates. You will also discover how to find all the points that are the same distance from one specified point as they are from another.

All the points that are the same distance from a *single* point form a circle. Circles are prevalent throughout our environment, and have been studied since ancient times. A circle is sometimes thought of as the most 'perfect' of shapes, since it can be turned through any angle around its centre, or reflected in any line that passes through the centre, and still occupy exactly the same position as the original shape.

In Section 2, you will learn how to find the equations of circles. Section 3 then extends the methods used in Unit 2 for finding the point of intersection of two lines, to obtain methods for finding the points of intersection of lines and other curves, including circles. You will also see how to use a computer to plot circles and some other curves.

All the geometry that you have studied so far in this module has been two-dimensional; that is, it lies within a plane. The world we live in, however, is three-dimensional: objects have length, breadth and depth. Section 4 extends the idea of coordinates to points in a three-dimensional space. You will see how to calculate the distance between two points in three dimensions and how a three-dimensional shape, the sphere, can be represented algebraically. Such representations form the basis of many computer graphics systems.

One way to specify the position of a point, which is often useful in practical situations, is to give both the distance and the direction of the point from a known reference point. For example, in Figure 1 the point B is 2 km north-west of the point A, where north is in the direction indicated.

Circles everywhere!

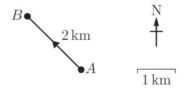

Figure 1 Specifying the position of B relative to A

The distance and direction of a point from a reference point is known as its *displacement*. Quantities such as displacement that have a size *and* a direction are called *vectors*. Vectors have many applications in physics and engineering; for example, specifying the velocity of an object or the force acting on an object requires the use of vectors. You will study vectors in the second part of this unit, starting in Section 5.

1 Distance

This first section is about finding distances in the plane.

1.1 The distance between two points in the plane

In this subsection you will meet a formula for the distance between any two points in the plane, in terms of their coordinates.

Consider any two points in the plane, say $A(x_1, y_1)$ and $B(x_2, y_2)$. To start with, let's look at the case where B lies above and to the right of A, as illustrated in Figure 2. Let C be the point that lies on the same horizontal line as A and the same vertical line as B, as shown in the figure.

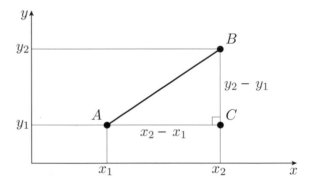

Figure 2 Two points A and B in the plane

The distance between A and B is the length of the hypotenuse of the right-angled triangle with vertices A, B and C. The two shorter sides of this triangle have lengths $x_2 - x_1$ and $y_2 - y_1$, so, by Pythagoras' theorem, the distance between A and B is given by the formula

$$\sqrt{(x_2 - x_1)^2 + (y_2 - y_1)^2}. \tag{1}$$

In fact, this formula for the distance between A and B holds *no matter where* in the plane A and B lie. For example, suppose that B lies above and to the left of A, as illustrated in Figure 3.

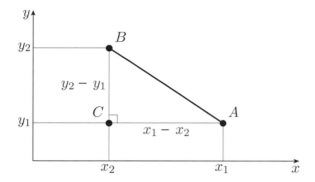

Figure 3 Another pair of points A and B in the plane

In this case, if you consider the point C that lies on the same horizontal line as A and the same vertical line as B, then you obtain a right-angled triangle whose two shorter sides have lengths $x_1 - x_2$ and $y_2 - y_1$. So the distance between A and B is given by

$$\sqrt{(x_1 - x_2)^2 + (y_2 - y_1)^2}.$$

This formula is slightly different from formula (1) (the only difference is that x_1 and x_2 are interchanged), but the two formulas are equivalent. To see this, notice that $x_1 - x_2 = -(x_2 - x_1)$, as you can check by removing the brackets, so $(x_1 - x_2)^2 = (x_2 - x_1)^2$.

You can see that if A and B lie anywhere in the plane, except on the same horizontal or vertical line, then you can form a right-angled triangle whose hypotenuse gives the distance between A and B, and whose two shorter sides have lengths $\pm(x_2 - x_1)$ and $\pm(y_2 - y_1)$. So in all these cases the distance between A and B is given by formula (1).

The formula also holds if A and B lie on the same horizontal or vertical line. For example, if B lies directly to the right of A, as illustrated in Figure 4, then $y_2 - y_1 = 0$, so formula (1) simplifies to $\sqrt{(x_2 - x_1)^2}$. This expression simplifies further to $x_2 - x_1$, since $x_2 - x_1$ is positive, and this is indeed the distance between A and B, as shown in Figure 4.

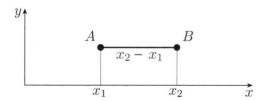

Figure 4 A third pair of points A and B in the plane

In summary, the following result holds in general.

Distance formula

The distance between the points (x_1, y_1) and (x_2, y_2) is
$$\sqrt{(x_2 - x_1)^2 + (y_2 - y_1)^2}.$$

Example 1   *Finding the distance between two points*

Find the distance between the points $(2, 4)$ and $(5, 3)$.

Solution

🔍 Take $(x_1, y_1) = (2, 4)$ and $(x_2, y_2) = (5, 3)$ in the formula above. 💬

The distance is
$$\sqrt{(5 - 2)^2 + (3 - 4)^2} = \sqrt{3^2 + (-1)^2}$$
$$= \sqrt{9 + 1}$$
$$= \sqrt{10}.$$

🔍 Leave the answer as a surd, since a decimal answer was not requested. 💬

Activity 1   *Finding the distance between two points*

Find the distance between the two points in each of the following pairs.

(a) $(3, 2)$ and $(7, 5)$ (b) $(-1, 4)$ and $(3, -2)$

1.2 Midpoints and perpendicular bisectors

In coordinate geometry, it is often useful to consider the collection of all the points that satisfy a particular property. You have already met some examples of this. For example, you have seen that the collection of all points whose y-coordinate is twice their x-coordinate is described by the equation $y = 2x$. The collection of all points that satisfy a particular property is called a **locus** of points. 'Locus' is the Latin word for 'place'.

Sometimes it is useful to consider the locus of points that satisfy a property involving distance. In the next activity you are asked to consider the locus of points that are **equidistant** from (the same distance from) each of two particular points.

Activity 2   *Finding points equidistant from two other points*

Mark two points on a piece of paper. Draw a third point such that its distance from each of the original points is the same. Then mark some more points with this property. Can you describe the geometrical object formed by all the points with this property?

The answer to Activity 2 is that all the points that are equidistant from the two original points form a straight line, which passes through the point halfway along the line segment that joins the two original points, and is perpendicular to this line segment. In the rest of this subsection you'll see one way to find the equation of this line, from the coordinates of the two original points.

The first step is to find the coordinates of the point halfway along the line segment that joins the two original points. This point is called the **midpoint** of the line segment.

Consider the midpoint M of the line segment joining two points $A(x_1, y_1)$ and $B(x_2, y_2)$, as shown in Figure 5. The figure shows B below and to the right of A, but the following argument applies in all cases.

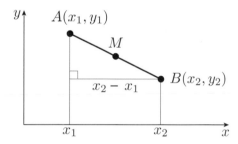

Figure 5   The midpoint M of the line segment AB

You can see from Figure 5 that the x-coordinate of M is equal to the x-coordinate of A plus half of the run from A to B. As you saw in Unit 2, the run from A to B is the value $x_2 - x_1$. It can be positive, negative or zero, depending on whether B lies to the right or left of A, or neither.

So the x-coordinate of M is
$$x_1 + \frac{x_2 - x_1}{2} = \frac{2x_1 + x_2 - x_1}{2} = \frac{x_1 + x_2}{2}.$$
A similar argument applies to the y-coordinate, so we have the following result.

> **Midpoint formula**
>
> The midpoint of the line segment joining the points (x_1, y_1) and (x_2, y_2) is
>
> $$\left(\frac{x_1 + x_2}{2}, \frac{y_1 + y_2}{2} \right).$$

That is, the x-coordinate of the midpoint is the mean of the x-coordinates of the two points, and the y-coordinate of the midpoint is the mean of the y-coordinates of the two points.

Activity 3   *Calculating the coordinates of a midpoint*

Find the midpoint of the line segment joining the points $(3, 4)$ and $(5, -3)$.

Earlier in this subsection you saw that if you choose any two points, then all the points equidistant from these two points form a straight line that passes through the midpoint of the line segment that joins the two points, and is perpendicular to this line segment.

The line that is perpendicular to a line segment and divides it into two equal parts is called its **perpendicular bisector**. (The word 'bisect' means to divide into two equal parts.) For example, Figure 6 shows the perpendicular bisector of a line segment AB.

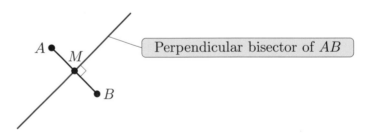

Figure 6   The midpoint M and perpendicular bisector of AB

In Subsection 2.3 of Unit 2, you saw that if two lines are perpendicular and are not parallel to the axes, then the product of their gradients is -1. So if A and B are points that do not lie on the same horizontal or vertical line, then the gradient of the perpendicular bisector of AB is

$$\frac{-1}{\text{gradient of } AB}.$$

You can use this fact to help you find the equation of a perpendicular bisector, as demonstrated in the next example.

Example 2 *Finding a perpendicular bisector*

Find the equation of the perpendicular bisector of the line segment joining the points $(4, 8)$ and $(1, -1)$.

Solution

🔍 Draw a diagram showing the given points, the midpoint and the perpendicular bisector. 💬

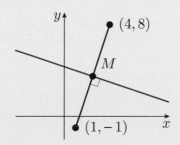

🔍 Find the midpoint of the line segment. 💬

The midpoint, M, has coordinates

$$\left(\frac{4+1}{2}, \frac{8+(-1)}{2}\right) = \left(\frac{5}{2}, \frac{7}{2}\right).$$

🔍 Find the gradient of the perpendicular bisector, by first finding the gradient of the line segment. Remember that the gradient of the line through (x_1, y_1) and (x_2, y_2) is $(y_2 - y_1)/(x_2 - x_1)$. 💬

The gradient of the line segment is $\dfrac{-1 - 8}{1 - 4} = \dfrac{-9}{-3} = 3$.

So the gradient of the perpendicular bisector is $-1/3 = -\frac{1}{3}$.

🔍 Now find the equation of the perpendicular bisector. Use the fact that the line with gradient m passing through the point (x_1, y_1) has equation $y - y_1 = m(x - x_1)$. 💬

Since M has coordinates $(\frac{5}{2}, \frac{7}{2})$, the perpendicular bisector has equation

$$y - \tfrac{7}{2} = -\tfrac{1}{3}\left(x - \tfrac{5}{2}\right).$$

Simplifying gives

$$y - \tfrac{7}{2} = -\tfrac{1}{3}x + \tfrac{5}{6}$$
$$y = -\tfrac{1}{3}x + \tfrac{13}{3}.$$

So the equation of the perpendicular bisector is $y = -\frac{1}{3}x + \frac{13}{3}$.

Here is an example for you to try.

Activity 4 *Finding a perpendicular bisector*

Find the equation of the perpendicular bisector of the line segment joining $(-3, 1)$ and $(1, -1)$.

There are often alternative ways to solve problems in coordinate geometry. For example, you can find the perpendicular bisector of the line segment joining two points, (a, b) and (c, d) say, as follows. The points (x, y) on this bisector are exactly those that are equidistant from (a, b) and (c, d); that is, those satisfying the equation $\sqrt{(x-a)^2 + (y-b)^2} = \sqrt{(x-c)^2 + (y-d)^2}$. So this is the equation of the perpendicular bisector. You can simplify it to obtain the equation of a line in the usual form.

You will use perpendicular bisectors to help you find the equations of circles in Subsection 2.2.

2 Circles

A **circle** can be defined as the locus of points that are at a particular distance from a specified point. The specified point is the **centre** of the circle, and the distance is its **radius**.

This definition of a circle corresponds to the usual way of drawing one, by using a pair of compasses, or by fixing one end of a taut piece of string and marking the curve swept out by the other end.

Figure 7 A circle

2.1 The equation of a circle

Just as lines and parabolas in the plane can be represented by equations, so can circles. For example, consider the circle with centre $C(4, 3)$ and radius 2 which is shown in Figure 8.

Marking out a circle in sand

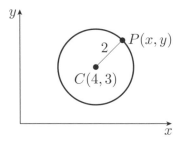

Figure 8 The circle with centre $(4, 3)$ and radius 2

Suppose that $P(x, y)$ is any point on this circle. The distance between the centre and P is equal to the radius, so, by the distance formula,

$$\sqrt{(x-4)^2 + (y-3)^2} = 2.$$

Squaring both sides of this equation, to remove the square root, gives the equivalent equation

$$(x-4)^2 + (y-3)^2 = 4.$$

Since this equation is satisfied by every point (x, y) on the circle, and only by these points, it is the equation of the circle.

In general, consider the circle with centre (a, b) and radius r, as illustrated in Figure 9.

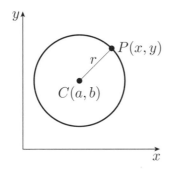

Figure 9   The circle with centre (a, b) and radius r

By the distance formula, every point (x, y) on the circle satisfies the equation

$$\sqrt{(x-a)^2 + (y-b)^2} = r.$$

Squaring this equation to remove the square root gives the **standard form of the equation of a circle** stated below. You will see other forms of this equation later.

> **Standard form of the equation of a circle**
>
> The circle with centre (a, b) and radius r has equation
>
> $$(x-a)^2 + (y-b)^2 = r^2.$$

Example 3   *Finding the equation of a circle*

Find the equation of the circle with centre $(2, -1)$ and radius 3.

Solution

Use the fact in the box above, with $(a, b) = (2, -1)$ and $r = 3$.

The equation is
$$(x - 2)^2 + (y - (-1))^2 = 3^2;$$
that is,
$$(x - 2)^2 + (y + 1)^2 = 9.$$

Activity 5   *Writing down equations of circles*

Write down the equations of the circles with the following centres and radii.

(a) Centre $(0, 0)$, radius 3   (b) Centre $(5, 7)$, radius $\sqrt{2}$

(c) Centre $(-3, -1)$, radius $\frac{1}{2}$ (d) Centre $(3, -\sqrt{3})$, radius $\dfrac{2}{\sqrt{5}}$

If you have the equation of a circle in standard form, then you can write down the centre and radius of the circle immediately.

Example 4   *Finding the centre and radius of a circle*

Find the centre and radius of the circle with equation
$$(x + 3)^2 + (y - 2)^2 = 16.$$

Solution

Comparing this particular equation with the general equation $(x - a)^2 + (y - b)^2 = r^2$ gives $a = -3$, $b = 2$ and $r^2 = 16$. Remember that r is *positive*, since it is a length.

The circle has centre $(-3, 2)$ and radius $\sqrt{16} = 4$.

Here are some examples for you to try.

Activity 6   *Finding centres and radii of circles*

Write down the centre and radius of the circle represented by each of the following equations.

(a) $(x-1)^2 + (y-2)^2 = 25$ (b) $(x+1)^2 + (y+2)^2 = 49$

(c) $(x-\pi)^2 + (y+\pi)^2 = \pi^2$ (d) $4x^2 + 4(y - \sqrt{3})^2 = 7$

You saw in Units 1 and 2 that the values that satisfy an equation do not change when the equation is rearranged into an equivalent form. So the points that satisfy the equation of a circle do not change when the equation is rearranged; that is, the circle represented does not change.

For example, consider the equation of the circle with centre $(4, 3)$ and radius 2, which is

$$(x-4)^2 + (y-3)^2 = 4.$$

Expanding the brackets gives

$$x^2 - 8x + 16 + y^2 - 6y + 9 = 4,$$

and simplifying gives

$$x^2 + y^2 - 8x - 6y + 21 = 0.$$

So this is an alternative form of the equation of the circle with centre $(4, 3)$ and radius 2.

If you have the equation of a circle written in an alternative form like this, then you can find the centre and radius of the circle by rearranging the equation into the standard form $(x-a)^2 + (y-b)^2 = r^2$. This allows you to read off the centre and radius in the usual way. To manipulate the equation into standard form, you can use the technique of completing the square, which you revised in Subsection 4.4 of Unit 2. The process is illustrated in the following example.

Example 5   *Finding the centre and radius of a circle whose equation is not in standard form*

Show that the equation

$$x^2 + y^2 + 4x - 12y - 9 = 0$$

represents a circle, and find its centre and radius.

Solution

🔍 Aim to express the equation in standard form. First concentrate on the subexpression formed by the terms in x^2 and x, and complete the square in this subexpression. 💬

The equation can be rearranged as

$$x^2 + 4x + y^2 - 12y - 9 = 0.$$

Completing the square gives

$$\boxed{x^2 + 4x} + y^2 - 12y - 9 = 0$$

$$\boxed{(x + 2)^2 - 4} + y^2 - 12y - 9 = 0$$

Then do the same for the subexpression formed by the terms in y^2 and y.

$$(x + 2)^2 - 4 + \boxed{y^2 - 12y} - 9 = 0$$

$$(x + 2)^2 - 4 + \boxed{(y - 6)^2 - 36} - 9 = 0$$

Gather the constants on the right, and combine them.

$$(x + 2)^2 + (y - 6)^2 = 49.$$

This is the equation of a circle in standard form, so the original equation represents a circle.

The centre is $(-2, 6)$ and the radius is $\sqrt{49} = 7$.

Activity 7 *Finding centres and radii of circles whose equations are not in standard form*

Show that each of the following equations represents a circle, and find the centre and radius in each case.

(a) $x^2 + y^2 - 6x + 8y = 0$ (b) $4x^2 + 4y^2 - 16x + 4y = 3$

You have seen that the equation of any circle can be written as an equation with terms in x^2, y^2, x and y and a constant term. However, not every equation of this form is the equation of a circle, because not every equation of this form can be rearranged into the form

$$(x - a)^2 + (y - b)^2 = r^2, \tag{2}$$

for some constants a, b and r.

First, any equation with terms as described above in which x^2 and y^2 have *different* coefficients is not the equation of a circle. This is because when you multiply out an equation of form (2), you always obtain an equation in which the coefficients of x^2 and y^2 are both 1, so if you multiply the equation through by a constant, then x^2 and y^2 always have the *same* coefficient. For example, the equation $3x^2 + 2y^2 + 4x + 4y - 5 = 0$ is not the equation of a circle.

Even if the coefficients of x^2 and y^2 are the same in an equation with terms as described above, it does not guarantee that the equation represents a circle. For example, consider the equation $x^2 + y^2 - 4x + 2y + 9 = 0$. Rearranging this equation by completing the squares gives $(x-2)^2 + (y+1)^2 = -4$. No point (x, y) satisfies this equation, because the square of every real number is non-negative. So this equation does not represent any curve. Similarly, the equation $(x-5)^2 + (y-3)^2 = 0$ is satisfied only by the single point $(5, 3)$ and hence is not the equation of a circle, since a single point is not usually regarded as a circle.

Some equations with terms in x^2, y^2, x and y and a constant term represent curves other than circles. For example, the equation $x^2 + 2y^2 = 4$ represents an *ellipse*, and the equation $x^2 - 2y^2 = 4$ represents a *hyperbola*. These curves are shown in Figure 10. You can learn more about ellipses and hyperbolas in the module *Essential mathematics 2* (MST125).

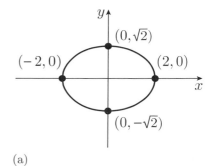

(a)

Activity 8　*Identifying the equations of circles*

Which of the following equations represent a circle? For each equation that represents a circle, find the centre and radius.

(a) $(x-2)^2 - (y+3)^2 = 4$　　(b) $(x+1)^2 + (y-2)^2 + 9 = 0$

(c) $(x+1)^2 + (y-3)^2 - 5 = 0$　　(d) $2x^2 + 2y^2 - 20x + 16y + 90 = 0$

(e) $x^2 + y^2 - 10x - 2y + 20 = 0$　　(f) $2x^2 + 3y^2 - 5x + 4y - 8 = 0$

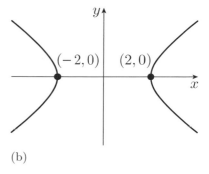

(b)

Figure 10　(a) The ellipse $x^2 + 2y^2 = 4$ (b) the hyperbola $x^2 - 2y^2 = 4$

Finding points that lie on a given circle is not as straightforward as finding points that lie on a line or a parabola, as you did in Unit 2, since the equation of a circle does not express either variable x or y as a function of the other variable.

However, you can substitute any particular value of x into the equation of a circle, and solve the resulting equation to find the corresponding values of y. The equation that you have to solve is quadratic, so you obtain two, one or no values of y, and each of these values gives a point on the circle. Similarly, you can substitute any particular value of y into the equation of a circle to find two, one or no corresponding values of x, and each of these values gives a point on the circle. Here's an example.

Example 6   *Finding points on a circle*

Find the points (if there are any) on the circle
$x^2 + y^2 - 2x - 6y + 8 = 0$ with each of the following x-coordinates.

(a) 0   (b) 4

Solution

🔍 In each case, substitute the value of x into the equation of the circle, and solve for y. 💬

(a) Putting $x = 0$ gives

$$y^2 - 6y + 8 = 0$$
$$(y - 4)(y - 2) = 0.$$

So $y = 4$ or $y = 2$.

The points with x-coordinate 0 on the circle are $(0, 2)$ and $(0, 4)$.

(b) Putting $x = 4$ gives

$$4^2 - 2 \times 4 + y^2 - 6y + 8 = 0$$
$$y^2 - 6y + 16 = 0.$$

🔍 Remember that the quadratic equation $ax^2 + bx + c = 0$ has no solutions if its discriminant $b^2 - 4ac$ is negative. 💬

The discriminant of this equation is $6^2 - 4 \times 1 \times 16 = -28$.

Hence the equation has no solutions, so there are no points on the circle with x-coordinate 4.

Note that we often shorten a phrase such as 'the circle with equation $x^2 + y^2 - 2x - 6y + 8 = 0$' to just 'the circle $x^2 + y^2 - 2x - 6y + 8 = 0$', as in Example 6.

You have seen that when you substitute a particular value of x into the equation of a circle and solve for y, you obtain two, one or no solutions. If there are two solutions, then one of them gives a point on the top half of the circle, and the other gives a point on the bottom half. If there is only one solution, then it gives the point at the extreme left or right of the circle. If there are no solutions, then there is no point on the circle with that value of x.

These three cases are illustrated in Figure 11(a). Similar cases occur when you substitute a particular value of y into the equation of a circle and solve for x, as illustrated in Figure 11(b).

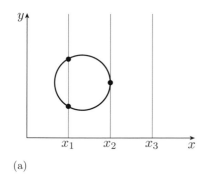
(a)

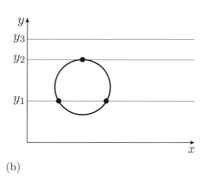
(b)

Figure 11   (a) There are two points on the circle corresponding to
$x = x_1$, one point corresponding to $x = x_2$ and no points corresponding to
$x = x_3$ (b) similar cases for three values of y

Activity 9   *Finding points on a circle*

(a) Find all points with y-coordinate 3 on the circle
$(x - 1)^2 + (y - 5)^2 = 9$.

(b) Find all points with x-coordinate 4 on the same circle.

The equation of a circle, such as

$$(x - 1)^2 + (y - 5)^2 = 9, \tag{3}$$

is said to be in **implicit form**, because it doesn't express either of the two
variables x and y explicitly in terms of the other variable.

By contrast, an equation such as

$$y - 3x^2 + 2,$$

which expresses the variable y explicitly as a function of the other
variable x, is said to be in **explicit form**. Some equations in the variables
x and y can be written in either implicit or explicit form. For example, the
equation $3y + 2x = 5$, which is in implicit form, can be rewritten in explicit
form as $y = \frac{1}{3}(5 - 2x)$.

The equation of a circle, however, can't be written in explicit form.
Although it's possible to rearrange the equation of a circle to obtain the
variable y by itself on the left-hand side, you can't rearrange it to express y
as a *function* of x. For example, you can rearrange equation (3) as follows:

$$(x - 1)^2 + (y - 5)^2 = 9$$
$$(y - 5)^2 = 9 - (x - 1)^2$$
$$y - 5 = \pm\sqrt{9 - (x - 1)^2}$$
$$y = 5 \pm \sqrt{9 - (x - 1)^2}.$$

This equation doesn't express y as a function of x, because each value of x
gives *two* values of y, due to the the $\pm$ sign.

2.2 The circle through three points

In Unit 2, you saw that if you choose any two points, then there is exactly one straight line that passes through both of them. This is not true of circles: there are many circles that pass through two chosen points, as illustrated in Figure 12.

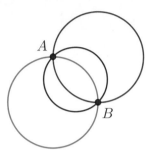

Figure 12   Circles passing through the points A and B

However, if you choose a third point, then as long as the three points do not all lie on the same straight line, there is only one circle that passes through all three points. If the three points *do* all lie on a straight line, then there is no circle that passes through them all. In this subsection you will see how to find the equation of the circle that passes through three chosen points.

Consider three points A, B and C, as illustrated in Figure 13. To find the equation of the circle passing through them, all you need to do is find the coordinates of the centre, labelled D in Figure 13. This is because once you know the coordinates of the centre, it is straightforward to calculate the radius, since it is the distance between the centre and any one of the points A, B and C. So how can you find the coordinates of the centre?

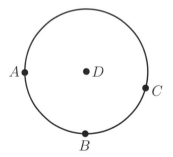

Figure 13   Three points A, B and C determine a circle

The centre of the circle is equidistant from A, B and C. In particular, it is equidistant from A and B, so it lies on the perpendicular bisector of AB. Similarly, it is equidistant from B and C, so it also lies on the perpendicular bisector of BC. It is the point at which the two perpendicular bisectors intersect. This is illustrated in Figure 14.

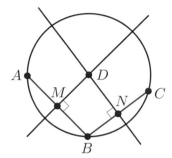

Figure 14 The centre of the circle is the point of intersection of the perpendicular bisectors of AB and BC

So you can use the following strategy to find the equation of the circle passing through three specified points.

> **Strategy:**
> **To find the equation of the circle passing through three points**
>
> 1. Find the equation of the perpendicular bisector of the line segment that joins any pair of the three points.
> 2. Find the equation of the perpendicular bisector of the line segment that joins a different pair of the three points.
> 3. Find the point of intersection of these two lines. This is the centre of the circle.
> 4. Find the radius of the circle, which is the distance from the centre to any of the three points.
>
> Hence write down the equation of the circle.

The strategy is illustrated in Example 7 below.

Example 7 *Finding the circle through three points*

Find the centre and radius of the circle that passes through the points $(4, 8)$, $(1, -1)$ and $(-3, 1)$. Hence write down the equation of the circle.

Solution

Let the points be $A(4,8)$, $B(1,-1)$ and $C(-3,1)$.

First sketch a diagram, showing the given points and the perpendicular bisectors.

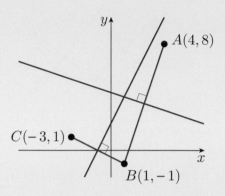

Find the perpendicular bisectors of the line segments joining two pairs of points. The perpendicular bisector of AB was found in Example 2 on page 109, and you were asked to find the perpendicular bisector of BC in Activity 4 on page 110.

The perpendicular bisector of AB is $y = -\frac{1}{3}x + \frac{13}{3}$.

The perpendicular bisector of BC is $y = 2x + 2$.

The centre of the circle lies on both these lines. To find it, solve the equations simultaneously, as explained in Subsection 3.1 of Unit 2.

The two expressions for y give
$$-\tfrac{1}{3}x + \tfrac{13}{3} = 2x + 2.$$
Simplifying gives
$$\tfrac{7}{3} = \tfrac{7}{3}x,$$
so $x = 1$. Substituting into $y = 2x + 2$ gives $y = 2 \times 1 + 2 = 4$.

The centre of the circle is $(1,4)$.

The radius is the distance between the centre and any one of the given points.

The radius is the distance between the centre and $(4,8)$, which is
$$\sqrt{(4-1)^2 + (8-4)^2} = \sqrt{3^2 + 4^2} = \sqrt{25} = 5.$$

Finally, write down the equation of the circle.

The equation of the circle is $(x-1)^2 + (y-4)^2 = 25$.

You can check the answer to Example 7 by confirming that each of the points A, B and C satisfies the equation found. Figure 15 shows the circle whose equation was found in Example 7.

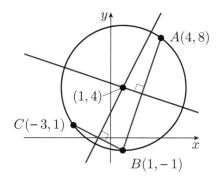

Figure 15   The circle in Example 7

Activity 10   *Finding the circle through three points*

Find the equation of the circle that passes through the points $(0,0)$, $(-4,2)$ and $(8,6)$.

Activity 11   *Finding the diameter of a plate from a fragment*

An archaeologist has uncovered a fragment of an ancient plate that she believes was circular. To help her find the diameter of the plate, she places a 1 cm grid over the fragment, as shown below.

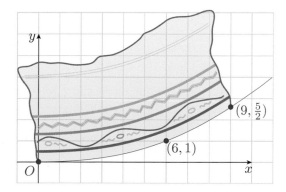

The outer edge of the fragment passes through the points $(0,0)$, $(6,1)$ and $(9, \frac{5}{2})$. Use this information to find the diameter of the plate.

3 Points of intersection

From Unit 2, you know that a point where two lines intersect can be found by solving the equations of the lines simultaneously. You can use a similar approach to find points where a line and a curve, such as a circle, intersect.

3.1 Points of intersection of a line and a curve

A line and a circle can have two, one or no points of intersection, as illustrated in Figure 16.

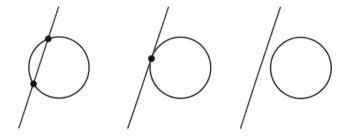

Figure 16   A line can intersect a circle twice, once or not at all

To find the points of intersection, you need to solve the equation of the line and the equation of the circle simultaneously. This leads to a *quadratic* equation, and the three cases that arise in solving such an equation (two solutions, one solution or no solutions) correspond to the three possibilities shown in Figure 16. The method is demonstrated in Example 8 below.

Example 8   *Finding the points of intersection of a line and a circle*

Find any points at which the line $y = 2x - 4$ intersects the circle $(x + 7)^2 + (y - 2)^2 = 80$.

Solution

🗨 The equation of the line gives y in terms of x, so use it to substitute for y in the equation of the circle. 🗩

Substituting $y = 2x - 4$ into the equation of the circle gives

$$(x + 7)^2 + (2x - 4 - 2)^2 = 80$$

🔍 Simplify. 💬

$$(x + 7)^2 + (2x - 6)^2 = 80$$
$$x^2 + 14x + 49 + 4x^2 - 24x + 36 = 80$$
$$5x^2 - 10x + 5 = 0$$
$$x^2 - 2x + 1 = 0.$$

🔍 Solve this quadratic equation. 💬

Factorising gives

$$(x - 1)^2 = 0$$
$$x - 1 = 0,$$

so the only solution is $x = 1$.

🔍 Find the corresponding value of y from the equation of the line. 💬

Substituting in $y = 2x - 4$ gives $y = 2 \times 1 - 4 = -2$.

There is only one point of intersection, namely $(1, -2)$.

🔍 As a check, you can confirm that the point $(1, -2)$ satisfies the equations of the line and the circle. 💬

Figure 17 shows the point of intersection of the line and the circle in Example 8.

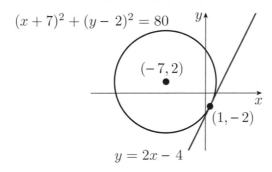

Figure 17 The line and circle in Example 8

Activity 12   *Finding the points of intersection of a line and a circle*

For each of the following lines, either find the point or points at which the line intersects the circle $(x+7)^2 + (y-2)^2 = 80$, or show that the line does not intersect the circle.

(a) $y = 2x$ (b) $y = 2x - 6$

You can use similar methods to find the points of intersection of a line and a parabola. (You studied parabolas in Unit 2.) As in the case of a line and a circle, a line and a parabola may intersect twice, once, or not at all, as illustrated in Figure 18.

Figure 18   A line can intersect a parabola twice, once or not at all

---

Activity 13   *Finding the points of intersection of a line and a parabola*

Find the points (if there are any) at which the line $y = x + 11$ intersects the parabola $y = -x^2 - 2x + 15$.

Supply and demand

In most economic models, the price of goods is assumed to be determined by the laws of supply and demand.

The *law of demand* states that the lower the selling price of the goods, the more consumers want to buy.

The *law of supply* states that the lower the selling price of the goods, the less producers want to produce.

The law of supply holds because when the price of a product is low, producers can make more profit by using the same materials and labour to produce different, higher-value products.

The selling price at which the supply of a particular item from producers is equal to the demand from consumers is called the **equilibrium price** for the item. Above this price, consumers buy less than sellers want to produce, so the price falls. Below this price consumers want to buy more than sellers produce, so the price rises.

Activity 14 *Working with supply and demand*

A commodity trader wishes to forecast the market price of wheat for the following year. Market research indicates that the relationship between the market demand and selling price for wheat can be modelled by the equation

$$p = 500 - 30q,$$

where q is the amount of wheat expected to be bought (in millions of tonnes), and p is the price of wheat (in £ per tonne).

The trader believes that the relationship between the market supply and selling price of wheat can be modelled by the equation

$$p = \frac{q^2}{2} + \frac{q}{2},$$

where q is the amount of wheat expected to be produced (in millions of tonnes) and p is the price of wheat (in £ per tonne).

Find the equilibrium price of wheat (to the nearest pound) and the quantity expected to be produced (to the nearest million tonnes) in the following year.

The price of wheat is often used to illustrate economic laws

3.2 Points of intersection of two circles

Sometimes it's useful to find the points where two curves, such as two circles, intersect.

Two circles may intersect at two points, one point or not at all, as illustrated in Figure 19.

  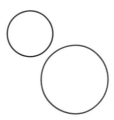

Figure 19 Two circles can intersect twice, once or not at all

To find the points of intersection of two circles, you need to solve their equations simultaneously. It's not straightforward to use one equation to find an expression for x or y to substitute into the other equation, because both equations have terms in x^2 and y^2. The next example illustrates a convenient method, based on first eliminating the terms in x^2 and y^2 by subtracting one equation from the other (or a multiple of one equation from a multiple of the other). This is always possible for the equations of two circles, because in the equation of a circle, x^2 and y^2 always have the same coefficient.

Example 9   *Finding the points of intersection of two circles*

Find the points of intersection (if there are any) of the circles with equations

$$(x - 3)^2 + (y + 4)^2 = 53 \quad \text{and} \quad (x + 2)^2 + (y - 1)^2 = 13.$$

Solution

🔍 First multiply out the brackets in each equation and simplify it. 💬

The equations can be written as

$$x^2 - 6x + 9 + y^2 + 8y + 16 = 53$$
$$x^2 + 4x + 4 + y^2 - 2y + 1 = 13;$$

that is,

$$x^2 + y^2 - 6x + 8y - 28 = 0 \tag{4}$$
$$x^2 + y^2 + 4x - 2y - 8 = 0. \tag{5}$$

🔍 Eliminate the terms in x^2 and y^2, by subtracting one equation from the other. 💬

Subtracting equation (5) from equation (4) gives

$$-10x + 10y - 20 = 0;$$

that is,

$$y = x + 2.$$

🔍 This tells you that if the point (x, y) satisfies both equation (4) and equation (5), then it also satisfies the equation $y = x + 2$. 💬

Using this equation to substitute for y in equation (4) gives

$$x^2 + (x + 2)^2 - 6x + 8(x + 2) - 28 = 0$$
$$2x^2 + 6x - 8 = 0$$
$$x^2 + 3x - 4 = 0.$$

🔍 Solve this quadratic equation. 💬

Factorising gives

$$(x + 4)(x - 1) = 0,$$

so the solutions are $x = -4$ and $x = 1$.

🔍 Use the equation $y = x + 2$ to find the corresponding values of y. 🗨

The corresponding values of y are

$$y = -4 + 2 = -2 \quad \text{and} \quad y = 1 + 2 = 3.$$

So the points of intersection of the two circles are $(-4, -2)$ and $(1, 3)$.

🔍 You can check that both points satisfy both original equations. 🗨

The linear equation $y = x + 2$ that appears in the solution to Example 9 is the equation of the line that passes through the two points of intersection $(-4, -2)$ and $(1, 3)$.

Activity 15   *Finding the points of intersection of two circles*

Find the points of intersection (if there are any) of the circles with equations

$$(x + 1)^2 + (y - 2)^2 = 9 \quad \text{and} \quad (x - 4)^2 + (y + 3)^2 = 36.$$

3.3   Using the computer for coordinate geometry

In this subsection you will use a computer to plot circles and calculate points of intersection.

Activity 16   *Plotting circles using a computer*

Work through Section 7 of the *Computer algebra guide*.

Activity 17   *Using a computer to calculate points of intersection*

(a) Use a computer to plot the parabola $y = 2x^2 - 10x + 14$ and the circle $x^2 - 6x + y^2 - 8y + 22 = 0$ on the same graph.

(b) By using the computer to solve the equations of the two curves in part (a) simultaneously (you saw how to do this in your study of Section 3 of the *Computer algebra guide*), calculate the coordinates of the points at which the two curves intersect, to two decimal places.

(c) What do you think is the maximum number of times that a parabola can intersect a circle?

4 Working in three dimensions

All the graphs and geometric diagrams that you have seen in this module up till now have been two-dimensional. As you know, the position of a point in two dimensions can be specified by using two coordinates, usually written as (x, y). However the real world is three-dimensional. In this section you will see how to specify the positions of points in three-dimensional space.

4.1 Three-dimensional coordinates

To allow us to specify the positions of points in three-dimensional space, we extend the usual two-dimensional Cartesian coordinate system, by introducing a third axis, the *z-axis*, at right angles to the x- and y-axes. This is illustrated in Figure 20, which shows two different views of the same system of axes. Different views of the axes can be useful because some diagrams are clearer in one view than in another. Of course, it is impossible to include a truly three-dimensional diagram within this page of text: the figure is actually a two-dimensional impression of a three-dimensional image! Although two-dimensional coordinate systems are usually drawn with the positive direction of the y-axis pointing up, three-dimensional systems are usually drawn with the positive direction of the z-axis pointing up.

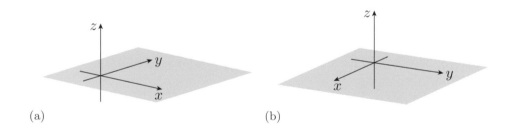

(a)   (b)

Figure 20   Two views of the same three-dimensional Cartesian coordinate system, with the x, y-plane shaded

In Figure 20 the plane that contains the x- and y-axes has been shaded. This plane is known as the x, y-plane. Similarly, the plane that contains the x- and z-axes is the x, z-plane, and the plane that contains the y- and z-axes is the y, z-plane. These three planes are known as the **coordinate planes**. The positive direction of the z-axis is called the **positive z-direction**, and similar terminology is used for the x- and y-axes.

There are in fact two different ways to introduce a z-axis perpendicular to both the x- and y-axes. The alternative way is for the positive direction of the z-axis to point down instead of up, as shown in Figure 21(a). If this system is rotated so that the z-axis points up, as shown in Figure 21(b), then the positions of the x- and y-axes are interchanged compared to those in Figure 20.

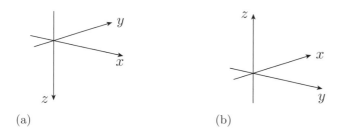

(a)   (b)

Figure 21   Two views of the alternative three-dimensional Cartesian coordinate system

The two different versions of a three-dimensional coordinate system are known as the **right-handed coordinate system** (Figure 20) and the **left-handed coordinate system** (Figure 21). One way of remembering which is which is to use the **right-hand rule**, which is illustrated in Figure 22.

You hold your right hand with the middle finger, first finger and thumb placed (roughly) perpendicular to each other, and the other two fingers closed. If your thumb and first finger point in the positive x- and y-directions, respectively, then your middle finger points in the positive z-direction of a right-handed coordinate system.

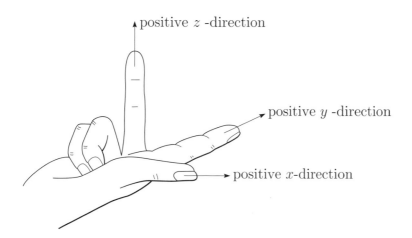

Figure 22   The right-hand rule

If you do the same with your left hand, then your middle finger points in the positive z-direction of a left-handed coordinate system.

Another way to remember which system is which is to use the **right-hand grip rule**, which is illustrated in Figure 23. If you hold your right hand in a fist, so that your fingers rotate from the positive part of the x-axis towards the positive part of the y-axis, then your thumb points in the positive z-direction of a right-handed coordinate system. Similarly, if you use your left hand, then your thumb points in the positive z-direction of a left-handed coordinate system.

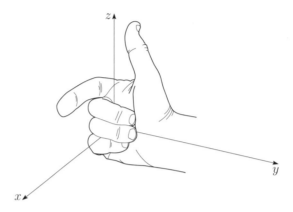

Figure 23   The right-hand grip rule

The right-handed coordinate system is usually used in preference to the left-handed one. In the rest of this module, wherever we use a three-dimensional coordinate system, we will assume that it is right-handed. Some mathematical formulas change slightly if a left-handed coordinate system is used, though none of the formulas in this module are affected by this.

The position of a point in three dimensions can be specified by three coordinates x, y and z, which are usually written as the triple (x, y, z). The first two numbers in the triple are the coordinates of the point in the x, y-plane that lies directly below or above the original point. The third number specifies how far above or below the x, y-plane the original point lies. For example, the point with coordinates $(3, 4, 2)$ is illustrated in Figure 24.

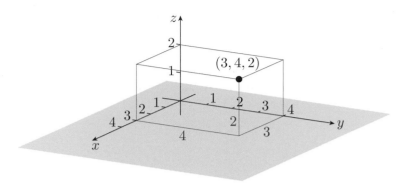

Figure 24   The point $(3, 4, 2)$; the x, y-plane is shaded

Activity 18   *Using three-dimensional coordinates*

The figure below shows a cuboid whose faces are parallel to the coordinate planes. Its bottom face lies in the x, y-plane, and its top face is 4 units above the x, y-plane.

What are the coordinates of the corners of the cuboid labelled A, B, C and D?

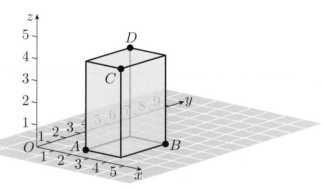

4.2   The distance between two points in three dimensions

In this subsection you will meet a formula for the distance between any two points in three-dimensional space, in terms of their coordinates. It's similar to the formula that you met earlier for the distance between any two points in two dimensions.

Consider two points, $A(x_1, y_1, z_1)$ and $B(x_2, y_2, z_2)$. For simplicity, let's consider the case in which $x_2 > x_1$, $y_2 > y_1$ and $z_2 > z_1$, as illustrated in Figure 25.

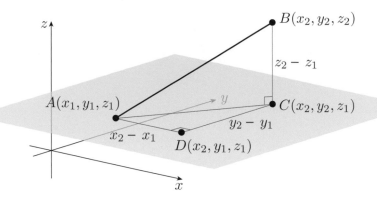

Figure 25   Two points in three dimensions

In the figure, the horizontal plane that contains the point A has been shaded. Let C be the point in this plane that lies directly below B, and let D be the point in the shaded plane such that AD is parallel to the x-axis and CD is parallel to the y-axis, as shown.

The distance AB is the length of the hypotenuse of the right-angled triangle with vertices A, B and C. So, by Pythagoras' theorem,

$$AB^2 = AC^2 + BC^2. \tag{6}$$

However the length AC that appears in this equation is itself the length of the hypotenuse of the right-angled triangle with vertices A, C and D. So, again by Pythagoras' theorem,

$$AC^2 = AD^2 + DC^2.$$

Using this equation to substitute for AC^2 in equation (6) gives

$$AB^2 = AD^2 + DC^2 + BC^2.$$

Since $AD = x_2 - x_1$, $DC = y_2 - y_1$ and $BC = z_2 - z_1$, this equation is

$$AB^2 = (x_2 - x_1)^2 + (y_2 - y_1)^2 + (z_2 - z_1)^2.$$

In fact this equation holds *no matter where* the points A and B lie, for similar reasons to those that you saw for the distance formula in two dimensions. So we have the following result.

> **Distance formula (three dimensions)**
>
> The distance between two points (x_1, y_1, z_1) and (x_2, y_2, z_2) is
>
> $$\sqrt{(x_2 - x_1)^2 + (y_2 - y_1)^2 + (z_2 - z_1)^2}.$$

Activity 19   *Finding distances between points in three dimensions*

Find the distance between the two points in each of the following pairs.

(a) $(1, 3, 5)$ and $(4, 1, 7)$ (b) $(-1, 2, 5)$ and $(4, -1, 3)$

4.3 The equation of a sphere

In Section 2 you saw that a circle is the locus of points in the plane that are equidistant from a particular point. In three dimensions, the locus of points equidistant from a particular point is a sphere. The particular point is the centre of the sphere, and the distance from the centre to each point on the sphere is the radius of the sphere.

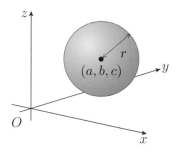

Figure 26   A sphere with centre (a, b, c) and radius r

If a sphere has centre (a, b, c), and (x, y, z) is any point on the sphere, then the distance between these two points is equal to the radius of the sphere. That is,

$$\sqrt{(x - a)^2 + (y - b)^2 + (z - c)^2} = r.$$

Squaring both sides of this equation gives the following fact.

The standard form of the equation of a sphere

The sphere with centre (a, b, c) and radius r has equation

$$(x - a)^2 + (y - b)^2 + (z - c)^2 = r^2.$$

Activity 20   *Writing down the equations of spheres*

Write down the standard form of the equation of each of the spheres below.

(a) The sphere with centre $(3, 5, 2)$ and radius 2

(b) The sphere with centre $(2, -1, -3)$ and radius $\sqrt{3}$

Activity 21   *Finding the centres and radii of spheres*

Write down the centre and radius of the sphere specified by each of the following equations.

(a) $(x-2)^2 + (y-3)^2 + (z-5)^2 = 16$

(b) $(x+2)^2 + (y-4)^2 + (z+1)^2 = 7$

As with the equations of circles, the equations of spheres can be written in forms other than the standard form. For example, multiplying out the equation

$$(x+1)^2 + (y-3)^2 + (z-2)^2 = 2$$

gives

$$x^2 + 2x + 1 + y^2 - 6y + 9 + z^2 - 4z + 4 = 2,$$

which simplifies to

$$x^2 + y^2 + z^2 + 2x - 6y - 4z + 12 = 0.$$

Each of the three equations above represents the same sphere.

If you have any equation for a sphere, then you can find its centre and radius by rearranging the equation into the standard form $(x-a)^2 + (y-b)^2 + (z-c)^2 = r^2$. To do this, you use the same procedure as you used to rearrange the equations of circles into standard form, except that as well as completing the square in the subexpression formed by the terms in x^2 and x, and in the subexpression formed by the terms in y^2 and y, you have to complete the square in the subexpression formed by the terms in z^2 and z.

Not every equation with terms in x^2, y^2, z^2, x, y, z and a constant term represents a sphere, because not every equation of this type can be rearranged into the form $(x-a)^2 + (y-b)^2 + (z-c)^2 = r^2$. For example, if the coefficients of x^2, y^2 and z^2 are not all the same, then the equation does not represent a sphere. Similarly, the equation $x^2 + y^2 + z^2 = -1$ does not represent a sphere, because no point (x, y, x) satisfies this equation.

Activity 22   *Identifying equations of spheres*

Which of the following equations represent a sphere? For each equation that represents a sphere, find the centre and radius of the sphere.

(a) $x^2 + y^2 + z^2 - 8x - 4y + 10z = -42$

(b) $x^2 - y^2 + 2z^2 + 2x + 4y - 4z - 2 = 0$

(c) $2x^2 + 2y^2 + 2z^2 + 4x - 12z + 12 = 0$

(d) $2x^2 + 2y^2 + 2z^2 + 8x - 4y + 13 = 0$

Non-spherical objects that are represented by equations with terms in x^2, y^2, z^2, x, y, z and a constant term include *ellipsoids* and *hyperboloids*, as illustrated in Figure 27.

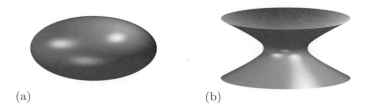

(a)   (b)

Figure 27   (a) The ellipsoid $x^2 + 2y^2 + 4z^2 = 1$ (b) the hyperboloid $x^2 + y^2 - 4z^2 = 1$

5 Vectors

This section marks the start of the second part of this unit, in which you'll learn about a type of mathematical object called a *vector*. Vectors play an important role in the study and analysis of phenomena in physics and engineering.

5.1 What is a vector?

Some mathematical quantities can't be specified just by stating their size – instead you need to state a size *and a direction*. For example, to fully describe the motion of a ship on the ocean at a point in time during its voyage, it's not enough to specify how fast the ship is moving – you also need to describe its direction of motion.

You saw other examples of this in Unit 2, when you considered objects moving along straight lines. To specify the position of a point P on a straight line relative to some other point, say O, on the line, you first choose one direction along the line to be the positive direction; then you state the distance between the two points, and attach a plus or minus sign to indicate the direction. The resulting quantity is called the *displacement* of P from O. For example, in Figure 28, if the positive direction is taken to be to the right, then the displacement of A from O is $-2\,\text{cm}$, and the displacement of B from O is $4\,\text{cm}$.

Figure 28   Positions along a straight line

Similarly, if an object is moving along a straight line, then you can describe its motion by giving its speed, and attaching a plus or minus sign to indicate its direction. The resulting quantity is called the *velocity* of the object.

Plus and minus signs provide a convenient way to specify direction when you're dealing with movement along a straight line – that is, in one dimension. Examples of movement of this type include the motion of a car along a straight road, or that of a tightrope walker along a tightrope. However, we often need to deal with movement in two or three dimensions. For example, someone standing in a flat field can move across the field in two dimensions, and a person in space can move in three dimensions.

In general, **displacement** is the position of one point relative to another, whether in one, two or three dimensions. To specify a displacement, you need to give both a distance and a direction. For example, consider the points O, P and Q in Figure 29. You can specify the displacement of P from O by saying that it is 1 km north-west of O. Similarly, you can specify the displacement of Q from O by saying that it is 1 km north-east of O.

You can move only in one dimension along a tightrope (unless you fall off!)

Figure 29   Points in a plane

Just as distance together with direction is called *displacement*, so speed together with direction is called **velocity**. For example, if you say that someone is walking at a speed of $5 \, \text{km} \, \text{h}^{-1}$ south, then you're specifying a velocity.

Quantities, such as displacement and velocity, that have both a size and a direction are called **vectors**, or **vector quantities**. (In Latin, the word *vector* means 'carrier'.) Another example of a vector quantity is *force*. The size of a vector is usually called its **magnitude**.

You can move in two dimensions across a flat field

In contrast to vectors, quantities that have size but no direction are called **scalars**, or **scalar quantities**. Examples of scalars include distance, speed, time, temperature and volume. So a scalar is a number, possibly with a unit.

Notice that the magnitude of the displacement of one point from another is the distance between the two points, and the magnitude of the velocity of an object is its speed. In everyday English the words 'speed' and 'velocity' are often used interchangeably, but in scientific and mathematical terminology there is an important difference: speed is a scalar and velocity is a vector.

You can move in three dimensions in space

The concept of vectors evolved over a long time. Isaac Newton (1642–1727) dealt extensively with vector quantities, but never formalised them. The first exposition of what we would today know as vectors was by Josiah Willard Gibbs in 1881, in his *Elements of vector analysis*. This work was derived from earlier ideas of William Rowan Hamilton (1805–1865).

Josiah Willard Gibbs
(1839–1903)

Any vector with non-zero magnitude can be represented by an *arrow*, which is a line segment with an associated direction, like the one in Figure 30. The length of the arrow represents the magnitude of the vector, according to some chosen scale, and the direction of the arrow represents the direction of the vector. Two-dimensional vectors are represented by arrows in a plane, and three-dimensional vectors are represented by arrows in three-dimensional space. For example, the arrow in Figure 30 might represent a displacement of 30 km north-west, if you're using a scale of 1 cm to represent 10 km. Alternatively, the same arrow might represent a velocity of 30 m s^{-1} north-west, if you're using a scale of 1 cm to represent 10 m s^{-1}.

Figure 30   An arrow that represents a vector

Once you've chosen a scale, any two arrows with the same length and the same direction represent the *same* vector. For example, all the arrows in Figure 31 represent the same vector.

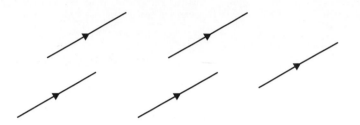

Figure 31   Several arrows representing the same vector

Vectors are often denoted by lower-case letters. We distinguish them from scalars by using a bold typeface in typed text, and by underlining them in handwritten text. For example, the vector in Figure 30 might be denoted by **v** in print, or handwritten as $\underline{v}$. These conventions prevent readers from confusing vector and scalar quantities.

> Remember to underline handwritten vectors (and make typed ones bold) in your own work.

Vectors that represent displacements are sometimes called **displacement vectors**. There is a useful alternative notation for such vectors. If P and Q are any two points, then the vector that specifies the displacement *from P to Q* (illustrated in Figure 32) is denoted by $\overrightarrow{PQ}$.

Figure 32   The vector $\overrightarrow{PQ}$

The magnitude of a vector **v** is a scalar quantity. It is denoted by $|\mathbf{v}|$, which is read as 'the magnitude of v', 'the modulus of v', or simply 'mod v'. For example, if the vector **v** represents a velocity of $30\,\mathrm{m\,s^{-1}}$ north-west, then $|\mathbf{v}| = 30\,\mathrm{m\,s^{-1}}$. Similarly, if the vector $\overrightarrow{PQ}$ represents a displacement of $3\,\mathrm{m}$ south-east, then $|\overrightarrow{PQ}| = 3\,\mathrm{m}$. Remember that the distance between the points P and Q can also be denoted by PQ, so

$$PQ = |\overrightarrow{PQ}|.$$

Notice that the notation for the magnitude of a vector is the same as the notation for the magnitude of a scalar that you met in Unit 3. For example, you saw there that $|-3| = 3$. So this notation can be applied to either vectors or scalars.

When we're working with vectors, it's often convenient, for simplicity, not to distinguish between vectors and the arrows that represent them. For example, we might say 'the vector shown in the diagram' rather than 'the vector represented by the arrow shown in the diagram'. This convention is used throughout the rest of this unit.

Over the next few pages you'll learn the basics of working with vectors.

Equal vectors

As you'd expect, two vectors are **equal** if they have the same magnitude and the same direction.

Activity 23   *Identifying equal vectors*

The following diagram shows several displacement vectors.

(a) Which vector is equal to the vector **a**?

(b) Which vector is equal to the vector $\overrightarrow{PQ}$?

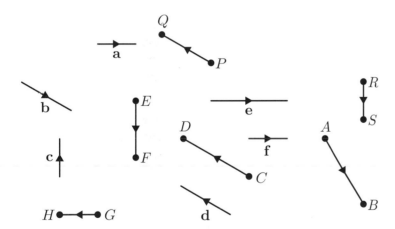

The zero vector

The *zero vector* is defined as follows.

Zero vector

The **zero vector**, denoted by **0** (bold zero), is the vector whose magnitude is zero. It has no direction.

The zero vector is handwritten as $\underline{0}$ (zero underlined).

For example, the displacement of a particular point from itself is the zero vector, as is the velocity of an object that is not moving.

Addition of vectors

To understand how to *add* two vectors, it's helpful to think about displacement vectors. For example, consider the situation shown in Figure 33. Suppose that an object is positioned at a point P and you first move it to the point Q, then you move it again to the point R. The two displacements are the vectors $\overrightarrow{PQ}$ and $\overrightarrow{QR}$, respectively, and the overall, combined displacement is the vector $\overrightarrow{PR}$. This method of combining two vectors to produce another vector is called **vector addition**.

We write
$$\overrightarrow{PQ} + \overrightarrow{QR} = \overrightarrow{PR}.$$

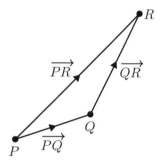

Figure 33   The result of adding two displacement vectors

Vectors are always added in this way. The general rule is called the *triangle law for vector addition*, and it can be stated as follows.

Triangle law for vector addition

To find the sum of two vectors **a** and **b**, place the tail of **b** at the tip of **a**. Then **a** + **b** is the vector from the tail of **a** to the tip of **b**.

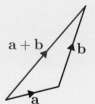

The sum of two vectors is also called their **resultant** or **resultant vector**.

You can add two vectors in either order, and you get the same result either way. This is illustrated in Figure 34. Diagrams (a) and (b) show how the vectors **a** + **b** and **b** + **a** are found using the triangle law for vector addition. When you place these two diagrams together, as shown in diagram (c), the two resultant vectors coincide, because they lie along the diagonal of the parallelogram formed by the two copies of **a** and **b**.

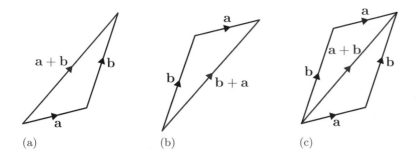

(a)   (b)   (c)

Figure 34   The vectors $\mathbf{a} + \mathbf{b}$ and $\mathbf{b} + \mathbf{a}$ are equal

In fact, Figure 34(c) gives an alternative way to add two vectors, the *parallelogram law for vector addition*, which can be stated as follows.

Parallelogram law for vector addition

To find the sum of two vectors $\mathbf{a}$ and $\mathbf{b}$, place their tails together, and complete the resulting figure to form a parallelogram. Then $\mathbf{a} + \mathbf{b}$ is the vector formed by the diagonal of the parallelogram, starting from the point where the tails of $\mathbf{a}$ and $\mathbf{b}$ meet.

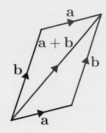

The parallelogram law is convenient in some contexts, and you'll use it in Unit 12. In this unit we'll always use the triangle law, as it's simpler in the sorts of situations that we'll deal with here.

You can add more than two vectors together. To add several vectors, you place them all tip to tail, one after another; then their sum is the vector from the tail of the first vector to the tip of the last vector. For example, Figure 35 illustrates how three vectors $\mathbf{a}$, $\mathbf{b}$ and $\mathbf{c}$ are added.

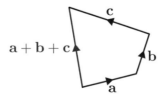

Figure 35   The sum of three vectors $\mathbf{a}$, $\mathbf{b}$ and $\mathbf{c}$

The order in which you add the vectors doesn't matter – you always get the same resultant vector.

Activity 24 *Adding vectors*

The diagram below shows three vectors **u**, **v** and **w** drawn on a grid.

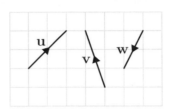

Draw arrows representing the following vector sums. (Use squared paper or sketch a grid.)

(a) $\mathbf{u} + \mathbf{v}$ (b) $\mathbf{u} + \mathbf{w}$ (c) $\mathbf{v} + \mathbf{w}$ (d) $\mathbf{u} + \mathbf{v} + \mathbf{w}$ (e) $\mathbf{u} + \mathbf{u}$

As you'd expect, adding the zero vector to any vector leaves it unchanged. That is, for any vector **a**,

$$\mathbf{a} + \mathbf{0} = \mathbf{a}.$$

Note that you can't add a vector to a scalar. Expressions such as $\mathbf{v} + x$, where **v** is a vector and x is a scalar, are meaningless.

Negative of a vector

The *negative* of a vector **a** is denoted by $-\mathbf{a}$, and is defined as follows.

> ### Negative of a vector
>
> The **negative** of a vector **a**, denoted by $-\mathbf{a}$, is the vector with the same magnitude as **a**, but the opposite direction.

For any points P and Q, the position vectors $\overrightarrow{PQ}$ and $\overrightarrow{QP}$ have the property that $-\overrightarrow{PQ} = \overrightarrow{QP}$, since $\overrightarrow{PQ}$ and $\overrightarrow{QP}$ have opposite directions.

If you add any vector **a** to its negative $-\mathbf{a}$, by placing the two vectors tip to tail in the usual way, then you get the zero vector. In other words, for any vector **a**,

$$\mathbf{a} + (-\mathbf{a}) = \mathbf{0},$$

as you'd expect.

The negative of the zero vector is the zero vector; that is, $-\mathbf{0} = \mathbf{0}$.

Subtraction of vectors

To see how vector *subtraction* is defined, first consider the subtraction of numbers. Subtracting a number is the same as adding the negative of the number. In other words, if a and b are numbers, then $a - b$ means the same as $a + (-b)$. We use this idea to define vector subtraction, as follows.

Vector subtraction

To subtract **b** from **a**, add $-\mathbf{b}$ to **a**.
That is,

$$\mathbf{a} - \mathbf{b} = \mathbf{a} + (-\mathbf{b}).$$

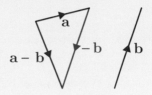

Activity 25 *Subtracting vectors*

The diagram below shows three vectors **u**, **v** and **w** drawn on a grid.

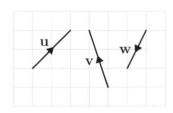

Draw arrows representing the following negatives and differences of vectors. (Use squared paper or sketch a grid.)

(a) $-\mathbf{v}$ (b) $-\mathbf{w}$ (c) $\mathbf{u} - \mathbf{v}$ (d) $\mathbf{v} - \mathbf{w}$ (e) $\mathbf{u} + \mathbf{v} - \mathbf{w}$

You have already seen that for any vector **a**, we have $\mathbf{a} + (-\mathbf{a}) = \mathbf{0}$. That is, for any vector **a**, we have $\mathbf{a} - \mathbf{a} = \mathbf{0}$, as you would expect.

Multiplication of vectors by scalars

You can multiply vectors by scalars. To understand what this means, first consider the effect of adding a vector **a** to itself, as illustrated in Figure 36.

Figure 36   A vector **a** added to itself

The resultant vector **a** + **a** has the same direction as **a**, but twice the magnitude. We denote it by 2**a**. We say that this vector is a **scalar multiple** of the vector **a**, since 2 is a scalar quantity. In general, scalar multiplication of vectors is defined as below. Note that in this box the notation $|m|$ means the magnitude of the *scalar m*.

> **Scalar multiple of a vector**
>
> Suppose that **a** is a vector. Then, for any non-zero real number m, the **scalar multiple** m**a** of **a** is the vector
>
> - whose magnitude is $|m|$ times the magnitude of **a**
> - that has the same direction as **a** if m is positive, and the opposite direction if m is negative.
>
> Also, 0**a** = **0**.
> (That is, the number zero times the vector **a** is the zero vector.)

Remember that a scalar multiple of a vector is a *vector*.

Various scalar multiples of a vector **a** are shown in Figure 37.

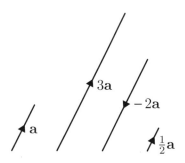

Figure 37   Scalar multiples of a vector **a**

By the definition above, if **a** is any vector, then (-1)**a** is the vector with the same magnitude as **a** but the opposite direction. In other words, as you would expect,

$$(-1)\mathbf{a} = -\mathbf{a}.$$

Activity 26   *Multiplying vectors by scalars*

The diagram below shows three vectors **u**, **v** and **w** drawn on a grid.

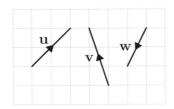

Draw arrows representing the following vectors. (Use squared paper or sketch a grid.)

(a) **3u**   (b) **−2v**   (c) $\frac{1}{2}\mathbf{v}$ (d) **3u − 2v**   (e) **−2v + w**

The next example illustrates how you can use scalar multiples of vectors to represent quantities in practical situations.

Example 10   *Scaling velocities*

Suppose that the vector **u** represents the velocity of a car travelling with speed $50\,\mathrm{km\,h^{-1}}$ along a straight road heading north. Write down, in terms of **u**, the velocity of a second car that is travelling in the same direction as the first with a speed of $75\,\mathrm{km\,h^{-1}}$.

Solution

🗨 The velocity of the second car has the same direction as **u**, and hence is a scalar multiple of it. The speed of the second car is 1.5 times the speed of the first. 🗨

The velocity of the second car is **1.5u**.

The activity below involves winds measured in *knots*. A knot is a unit of speed often used in meteorology, and in air and maritime navigation. Its usual abbreviation is kn, and $1\,\mathrm{kn} = 1.852\,\mathrm{km\,h^{-1}}$.

Conventionally, the direction of a wind is usually given as the direction *from* which it blows, rather than the direction that it blows towards. So, for example, a southerly wind is one blowing from the south, towards the north.

Activity 27   *Scaling velocities*

Suppose that the vector **v** represents the velocity of a wind of 35 knots blowing from the north-east. Express the following vectors in terms of **v**.

(a) The velocity of a wind of 70 knots blowing from the north-east.

(b) The velocity of a wind of 35 knots blowing from the south-west.

5.2 Vector algebra

In Subsection 5.1, you met some properties of the addition, subtraction and scalar multiplication of vectors. For example, you saw that for any vectors **a** and **b**,

$$\mathbf{a} + \mathbf{b} = \mathbf{b} + \mathbf{a}, \quad \mathbf{a} + \mathbf{0} = \mathbf{a}, \quad \mathbf{a} - \mathbf{a} = \mathbf{0} \quad \text{and} \quad \mathbf{a} + \mathbf{a} = 2\mathbf{a}.$$

All the properties that you met can be deduced from the eight basic algebraic properties of vectors listed below.

Properties of vector algebra

The following properties hold for all vectors **a**, **b** and **c**, and all scalars m and n.

1. $\mathbf{a} + \mathbf{b} = \mathbf{b} + \mathbf{a}$

2. $(\mathbf{a} + \mathbf{b}) + \mathbf{c} = \mathbf{a} + (\mathbf{b} + \mathbf{c})$

3. $\mathbf{a} + \mathbf{0} = \mathbf{a}$

4. $\mathbf{a} + (-\mathbf{a}) = \mathbf{0}$

5. $m(\mathbf{a} + \mathbf{b}) = m\mathbf{a} + m\mathbf{b}$

6. $(m + n)\mathbf{a} = m\mathbf{a} + n\mathbf{a}$

7. $m(n\mathbf{a}) = (mn)\mathbf{a}$

8. $1\mathbf{a} = \mathbf{a}$

These properties are similar to properties that hold for addition, subtraction and multiplication of real numbers. Similar properties also hold for many different systems of mathematical objects. You'll meet further examples of such systems later in the module.

Property 1 says that the order in which two vectors are added does not matter. This property can be described by saying that vector addition is **commutative**. Similarly, addition of real numbers is commutative, because $a + b = b + a$ for all real numbers a and b, and multiplication of real numbers is commutative, because $ab = ba$ for all real numbers a and b. Subtraction of real numbers is not commutative, because it is not true that $a - b = b - a$ for all real numbers a and b.

Property 2 says that finding $\mathbf{a} + \mathbf{b}$ and then adding $\mathbf{c}$ to the result gives the same final answer as finding $\mathbf{b} + \mathbf{c}$ and then adding $\mathbf{a}$ to the result. You might like to check this for a particular case, by drawing the vectors as arrows. This property is described by saying that vector addition is **associative**. It allows us to write the expression $\mathbf{a} + \mathbf{b} + \mathbf{c}$ without there being any ambiguity in what is meant – you can interpret it as either $(\mathbf{a} + \mathbf{b}) + \mathbf{c}$ or $\mathbf{a} + (\mathbf{b} + \mathbf{c})$, because both mean the same. Addition and multiplication of real numbers are also associative operations.

Property 5 says that adding two vectors and then multiplying the result by a scalar gives the same final answer as multiplying each of the two vectors individually by the scalar and then adding the two resulting vectors. This property is described by saying that scalar multiplication is **distributive** over the addition of vectors.

Similarly, property 6 says that scalar multiplication is distributive over the addition of scalars.

You will notice that nothing has been said about whether vectors can be multiplied or divided by other vectors. There is a useful way to define multiplication of two vectors – two different ways, in fact! You will meet one of these ways in Section 7. Division of a vector by another vector is not possible.

The properties in the box above allow you to perform some operations on vector expressions in a similar way to real numbers, as illustrated in the following example.

Example 11 *Simplifying a vector expression*

Simplify the vector expression

$$2(\mathbf{a} + \mathbf{b}) + 3(\mathbf{b} + \mathbf{c}) - 5(\mathbf{a} + \mathbf{b} - \mathbf{c}).$$

Solution

Expand the brackets, using property 5 above.

$$2(\mathbf{a} + \mathbf{b}) + 3(\mathbf{b} + \mathbf{c}) - 5(\mathbf{a} + \mathbf{b} - \mathbf{c})$$
$$= 2\mathbf{a} + 2\mathbf{b} + 3\mathbf{b} + 3\mathbf{c} - 5\mathbf{a} - 5\mathbf{b} + 5\mathbf{c}$$

Collect like terms, using property 6 above.

$$= 2\mathbf{a} - 5\mathbf{a} + 2\mathbf{b} + 3\mathbf{b} - 5\mathbf{b} + 3\mathbf{c} + 5\mathbf{c}$$
$$= 8\mathbf{c} - 3\mathbf{a}.$$

The properties in the box above also allow you to manipulate equations containing vectors, which are known as **vector equations**, in a similar way to ordinary equations. For example, you can add or subtract vectors on both sides of such an equation, and you can multiply or divide both sides by a non-zero scalar. You can use these methods to rearrange a vector equation to make a particular vector the subject, or to solve a vector equation for an unknown vector.

Activity 28   *Manipulating vector expressions and equations*

(a) Simplify the vector expression $4(\mathbf{a} - \mathbf{c}) + 3(\mathbf{c} - \mathbf{b}) + 2(2\mathbf{a} - \mathbf{b} - 3\mathbf{c})$.

(b) Rearrange each of the following vector equations to express $\mathbf{x}$ in terms of $\mathbf{a}$ and $\mathbf{b}$.

   (i) $2\mathbf{b} + 4\mathbf{x} = 7\mathbf{a}$ (ii) $3(\mathbf{b} - \mathbf{a}) + 5\mathbf{x} = 2(\mathbf{a} - \mathbf{b})$

5.3 Using vectors

In this subsection you'll see some examples of how you can use two-dimensional vectors in practical situations.

When you use a vector to represent a real-world quantity, you need a means of expressing its direction. For a two-dimensional vector, one way to do this is to state the angle measured from some chosen reference direction to the direction of the vector. You have to make it clear whether the angle is measured clockwise or anticlockwise.

If the vector represents the displacement or velocity of an object such as a ship or an aircraft, then its direction is often given as a *compass bearing*. There are various different types of compass bearings, but in this module we will use the following type.

A **bearing** is an angle between $0°$ and $360°$, measured clockwise in degrees from north to the direction of interest.

For example, Figure 38 shows a vector $\mathbf{v}$ with a bearing of $150°$.

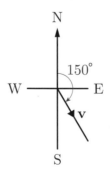

Figure 38   A vector with a bearing of $150°$

A navigational compass

When bearings are used in practice, there are various possibilities for the meaning of 'north'. It can mean magnetic north (the direction in which a compass points), true north (the direction to the North Pole) or grid north (the direction marked as north on a particular map). We'll assume that one of these has been chosen in any particular situation.

Notice that the rotational direction in which bearings are measured is *opposite* to that in which angles are usually measured in mathematics.

Bearings are measured *clockwise* (from north), whereas in Unit 4 you saw angles measured *anticlockwise* (from the positive direction of the x-axis).

Activity 29 *Working with bearings*

(a) Write down the bearings that specify the directions of the following vectors. (The acute angle between each vector and the gridlines is 45°.)

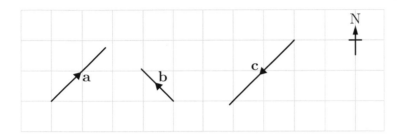

(b) Draw arrows to represent vectors (of any magnitude) with directions given by the following bearings.

(i) 90°   (ii) 135°   (iii) 270°

When you work with the directions of vectors expressed using angles, you often need to use trigonometry, as illustrated in the next example.

Example 12   *Adding two perpendicular vectors*

An explorer walks for 3 km on a bearing of 90°, then turns and walks for 4 km on a bearing of 0°.

Find the magnitude and bearing of his resultant displacement, giving the bearing to the nearest degree.

Solution

Represent the first part of the walk by the vector **a**, and the second part by the vector **b**. Then the resultant displacement is **a** + **b**.

🔍 Draw a diagram showing **a**, **b** and **a** + **b**. Since **a** and **b** are perpendicular, you obtain a right-angled triangle. 💭

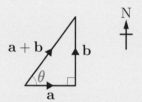

🔍 Use Pythagoras' theorem to find the magnitude of **a** + **b**. 💭

Since $|\mathbf{a}| = 3$ km, $|\mathbf{b}| = 4$ km and the triangle is right-angled,

$$|\mathbf{a} + \mathbf{b}| = \sqrt{|\mathbf{a}|^2 + |\mathbf{b}|^2} = \sqrt{3^2 + 4^2} = \sqrt{25} = 5 \text{ km}.$$

🔍 Use basic trigonometry to find one of the acute angles in the triangle. 💭

From the diagram,

$$\tan\theta = \frac{|\mathbf{b}|}{|\mathbf{a}|} = \frac{4}{3},$$

so $\theta = \tan^{-1}\left(\frac{4}{3}\right) = 53°$ (to the nearest degree).

🔍 Hence find the bearing of **a** + **b**. 💭

The bearing of **a** + **b** is $90° - \theta = 37°$ (to the nearest degree).

🔍 State a conclusion, remembering to include units. 💭

So the resultant displacement has magnitude 5 km and a bearing of approximately 37°.

Activity 30   *Adding two perpendicular vectors*

A yacht sails on a bearing of 60° for 5.3 km, then turns through 90° and sails on a bearing of 150° for a further 2.1 km.

Find the magnitude and bearing of the yacht's resultant displacement. Give the magnitude of the displacement in km to one decimal place, and the bearing to the nearest degree.

The vectors that were added in Example 12 and Activity 30 were perpendicular, so only basic trigonometry was needed. In the next activity, you're asked to add two displacement vectors that aren't perpendicular. You need to draw a clear diagram and use the sine and cosine rules to find the required lengths and angles.

Activity 31   *Adding two non-perpendicular vectors*

The grab of a robotic arm moves 40 cm from its starting point on a bearing of 90° to pick up an object, and then moves the object 20 cm on a bearing of 315°.

Find the resultant displacement of the grab, giving the magnitude to the nearest centimetre, and the bearing to the nearest degree.

In some examples involving vectors, it can be quite complicated to work out the angles that you need to know from the information that you have. You often need to use the following geometric properties.

Opposite, corresponding and alternate angles

Where two lines intersect:

    opposite angles are equal
    (for example, $\theta = \phi$).

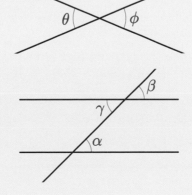

Where a line intersects parallel lines:

    corresponding angles are equal
    (for example, $\alpha = \beta$);

    alternate angles are equal
    (for example, $\alpha = \gamma$).

Figure 39 $\angle ABC$

The next example illustrates how to use some of these geometric properties. You should find the tutorial clip for this example particularly helpful.

The example uses the standard notation $\angle ABC$ (read as 'angle ABC') for the acute angle at the point B between the line segments AB and BC. This is illustrated in Figure 39.

Example 13   *Adding two non-perpendicular vectors*

The displacement from Exeter to Belfast is 460 km with a bearing of 340°, and the displacement from Belfast to Glasgow is 173 km with a bearing of 36°. Use this information to find the magnitude (to the nearest kilometre) and direction (as a bearing, to the nearest degree) of the displacement from Exeter to Glasgow.

Solution

Denote Exeter by E, Belfast by B, and Glasgow by G.

Draw a diagram showing the displacement vectors $\overrightarrow{EB}$, $\overrightarrow{BG}$ and their resultant $\overrightarrow{EG}$. Mark the angles that you know. Mark or state any magnitudes that you know.

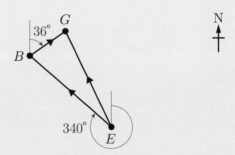

We know that $EB = 460$ km and $BG = 173$ km.

To enable you to calculate the magnitude and bearing of $\overrightarrow{EG}$, you need to find an angle in triangle BEG. Use geometric properties to find $\angle EBG$.

Since the bearing of $\overrightarrow{EB}$ is 340°, the acute angle at E between $\overrightarrow{EB}$ and north is $360° - 340° = 20°$, as shown in the diagram below.

Hence, since alternate angles are equal, the acute angle at B between $\overrightarrow{EB}$ and south is also 20°.

So $\angle EBG = 180° - 36° - 20° = 124°$.

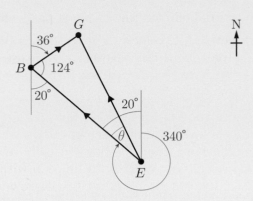

🗨 Now use the cosine rule to calculate EG. 🗨

Applying the cosine rule in triangle EBG gives

$$EG^2 = EB^2 + BG^2 - 2 \times EB \times BG \times \cos 124°,$$

so

$$EG = \sqrt{460^2 + 173^2 - 2 \times 460 \times 173 \times \cos 124°}$$
$$= 574.91\ldots = 575\,\text{km (to the nearest km)}.$$

🗨 To find the bearing of $\overrightarrow{EG}$, first find $\angle BEG$. 🗨

Let $\angle BEG = \theta$, as marked in the diagram. Then, by the sine rule,

$$\frac{BG}{\sin \theta} = \frac{EG}{\sin 124°}$$

$$\sin \theta = \frac{BG \sin 124°}{EG}$$
$$= \frac{173 \sin 124°}{574.91\ldots}.$$

Now

$$\sin^{-1}\left(\frac{173 \sin 124°}{574.91\ldots}\right) = 14.44\ldots°,$$

so

$$\theta = 14.44\ldots° \quad \text{or} \quad \theta = 180° - 14.44\ldots° = 165.55\ldots°.$$

If $\theta = 165.55\ldots°$, then the sum of θ and $\angle EBG$ (two of the angles in triangle EBG) is greater than $180°$, which is impossible. So $\theta = 14.44\ldots°$.

Hence the bearing of $\overrightarrow{EG}$ is

$$340° + \theta = 340° + 14.44\ldots° = 354.44\ldots°.$$

🗨 State a conclusion. 🗨

The displacement of Glasgow from Exeter is $575\,\text{km}$ (to the nearest km) on a bearing of $354°$ (to the nearest degree).

As mentioned in Subsection 5.1, velocity is a vector quantity, since it is the speed with which an object is moving together with its direction of motion. So the methods that you have seen for adding displacements can also be applied to velocities.

It may at first seem strange to add velocities, but consider the following situation. Suppose that a boy is running across the deck of a ship. If the ship is motionless in a harbour, then the boy's velocity relative to the sea bed is the same as his velocity relative to the ship.

However, if the ship is moving, then the boy's velocity relative to the sea bed is a combination of his velocity relative to the ship and the ship's velocity relative to the sea bed. In fact, the boy's resultant velocity relative to the sea bed is the vector sum of the two individual velocities.

Activity 32 *Adding velocities*

A ship is steaming at a speed of 10.0 m s^{-1} on a bearing of $30°$ in still water. A boy runs across the deck of the ship from the port side to the starboard side, perpendicular to the direction of motion of the ship, with a speed of 4.0 m s^{-1} relative to the ship. (The port and starboard sides of a ship are the sides on the left and right, respectively, of a person on board facing the front.)

Find the resultant velocity of the boy, giving the speed in m s^{-1} to one decimal place and the bearing to the nearest degree.

When a ship sails in a current, or an aircraft flies through a wind, its actual velocity is the resultant of the velocity that it would have if the water or air were still, and the velocity of the current or wind. In particular, the direction in which the ship or aircraft is *pointing* – this is called its **heading**, when it is given as a bearing – may be different from the direction in which it is actually moving, which is called its **course**. This is because the current or wind may cause it to continuously drift to one side.

A ship has a speed in still water of $5.7\,\mathrm{m\,s^{-1}}$ and is sailing on a heading of $230°$. However, there is a current in the water of speed $2.5\,\mathrm{m\,s^{-1}}$ flowing on a bearing of $330°$. Find the resultant velocity of the ship, giving the speed in $\mathrm{m\,s^{-1}}$ to one decimal place and the bearing to the nearest degree.

6 Component form of a vector

In Section 5, you saw how to specify two-dimensional vectors by stating their magnitudes and directions, and how to work with them using trigonometry. The calculations involved can be quite complicated, especially when you want to find a sum of more than two vectors. Three-dimensional vectors can be dealt with in a similar way, though the calculations are usually even more complicated. Fortunately, there is an alternative way to represent and manipulate vectors, which makes them easier to work with. This involves expressing them in terms of *components*.

6.1 Representing vectors using components

To express a vector in terms of components, you first introduce a system of coordinate axes with which to work, as shown in Figure 40. You can choose any perpendicular directions for the axes, but usually you choose them to be horizontal and vertical, or you align them with directions intrinsic to the situation that you're dealing with. You label the axes x and y (in two dimensions), or x, y and z (in three dimensions), in the usual way.

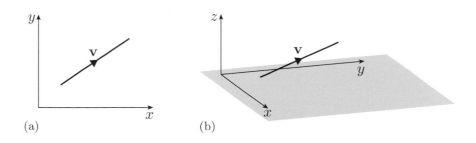

(a)   (b)

Figure 40   A vector in a coordinate system (a) in two dimensions (b) in three dimensions

We denote the vectors of magnitude 1 in the directions of the x-, y- and z-axes by $\mathbf{i}$, $\mathbf{j}$ and $\mathbf{k}$, respectively, as shown in Figure 41. These vectors are called the **Cartesian unit vectors**. In general, a **unit vector** is a vector with magnitude 1.

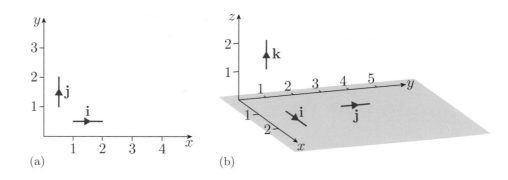

(a)   (b)

Figure 41   The Cartesian unit vectors (a) in two dimensions (b) in three dimensions

Every vector can be expressed as the sum of scalar multiples of the Cartesian unit vectors. For example, in Figure 42(a), $\mathbf{u} = 3\mathbf{i} + (-2\mathbf{j}) = 3\mathbf{i} - 2\mathbf{j}$, and in Figure 42(b), $\mathbf{v} = \frac{3}{2}\mathbf{i} + 2\mathbf{j} + 3\mathbf{k}$.

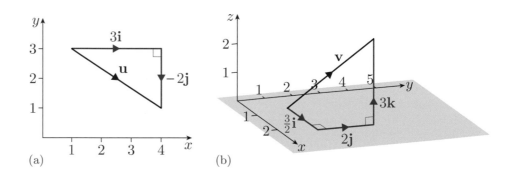

(a)   (b)

Figure 42   Vectors expressed as sums of scalar multiples of the Cartesian unit vectors

We make the following definitions, illustrated in Figure 43.

Component form of a vector

If $\mathbf{v} = a\mathbf{i} + b\mathbf{j}$, then the expression $a\mathbf{i} + b\mathbf{j}$ is called the **component form** of $\mathbf{v}$. The scalars a and b are called the **i-component** and **j-component**, respectively, of $\mathbf{v}$.

Similarly, if $\mathbf{v} = a\mathbf{i} + b\mathbf{j} + c\mathbf{k}$, then the expression $a\mathbf{i} + b\mathbf{j} + c\mathbf{k}$ is called the **component form** of $\mathbf{v}$. The scalars a, b and c are called the **i-component**, **j-component** and **k-component**, respectively, of $\mathbf{v}$.

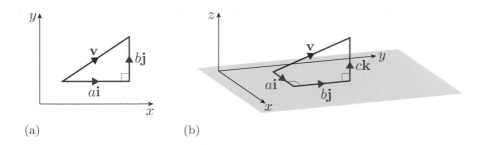

(a)   (b)

Figure 43 General vectors expressed as sums of scalar multiples of the Cartesian unit vectors

For example, the component form of the vector **u** in Figure 42 on the previous page is $\mathbf{u} = 3\mathbf{i} - 2\mathbf{j}$, and its **i**- and **j**- components are 3 and -2, respectively.

The components of a vector represent the 'amount of the vector' in the positive direction of each axis.

The **i**- and **j**-components of a two-dimensional vector are alternatively called the x-component and y-component, respectively. Similarly, the **i**-, **j**- and **k**-components of a three-dimensional vector are alternatively called the x-component, y-component and z-component, respectively.

Activity 34 *Expressing vectors in component form*

Express each of the vectors in the diagram below in component form.

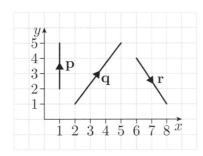

There is a useful alternative notation for expressing a vector in component form, as follows.

> **Alternative component form of a vector**
>
> The vector $a\mathbf{i} + b\mathbf{j}$ can be written as $\begin{pmatrix} a \\ b \end{pmatrix}$.
>
> The vector $\mathbf{a}\mathbf{i} + b\mathbf{j} + c\mathbf{k}$ can be written as $\begin{pmatrix} a \\ b \\ c \end{pmatrix}$.
>
> A vector written in this form is called a **column vector**.

For example,

$$3\mathbf{i} - 2\mathbf{j} = \begin{pmatrix} 3 \\ -2 \end{pmatrix}.$$

The first number in a column vector is its **i**-component, the second number is its **j**-component, and, in three dimensions, the third number is its **k**-component.

Activity 35 *Writing vectors as column vectors*

Write the vectors in Activity 34 as column vectors.

In general, if you are asked to write a vector in component form, then you can use either of the two types of component form. Both forms are used in this module. Sometimes one form is more convenient than the other.

Notice that, in two dimensions,

$$\mathbf{i} = \begin{pmatrix} 1 \\ 0 \end{pmatrix} \quad \text{and} \quad \mathbf{j} = \begin{pmatrix} 0 \\ 1 \end{pmatrix},$$

and, in three dimensions,

$$\mathbf{i} = \begin{pmatrix} 1 \\ 0 \\ 0 \end{pmatrix}, \quad \mathbf{j} = \begin{pmatrix} 0 \\ 1 \\ 0 \end{pmatrix} \quad \text{and} \quad \mathbf{k} = \begin{pmatrix} 0 \\ 0 \\ 1 \end{pmatrix}.$$

The zero vector, like any other vector, can be expressed in component form. In two dimensions,

$$\mathbf{0} = 0\mathbf{i} + 0\mathbf{j} = \begin{pmatrix} 0 \\ 0 \end{pmatrix},$$

and, in three dimensions,

$$\mathbf{0} = 0\mathbf{i} + 0\mathbf{j} + 0\mathbf{k} = \begin{pmatrix} 0 \\ 0 \\ 0 \end{pmatrix}.$$

It is often convenient to denote the components of a vector by the same letter as the vector (but not bold or underlined), with subscripts. For example, we can write

$$\mathbf{a} = a_1\mathbf{i} + a_2\mathbf{j} = \begin{pmatrix} a_1 \\ a_2 \end{pmatrix} \quad \text{or} \quad \mathbf{u} = u_1\mathbf{i} + u_2\mathbf{j} + u_3\mathbf{k} = \begin{pmatrix} u_1 \\ u_2 \\ u_3 \end{pmatrix}.$$

If a vector represents a displacement whose magnitude is measured in metres, for example, then its components are also measured in metres. Similarly, if a vector represents a velocity whose magnitude is measured in m s^{-1}, for example, then its components are also measured in m s^{-1}.

6.2 Vector algebra using components

In Subsection 5.1 you saw how to add and subtract vectors using the triangle law, and how to multiply a vector by a scalar. Here you will see how to carry out these operations when vectors are expressed in component form.

Addition of vectors

By the properties of vector algebra that you met in Subsection 5.2, if $\mathbf{a} = a_1\mathbf{i} + a_2\mathbf{j}$ and $\mathbf{b} = b_1\mathbf{i} + b_2\mathbf{j}$, then

$$\begin{aligned} \mathbf{a} + \mathbf{b} &= a_1\mathbf{i} + a_2\mathbf{j} + b_1\mathbf{i} + b_2\mathbf{j} \\ &= (a_1 + b_1)\mathbf{i} + (a_2 + b_2)\mathbf{j}. \end{aligned}$$

This is illustrated in Figure 44.

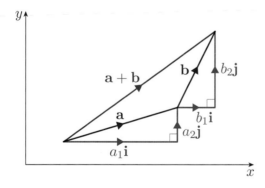

Figure 44 The sum $\mathbf{a} + \mathbf{b}$ of two vectors $\mathbf{a}$ and $\mathbf{b}$

So, to add two two-dimensional vectors, you just add their corresponding components.

Addition of two-dimensional vectors in component form

If $\mathbf{a} = a_1\mathbf{i} + a_2\mathbf{j}$ and $\mathbf{b} = b_1\mathbf{i} + b_2\mathbf{j}$, then

$$\mathbf{a} + \mathbf{b} = (a_1 + b_1)\mathbf{i} + (a_2 + b_2)\mathbf{j}.$$

In column notation,

$$\text{if } \mathbf{a} = \begin{pmatrix} a_1 \\ a_2 \end{pmatrix} \text{ and } \mathbf{b} = \begin{pmatrix} b_1 \\ b_2 \end{pmatrix}, \text{ then } \mathbf{a} + \mathbf{b} = \begin{pmatrix} a_1 + b_1 \\ a_2 + b_2 \end{pmatrix}.$$

For example,

$$\begin{pmatrix} 2 \\ 3 \end{pmatrix} + \begin{pmatrix} 3 \\ -1 \end{pmatrix} = \begin{pmatrix} 2+3 \\ 3 + (-1) \end{pmatrix} = \begin{pmatrix} 5 \\ 2 \end{pmatrix}.$$

Vectors in three dimensions are added in a similar way, as follows.

Addition of three-dimensional vectors in component form

If $\mathbf{a} = a_1\mathbf{i} + a_2\mathbf{j} + a_3\mathbf{k}$ and $\mathbf{b} = b_1\mathbf{i} + b_2\mathbf{j} + b_3\mathbf{k}$, then

$$\mathbf{a} + \mathbf{b} = (a_1 + b_1)\mathbf{i} + (a_2 + b_2)\mathbf{j} + (a_3 + b_3)\mathbf{k}.$$

In column notation,

$$\text{if } \mathbf{a} = \begin{pmatrix} a_1 \\ a_2 \\ a_3 \end{pmatrix} \text{ and } \mathbf{b} = \begin{pmatrix} b_1 \\ b_2 \\ b_3 \end{pmatrix}, \text{ then } \mathbf{a} + \mathbf{b} = \begin{pmatrix} a_1 + b_1 \\ a_2 + b_2 \\ a_3 + b_3 \end{pmatrix}.$$

The facts in the boxes above extend to sums of more than two vectors. That is, the $\mathbf{i}$-component of the sum of several vectors is the sum of the $\mathbf{i}$-components of the individual vectors, and similarly for the other components.

Example 14   *Adding vectors in component form*

Let $\mathbf{a} = 4\mathbf{i} + \mathbf{j}$, $\mathbf{b} = -3\mathbf{i} + 2\mathbf{j}$ and $\mathbf{c} = 2\mathbf{i} - 2\mathbf{j}$. Find the vector $\mathbf{a} + \mathbf{b} + \mathbf{c}$.

Solution

Add corresponding components.

$$\begin{aligned}
\mathbf{a} + \mathbf{b} + \mathbf{c} &= (4\mathbf{i} + \mathbf{j}) + (-3\mathbf{i} + 2\mathbf{j}) + (2\mathbf{i} - 2\mathbf{j}) \\
&= 4\mathbf{i} - 3\mathbf{i} + 2\mathbf{i} + \mathbf{j} + 2\mathbf{j} - 2\mathbf{j} \\
&= 3\mathbf{i} + \mathbf{j}.
\end{aligned}$$

Activity 36   *Adding vectors in component form*

Find the following vector sums.

(a) $(4\mathbf{i} - 2\mathbf{j}) + (-3\mathbf{i} + \mathbf{j})$ (b) $\begin{pmatrix} 5 \\ 3 \end{pmatrix} + \begin{pmatrix} -4 \\ -3 \end{pmatrix}$

(c) $\begin{pmatrix} -7 \\ -4 \\ 1 \end{pmatrix} + \begin{pmatrix} 2 \\ 7 \\ -3 \end{pmatrix} + \begin{pmatrix} 5 \\ 1 \\ 4 \end{pmatrix}$

Negative of a vector in component form

By the properties of vector algebra, if $\mathbf{b} = b_1\mathbf{i} + b_2\mathbf{j}$, then $-\mathbf{b} = -b_1\mathbf{i} - b_2\mathbf{j}$. This is illustrated in Figure 45.

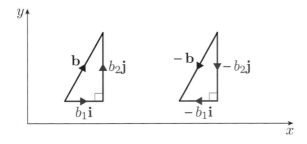

Figure 45   A vector $\mathbf{b}$ and its negative $-\mathbf{b}$

In general we have the following.

Negative of a two-dimensional vector in component form

If $\mathbf{b} = b_1\mathbf{i} + b_2\mathbf{j}$, then $-\mathbf{b} = -b_1\mathbf{i} - b_2\mathbf{j}$.

In column notation,

$$\text{if } \mathbf{b} = \begin{pmatrix} b_1 \\ b_2 \end{pmatrix}, \text{ then } -\mathbf{b} = \begin{pmatrix} -b_1 \\ -b_2 \end{pmatrix}.$$

Negative of a three-dimensional vector in component form

If $\mathbf{b} = b_1\mathbf{i} + b_2\mathbf{j} + b_3\mathbf{k}$, then $-\mathbf{b} = -b_1\mathbf{i} - b_2\mathbf{j} - b_3\mathbf{k}$.

In column notation,

$$\text{if } \mathbf{b} = \begin{pmatrix} b_1 \\ b_2 \\ b_3 \end{pmatrix}, \text{ then } -\mathbf{b} = \begin{pmatrix} -b_1 \\ -b_2 \\ -b_3 \end{pmatrix}.$$

Subtraction of vectors in component form

By the properties of vector algebra, if $\mathbf{a} = a_1\mathbf{i} + a_2\mathbf{j}$ and $\mathbf{b} = b_1\mathbf{i} + b_2\mathbf{j}$, then

$$\mathbf{a} - \mathbf{b} = (a_1\mathbf{i} + a_2\mathbf{j}) - (b_1\mathbf{i} + b_2\mathbf{j})$$
$$= (a_1 - b_1)\mathbf{i} + (a_2 - b_2)\mathbf{j}.$$

So, to subtract one two-dimensional vector in component form from another, you subtract each component of the first vector from the corresponding component of the other vector.

Subtraction of two-dimensional vectors in component form

If $\mathbf{a} = a_1\mathbf{i} + a_2\mathbf{j}$ and $\mathbf{b} = b_1\mathbf{i} + b_2\mathbf{j}$, then

$$\mathbf{a} - \mathbf{b} = (a_1 - b_1)\mathbf{i} + (a_2 - b_2)\mathbf{j}.$$

In column notation,

$$\text{if } \mathbf{a} = \begin{pmatrix} a_1 \\ a_2 \end{pmatrix} \text{ and } \mathbf{b} = \begin{pmatrix} b_1 \\ b_2 \end{pmatrix}, \text{ then } \mathbf{a} - \mathbf{b} = \begin{pmatrix} a_1 - b_1 \\ a_2 - b_2 \end{pmatrix}.$$

A similar fact holds in three dimensions.

Subtraction of three-dimensional vectors in component form

If $\mathbf{a} = a_1\mathbf{i} + a_2\mathbf{j} + a_3\mathbf{k}$ and $\mathbf{b} = b_1\mathbf{i} + b_2\mathbf{j} + b_3\mathbf{k}$, then

$$\mathbf{a} - \mathbf{b} = (a_1 - b_1)\mathbf{i} + (a_2 - b_2)\mathbf{j} + (a_3 - b_3)\mathbf{k}.$$

In column notation,

$$\text{if } \mathbf{a} = \begin{pmatrix} a_1 \\ a_2 \\ a_3 \end{pmatrix} \text{ and } \mathbf{b} = \begin{pmatrix} b_1 \\ b_2 \\ b_3 \end{pmatrix}, \text{ then } \mathbf{a} - \mathbf{b} = \begin{pmatrix} a_1 - b_1 \\ a_2 - b_2 \\ a_3 - b_3 \end{pmatrix}.$$

Example 15   *Subtracting vectors in component form*

Let $\mathbf{a} = 5\mathbf{i} - 2\mathbf{j}$ and $\mathbf{b} = -\mathbf{i} + 3\mathbf{j}$. Find $\mathbf{a} - \mathbf{b}$.

Solution

🔍 Subtract the corresponding components. 💬

$$\begin{aligned} \mathbf{a} - \mathbf{b} &= (5\mathbf{i} - 2\mathbf{j}) - (-\mathbf{i} + 3\mathbf{j}) \\ &= 5\mathbf{i} + \mathbf{i} - 2\mathbf{j} - 3\mathbf{j} \\ &= 6\mathbf{i} - 5\mathbf{j}. \end{aligned}$$

Activity 37   *Subtracting vectors in component form*

Find the following vectors.

(a) $(2\mathbf{i} + \mathbf{j}) - (3\mathbf{i} + 2\mathbf{j})$ (b) $(3\mathbf{i} + 2\mathbf{j} - 4\mathbf{k}) - (-2\mathbf{i} + 4\mathbf{j} + 2\mathbf{k})$

(c) $\begin{pmatrix} 3 \\ 4 \\ -1 \end{pmatrix} - \begin{pmatrix} 2 \\ -1 \\ 3 \end{pmatrix}$

Multiplication of vectors by scalars

By the properties of vector algebra, if $\mathbf{a} = a_1\mathbf{i} + a_2\mathbf{j}$ and m is a scalar, then

$$m\mathbf{a} = m(a_1\mathbf{i} + a_2\mathbf{j})$$
$$= ma_1\mathbf{i} + ma_2\mathbf{j}.$$

This is illustrated in Figure 46.

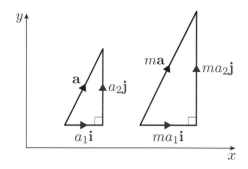

Figure 46   Scaling the vector $\mathbf{a}$ by m

So, to multiply a two-dimensional vector by a scalar m, you simply multiply each component by m.

Scalar multiplication of a two-dimensional vector in component form

If $\mathbf{a} = a_1\mathbf{i} + a_2\mathbf{j}$ and m is a scalar, then

$$m\mathbf{a} = ma_1\mathbf{i} + ma_2\mathbf{j}.$$

In column notation,

$$\text{if } \mathbf{a} = \begin{pmatrix} a_1 \\ a_2 \end{pmatrix}, \text{ then } m\mathbf{a} = \begin{pmatrix} ma_1 \\ ma_2 \end{pmatrix}.$$

For example, $3(4\mathbf{i} - 5\mathbf{j}) = 12\mathbf{i} - 15\mathbf{j}$.

A similar result applies in three dimensions.

Scalar multiplication of a three-dimensional vector in component form

If $\mathbf{a} = a_1\mathbf{i} + a_2\mathbf{j} + a_3\mathbf{k}$ and m is a scalar, then

$$m\mathbf{a} = ma_1\mathbf{i} + ma_2\mathbf{j} + ma_3\mathbf{k}.$$

In column notation,

$$\text{if } \mathbf{a} = \begin{pmatrix} a_1 \\ a_2 \\ a_3 \end{pmatrix}, \text{ then } m\mathbf{a} = \begin{pmatrix} ma_1 \\ ma_2 \\ ma_3 \end{pmatrix}.$$

Activity 38 *Multiplying a vector in component form by a scalar*

Let $\mathbf{a} = \begin{pmatrix} 2 \\ -1 \end{pmatrix}$ and $\mathbf{b} = \mathbf{i} + 3\mathbf{j} - 6\mathbf{k}$.

Find each of the following scalar multiples.

(a) $4\mathbf{a}$ (b) $-2\mathbf{a}$ (c) $\frac{1}{2}\mathbf{a}$ (d) $3\mathbf{b}$ (e) $-4\mathbf{b}$ (f) $\frac{1}{3}\mathbf{b}$

Combining vector operations

In the next example, the vector operations of addition, subtraction and scalar multiplication are combined.

Example 16 *Simplifying a combination of vectors in component form*

Let $\mathbf{t} = 5\mathbf{i} + 3\mathbf{j}$, $\mathbf{u} = -2\mathbf{i} + 7\mathbf{j}$ and $\mathbf{v} = 4\mathbf{i} - 4\mathbf{j}$. Find $3\mathbf{t} - \mathbf{u} - 5\mathbf{v}$ in component form.

Solution

🗨 Substitute in the expressions for $\mathbf{t}$, $\mathbf{u}$ and $\mathbf{v}$ in terms of $\mathbf{i}$ and $\mathbf{j}$, and simplify. 🗨

$$\begin{aligned} 3\mathbf{t} - \mathbf{u} - 5\mathbf{v} &= 3(5\mathbf{i} + 3\mathbf{j}) - (-2\mathbf{i} + 7\mathbf{j}) - 5(4\mathbf{i} - 4\mathbf{j}) \\ &= 15\mathbf{i} + 9\mathbf{j} + 2\mathbf{i} - 7\mathbf{j} - 20\mathbf{i} + 20\mathbf{j} \\ &= -3\mathbf{i} + 22\mathbf{j}. \end{aligned}$$

> **Activity 39**   *Simplifying combinations of vectors in component form*
>
> Find each of the following vectors in component form.
>
> (a) $-2\mathbf{a} + 3\mathbf{b} + 4\mathbf{c}$, where $\mathbf{a} = 2\mathbf{i} + 3\mathbf{j}$, $\mathbf{b} = \mathbf{i} - 4\mathbf{j}$ and $\mathbf{c} = -5\mathbf{i} + 7\mathbf{j}$
>
> (b) $2 \begin{pmatrix} 6 \\ -3 \end{pmatrix} - 7 \begin{pmatrix} 1 \\ 2 \end{pmatrix} + 5 \begin{pmatrix} -1 \\ 4 \end{pmatrix}$
>
> (c) $a_1 \begin{pmatrix} 1 \\ 0 \end{pmatrix} + a_2 \begin{pmatrix} 0 \\ 1 \end{pmatrix}$, where a_1 and a_2 are any scalars
>
> (d) $2 \begin{pmatrix} 1 \\ 3 \\ 4 \end{pmatrix} + 3 \begin{pmatrix} 0 \\ 3 \\ 1 \end{pmatrix} - 2 \begin{pmatrix} 1 \\ 4 \\ 2 \end{pmatrix}$

6.3 Position vectors

If P is any point, either in the plane or in three-dimensional space, then the **position vector** of P is the displacement vector $\overrightarrow{OP}$, where O is the origin. This is illustrated in Figure 47, in the case of two dimensions.

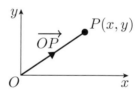

Figure 47   The position vector $\overrightarrow{OP}$ in two dimensions

The components of the position vector of a point are the same as the coordinates of the point. That is, the position vector of the point $P(x, y)$ in two dimensions is

$$\overrightarrow{OP} = x\mathbf{i} + y\mathbf{j} = \begin{pmatrix} x \\ y \end{pmatrix},$$

and similarly the position vector of the point $Q(x, y, z)$ in three dimensions is

$$\overrightarrow{OQ} = x\mathbf{i} + y\mathbf{j} + z\mathbf{k} = \begin{pmatrix} x \\ y \\ z \end{pmatrix}.$$

If a point is denoted by a capital letter, as is usual, then it's often convenient to denote its position vector by the corresponding lower-case, bold (or underlined) letter. For example, we often denote the position vector of the point P by $\mathbf{p}$, the position vector of the point A by $\mathbf{a}$, and so on.

There is a simple equation that expresses any displacement vector $\overrightarrow{AB}$ in terms of the position vectors of the points A and B. Consider Figure 48, which shows two points A and B, the displacement vector $\overrightarrow{AB}$, and the position vectors of A and B.

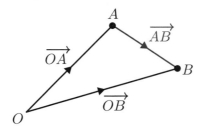

Figure 48 A vector $\overrightarrow{AB}$, and the position vectors of A and B

Since

$$\overrightarrow{AB} = \overrightarrow{AO} + \overrightarrow{OB},$$

it follows that

$$\overrightarrow{AB} = -\overrightarrow{OA} + \overrightarrow{OB};$$

that is,

$$\overrightarrow{AB} = \overrightarrow{OB} - \overrightarrow{OA}.$$

This equation, which applies in either two or three dimensions, can be stated as below.

> If the points A and B have position vectors $\mathbf{a}$ and $\mathbf{b}$, respectively, then
> $$\overrightarrow{AB} = \mathbf{b} - \mathbf{a}.$$

For example, Figure 49 shows two points A and B, with position vectors $2\mathbf{i} + \mathbf{j}$ and $3\mathbf{i} + 5\mathbf{j}$, respectively. The vector $\overrightarrow{AB}$ is $(3\mathbf{i} + 5\mathbf{j}) - (2\mathbf{i} + \mathbf{j}) = \mathbf{i} + 4\mathbf{j}$.

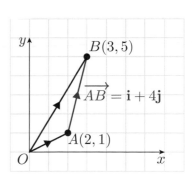

Figure 49 A particular vector $\overrightarrow{AB}$, and the position vectors of A and B

Activity 40   *Using position vectors*

Consider the points $A(5,3)$ and $B(-2,4)$. Find the vector $\overrightarrow{AB}$ in component form.

Vectors, and position vectors in particular, often provide a convenient means of solving problems and proving facts in coordinate geometry. The next example gives an alternative proof of the formula that you met earlier for the coordinates of the midpoint of a line segment in terms of the coordinates of the endpoints.

Example 17   *Working with position vectors*

Consider the points $A(x_1, y_1)$ and $B(x_2, y_2)$. Let M be the midpoint of the line segment AB, and let $\mathbf{a}$, $\mathbf{b}$ and $\mathbf{m}$ be the position vectors of A, B and M, respectively.

(a) Express $\mathbf{m}$ in terms of $\mathbf{a}$ and $\mathbf{b}$.

(b) Hence find the coordinates of M, in terms of the coordinates of A and B.

Solution

(a)

🗨 First draw a diagram. 🗨

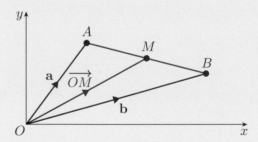

We have
$$\overrightarrow{OM} = \overrightarrow{OA} + \overrightarrow{AM};$$
that is,
$$\mathbf{m} = \mathbf{a} + \overrightarrow{AM}.$$
Also, $\overrightarrow{AM}$ has the same direction as $\overrightarrow{AB}$ but half its magnitude. So
$$\overrightarrow{AM} = \tfrac{1}{2}\overrightarrow{AB} = \tfrac{1}{2}(\mathbf{b} - \mathbf{a}).$$

Hence

$$\mathbf{m} = \mathbf{a} + \tfrac{1}{2}(\mathbf{b} - \mathbf{a})$$
$$= \mathbf{a} + \tfrac{1}{2}\mathbf{b} - \tfrac{1}{2}\mathbf{a}$$
$$= \tfrac{1}{2}\mathbf{a} + \tfrac{1}{2}\mathbf{b}$$
$$= \tfrac{1}{2}(\mathbf{a} + \mathbf{b}).$$

(b)

💬 Use the components of $\mathbf{a}$ and $\mathbf{b}$ to find the components of $\mathbf{m}$ and hence the coordinates of M. 💬

Since $\mathbf{a} = x_1\mathbf{i} + y_1\mathbf{j}$ and $\mathbf{b} = x_2\mathbf{i} + y_2\mathbf{j}$, we have

$$\mathbf{m} = \tfrac{1}{2}\left(x_1\mathbf{i} + y_1\mathbf{j} + x_2\mathbf{i} + y_2\mathbf{j}\right)$$
$$= \left(\frac{x_1 + x_2}{2}\right)\mathbf{i} + \left(\frac{y_1 + y_2}{2}\right)\mathbf{j}.$$

Hence the coordinates of M are $\left(\dfrac{x_1 + x_2}{2}, \dfrac{y_1 + y_2}{2}\right)$.

Example 17 gives the following useful fact.

Midpoint formula in terms of position vectors

If the points A and B have position vectors $\mathbf{a}$ and $\mathbf{b}$, respectively, then the midpoint of the line segment AB has position vector $\tfrac{1}{2}(\mathbf{a} + \mathbf{b})$.

Here is a similar example for you to try.

Activity 41   *Working with position vectors*

Consider the regular hexagon $ABCDEF$, with centre the origin, shown below. Here $\overrightarrow{OA} = \mathbf{a}$ and $\overrightarrow{OB} = \mathbf{b}$.

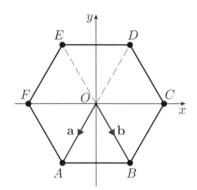

Express the following vectors in terms of $\mathbf{a}$ and $\mathbf{b}$.

(a) $\overrightarrow{AB}$ (b) $\overrightarrow{OC}$ (c) $\overrightarrow{BC}$ (d) $\overrightarrow{AD}$ (e) $\overrightarrow{AE}$

(Remember that each of the six triangles OAB, OBC, OCD, ODE, OEF and OFA is equilateral.)

In the next activity you are asked to use position vectors to prove the following basic property of every triangle: the three lines that each join a vertex to the midpoint of the opposite side meet at a common point.

Activity 42   *Proving a geometric property of triangles*

In the triangle OAB shown below, the points C, D and E are the midpoints of the sides of the triangle. Let $\overrightarrow{OA} = \mathbf{a}$ and $\overrightarrow{OB} = \mathbf{b}$.

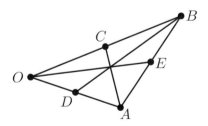

(a) Show that

$$\overrightarrow{AC} = \tfrac{1}{2}\mathbf{b} - \mathbf{a} \quad \text{and} \quad \overrightarrow{BD} = \tfrac{1}{2}\mathbf{a} - \mathbf{b}.$$

(b) Find the position vectors of each of the following points, expressed in terms of the position vectors **a** and **b**.

    (i)   The point two-thirds of the way along OE from O.

    (ii)   The point two-thirds of the way along AC from A.

    (iii) The point two-thirds of the way along BD from B.

(c) Deduce that the lines OE, AC and BD are concurrent; that is, they meet at a common point.

6.4 Converting from component form to magnitude and direction, and vice versa

In this subsection you will learn how to find the magnitude and direction of a two-dimensional vector from its components, and how to find the components of a two-dimensional vector from its magnitude and direction. These skills will enable you to use components to solve problems specified in terms of magnitudes and directions. You will see some examples of this in Subsection 6.5.

You'll also learn here how to calculate the magnitude of a three-dimensional vector from its components. Techniques involving the directions of three-dimensional vectors are more complicated, and are not covered in this module.

Finding the magnitude of a vector from its components

Consider any two-dimensional vector **v**, not parallel to an axis. If you draw a right-angled triangle whose hypotenuse is **v**, and whose two shorter sides are parallel to the axes, then the lengths of these two shorter sides are the *magnitudes* of the components of **v**. This is illustrated in Figure 50, for a vector $\mathbf{v} = a\mathbf{i} + b\mathbf{j}$ whose components a and b are positive.

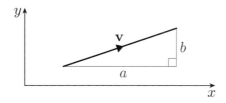

Figure 50   A two-dimensional vector with positive components

By Pythagoras' theorem, the magnitude of the vector **v** in Figure 50 is given by

$$|\mathbf{v}| = \sqrt{a^2 + b^2}.$$

You can see that this formula will hold for any vector $\mathbf{v} = a\mathbf{i} + b\mathbf{j}$, no matter whether the components a and b are positive, negative or zero, for reasons similar to those that you saw for the distance formula in Subsection 1.1. So we have the following fact.

> **The magnitude of a two-dimensional vector in terms of its components**
>
> The magnitude of the vector $a\mathbf{i} + b\mathbf{j}$ is $\sqrt{a^2 + b^2}$.

There is a similar formula for three-dimensional vectors.

> **The magnitude of a three-dimensional vector in terms of its components**
>
> The magnitude of the vector $a\mathbf{i} + b\mathbf{j} + c\mathbf{k}$ is $\sqrt{a^2 + b^2 + c^2}$.

Activity 43 *Finding the magnitudes of vectors from their components*

Find the magnitudes of the following vectors. Give exact answers.

(a) $-3\mathbf{i} + \mathbf{j}$ (b) $2\mathbf{i} + 4\mathbf{j} - 3\mathbf{k}$ (c) $\begin{pmatrix} -2 \\ 0 \end{pmatrix}$ (d) $\begin{pmatrix} 3 \\ -1 \\ 3 \end{pmatrix}$

Finding the direction of a two dimensional vector from its components

As you saw earlier, you can specify the direction of a two-dimensional vector by stating the angle (measured clockwise or anticlockwise) from some chosen reference direction to the direction of the vector.

You saw that one way to do this, which is common in air and maritime navigation, is to use *bearings*. To express the direction of a vector as a bearing, you state the angle measured clockwise from north to the direction of the vector. In this module, bearings are always stated as angles between $0°$ and $360°$.

Another method of expressing the direction of a two-dimensional vector, which is often used when components are involved, is to state the angle measured from the positive x-direction to the direction of the vector. The angle is always measured *anticlockwise*, and this is usually assumed rather than being stated explicitly. This way of measuring angles is the standard way that you met in Unit 4. For example, Figure 51 shows two vectors making angles of $35°$ and $200°$, respectively, with the positive x-direction.

With this method, you can state the angles in any convenient way – they don't need to be between 0° and 360°, and they could be measured in radians, rather than degrees. Sometimes it is helpful to use negative angles – for example, you can say that the vector **b** in Figure 51 makes an angle of −160° with the positive direction of the x-axis.

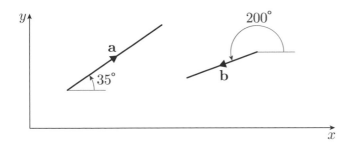

Figure 51 A vector **a** that makes an angle of 35° with the positive x-direction, and a vector **b** that makes an angle of 200° with the positive x-direction

Suppose that you have a two-dimensional vector in component form, and you want to find the angle that it makes with some reference direction, such as north or the positive x-direction. The first thing to do is to sketch the vector. If it is parallel to an axis, then it should be straightforward to find the angle that you want. Otherwise, you can sketch a right-angled triangle whose hypotenuse is the vector, and whose shorter sides are parallel to the axes. The lengths of the shorter sides are the magnitudes of the components of the vector.

You can use basic trigonometry to find an acute angle in the triangle, and you can then use this acute angle to find the angle that you want. This method is demonstrated in the following example.

Example 18   *Finding the magnitude and direction of a vector from its components*

Find the magnitude of the vector $4\mathbf{i} - 3\mathbf{j}$, and the angle that it makes with the positive x-direction. Give the angle to the nearest degree.

Solution

◖ Use the standard formula to find the magnitude. ◗

The magnitude of the vector is

$$\sqrt{4^2 + (-3)^2} = \sqrt{16 + 9} = \sqrt{25} = 5.$$

◖ To find the required angle, first draw a diagram. ◗

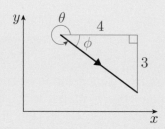

◖ Find the acute angle ϕ, and hence find the required angle. ◗

From the diagram,

$$\tan \phi = \tfrac{3}{4},$$

so

$$\phi = \tan^{-1} \tfrac{3}{4} = 36.86\ldots°.$$

Hence the angle, labelled θ, that the vector makes with the positive x-direction is

$$360° - 36.86\ldots° = 323.13\ldots°$$
$$= 323° \text{ (to the nearest degree)}.$$

Find the magnitudes and directions of the following vectors. Give the magnitudes as exact values, and give the directions as the angles that the vectors make with the positive x-direction, to the nearest degree.

(a) $\mathbf{a} = -2\mathbf{i} + 3\mathbf{j}$ (b) $\mathbf{b} = \begin{pmatrix} 0 \\ -3.5 \end{pmatrix}$

To find the direction of a vector as a *bearing*, you can use methods similar to those in Example 18. The only difference is that in the last step you need to find the angle measured clockwise from north to the direction of the vector. You can try this in the next activity.

Find the magnitude and bearing of each of the following velocity vectors. Assume that $\mathbf{i}$ and $\mathbf{j}$ are taken to point east and north, respectively, and that the units are $\mathrm{m\,s}^{-1}$. Give the magnitudes of the vectors in $\mathrm{m\,s}^{-1}$ to one decimal place, and their bearings to the nearest degree.

(a) $\mathbf{u} = 4\mathbf{i} - 2\mathbf{j}$ (b) $\mathbf{v} = \begin{pmatrix} -1 \\ -4 \end{pmatrix}$

Finding the components of a two-dimensional vector from its magnitude and direction

To find the components of a two-dimensional vector from its magnitude and direction, again the key is to first sketch the vector. If it is parallel to an axis, then it is straightforward to find its components. Otherwise, as before, you can sketch a right-angled triangle whose hypotenuse is the vector, and whose shorter sides are parallel to the axes. You can use basic trigonometry in this triangle to find the *magnitudes* of the components, and you can find their *signs* by using the direction of the vector. This method is demonstrated in the following example.

Example 19 *Finding the components of a vector from its magnitude and direction*

Express in component form the vector **v** with magnitude 4 that makes an angle of 120° with the positive x-direction.

Solution

🔍 First sketch the vector and a right-angled triangle whose shorter sides represent the magnitudes of the components. 💬

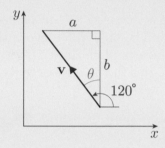

🔍 Find the size of an acute angle in the triangle. 💬

The angle marked θ is given by $\theta = 120° - 90° = 30°$.

🔍 Calculate the side lengths a and b, which are the *magnitudes* of the components. 💬

From the triangle,

$$\sin \theta = \frac{a}{|\mathbf{v}|}.$$

So, since $|\mathbf{v}| = 4$,

$$a = |\mathbf{v}| \sin \theta = 4 \sin 30° = 4 \times \tfrac{1}{2} = 2.$$

Similarly,

$$\cos \theta = \frac{b}{|\mathbf{v}|}.$$

So

$$b = |\mathbf{v}| \cos \theta = 4 \cos 30° = 4 \times \frac{\sqrt{3}}{2} = 2\sqrt{3}.$$

🔍 Find the signs of the components. You can see from the diagram that the **i**-component is negative, and the **j**-component is positive. Hence write the vector in component form. 💬

Hence

$$\mathbf{v} = -2\mathbf{i} + 2\sqrt{3}\mathbf{j}.$$

💬 You can check that the magnitude of this vector is as given in the question. 💬

Here are some vectors for you to express in component form.

Activity 46 *Calculating the components of vectors from their magnitudes and directions*

Express the following vectors in component form, giving each component to one decimal place.

(a) The vector **p** with magnitude 1 that makes an angle of 45° with the positive x-direction.

(b) The vector **q** with magnitude 2.5 that makes an angle of 340° with the positive x-direction.

In the next activity the directions of the vectors are given as bearings.

Activity 47 *Calculating the components of more vectors from their magnitudes and directions*

Express the following vectors in component form. Assume that **i** and **j** are taken to point east and north, respectively. Give each component to one decimal place.

(a) The displacement vector **p**, with magnitude 3.5 m, and bearing 340°.

(b) The velocity vector **u**, with magnitude 5.2 m s^{-1} and bearing 240°.

There is a useful standard formula for calculating the components of a vector from its magnitude and direction, when its direction is given as the angle that it makes with the positive x-direction. You can use this formula instead of the method in Example 19, when it is convenient to do so.

To obtain this formula, consider any non-zero vector $\mathbf{v}$, and let the angle that it makes with the positive x-direction be θ.

Let $\mathbf{u}$ be the vector in the same direction as $\mathbf{v}$, but with magnitude 1. If you draw $\mathbf{u}$ with its tail at the origin, as shown in Figure 52(a), then its tip lies on the unit circle, and hence, by what you saw in Subsection 2.2 of Unit 4, its tip has coordinates $(\cos\theta, \sin\theta)$. This is true whatever the size of the angle θ.

Hence $\mathbf{u} = \cos\theta\,\mathbf{i} + \sin\theta\,\mathbf{j}$. Multiplying $\mathbf{u}$ by the magnitude of the vector $\mathbf{v}$ gives the vector $\mathbf{v}$, so

$$\mathbf{v} = |\mathbf{v}|(\cos\theta\,\mathbf{i} + \sin\theta\,\mathbf{j}) = |\mathbf{v}|\cos\theta\,\mathbf{i} + |\mathbf{v}|\sin\theta\,\mathbf{j},$$

as illustrated in Figure 52(b). This is a formula for the components of $\mathbf{v}$.

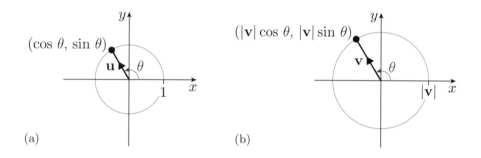

(a)   (b)

Figure 52   (a) A vector $\mathbf{u}$ of magnitude 1 with its tail at the origin (b) a vector $\mathbf{v}$ of any magnitude, in the same direction as $\mathbf{u}$, with its tail at the origin

So we have the following general fact.

Component form of a two-dimensional vector in terms of its magnitude and its angle with the positive x-direction

If the two-dimensional vector $\mathbf{v}$ makes the angle θ with the positive x-direction, then

$$\mathbf{v} = |\mathbf{v}|\cos\theta\,\mathbf{i} + |\mathbf{v}|\sin\theta\,\mathbf{j}.$$

This fact is illustrated in Figure 53.

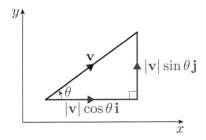

Figure 53 A vector **v** and its components

You can practise using this formula in the next activity. Remember that where the direction of a vector is given as a bearing, you need to start by finding the angle that it makes with the positive x-direction.

Activity 48 *Using the formula for the component form of a vector*

Use the formula above to find the component forms of the following vectors. In part (b), assume that **i** and **j** are taken to point east and north, respectively. Give each component to two significant figures.

(a) The vector **a** with magnitude 78 that makes an angle of 216° with the positive x-direction.

(b) The velocity vector **w** with magnitude $4.4\,\mathrm{m\,s^{-1}}$ and bearing 119°.

6.5 Using vectors in component form

When you're using vectors to help you solve a practical problem, you often have to find the sum of two or more vectors. If you know the magnitudes and directions of the vectors, then you can do this by using the triangle rule for vector addition and applying trigonometry, as you saw in Subsection 5.3.

However, as you saw, the calculations involved can be complicated. It is often easier to write the vectors in component form, add them in this form, and then find the magnitude and direction of the resultant vector.

This method is demonstrated in the next example.

Example 20 *Combining displacements using components*

A metal detectorist walks $200\,\text{m}$ on a bearing of $30°$, turns and walks $150\,\text{m}$ due west, then walks $50\,\text{m}$ due south.

Find the magnitude and bearing of his resultant displacement from his initial position. Give the magnitude to the nearest metre, and the bearing to the nearest degree.

Solution

Let the three parts of the metal detectorist's walk be the vectors **a**, **b** and **c**, and let the resultant displacement be the vector **d**.

💬 Choose a convenient coordinate system. Since the problem involves bearings, choose the y-axis to point north and the x-axis to point east. Draw a diagram showing the vectors. Mark any angles that you know, and mark or state any magnitudes that you know. 💬

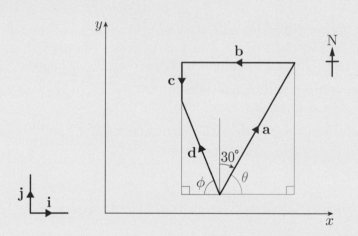

We know that $|\mathbf{a}| = 200\,\text{m}$, $|\mathbf{b}| = 150\,\text{m}$ and $|\mathbf{c}| = 50\,\text{m}$.

💬 Express the vectors representing the parts of the walk in component form. To find the components of a, first find the angle marked θ. 💬

In the diagram, $\theta = 90° - 30° = 60°$. Hence

$$\mathbf{a} = |\mathbf{a}| \cos\theta\,\mathbf{i} + |\mathbf{a}| \sin\theta\,\mathbf{j}$$
$$= 200 \cos 60°\mathbf{i} + 200 \sin 60°\mathbf{j}$$
$$= 100\mathbf{i} + 100\sqrt{3}\mathbf{j}.$$

Also, $\mathbf{b} = -150\mathbf{i}$ and $\mathbf{c} = -50\mathbf{j}$.

🔍 Find the resultant displacement **d**, and hence calculate its magnitude and direction. 💬

Hence the resultant displacement **d** is

$$\mathbf{d} = \mathbf{a} + \mathbf{b} + \mathbf{c}$$
$$= 100\mathbf{i} + 100\sqrt{3}\mathbf{j} - 150\mathbf{i} - 50\mathbf{j}$$
$$= -50\mathbf{i} + (100\sqrt{3} - 50)\mathbf{j}.$$

The magnitude of **d** is given by

$$|\mathbf{d}| = \sqrt{(-50)^2 + (100\sqrt{3} - 50)^2} = 132.964\ldots \text{ m.}$$

The angle ϕ shown on the diagram can be found by using the components of **d**, as follows:

$$\tan\phi = \frac{100\sqrt{3} - 50}{50},$$

so

$$\phi = \tan^{-1}\left(\frac{100\sqrt{3} - 50}{50}\right) = 67.91\ldots^\circ.$$

So the bearing of **d** is $270^\circ + 67.91\ldots^\circ = 337.91\ldots^\circ$.

🔍 Write down a conclusion, including units. 💬

The resultant displacement has magnitude $133\,\text{m}$ (to the nearest metre) and bearing 338° (to the nearest degree).

Here are two problems for you to try. You might recognise the first of them: it was solved in Example 13 on page 152 by using the triangle law for vector addition. You should find that using components is less complicated, but gives the same answers!

Activity 49   *Combining displacements using components*

The displacement from Exeter to Belfast is $460\,\text{km}$ with a bearing of 340°, and the displacement from Belfast to Glasgow is $173\,\text{km}$ with a bearing of 36°. By using components, find the magnitude (to the nearest kilometre) and direction (as a bearing, to the nearest degree) of the displacement from Exeter to Glasgow.

Activity 50 *Combining velocities using components*

An aircraft flies on a course with a bearing of 80°, and with a horizontal ground speed of 600 mph. (This is its horizontal speed relative to the ground – you can think of it as the speed of a point directly underneath the plane on horizontal ground.)

(a) Express the horizontal ground velocity of the aircraft in component form. Take **i** and **j** to point east and north, respectively, and state each component to the nearest mph.

(b) In addition to this horizontal ground velocity, the aircraft is also climbing at a rate of 30 mph. Find the resultant velocity of the aircraft in component form and the magnitude of the resultant velocity (to the nearest mph).

(c) The resultant velocity of the aircraft found in part (b) is actually a combination of its velocity relative to the air in which it is flying, which is called its *air velocity*, and the velocity of the air itself, which is called the *wind velocity*. Suppose that the wind velocity is horizontal, with a speed of 100 mph *from* a bearing of 290°. Find the air velocity of the aircraft, in component form, and the magnitude of the air velocity (to the nearest mph).

7 Scalar product of two vectors

In this section you'll learn a way to multiply two vectors, called the *scalar product*, also known as the *dot product*, of the two vectors, and you'll see that this quantity provides a convenient method for finding the angle between any two vectors.

7.1 Calculating scalar products

First, let's clarify what's meant by the angle between two vectors. The **angle between** two vectors **a** and **b** is the angle θ in the range $0 \le \theta \le 180°$ between their directions when the vectors are placed tail-to-tail, as illustrated in Figure 54. This definition applies to both two-dimensional and three-dimensional vectors.

Here's the definition of the scalar product.

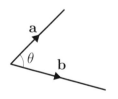

Figure 54 The angle between two vectors **a** and **b**

Scalar product of two vectors

The **scalar product** of the non-zero vectors
a and **b** is

$$\mathbf{a} \cdot \mathbf{b} = |\mathbf{a}|\,|\mathbf{b}| \cos\theta,$$

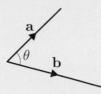

where θ is the angle between **a** and **b**.

If **a** or **b** is the zero vector, then $\mathbf{a} \cdot \mathbf{b} = 0$.

The notation $\mathbf{a} \cdot \mathbf{b}$ is read as 'a dot b'. The scalar product $\mathbf{a} \cdot \mathbf{b}$ of two
vectors **a** and **b** is a *scalar*, since none of the quantities $|\mathbf{a}|$, $|\mathbf{b}|$ and $\cos\theta$
has a direction. This is why it is called the *scalar* product. The alternative
name of *dot product* arises from the notation used. When you are writing a
scalar product, it is important to make sure that the dot between the
vectors is clear.

The definition of scalar product applies to both two-dimensional and
three-dimensional vectors. It has a geometric interpretation, as follows.
Figure 55 shows two non-zero vectors **a** and **b** placed tail-to-tail, and the
right-angled triangle formed by drawing a line from the tip of **a**,
perpendicular to **b**. The vector **p** in the diagram is called the **projection**
of **a** on **b**. You can see that if θ is an acute angle, then this projection has
magnitude $|\mathbf{a}| \cos\theta$, and hence

$$\mathbf{a} \cdot \mathbf{b} = |\mathbf{b}| \times (\text{magnitude of projection of } \mathbf{a} \text{ on } \mathbf{b}).$$

Similarly, by considering the projection of **b** on **a**, you can see that

$$\mathbf{a} \cdot \mathbf{b} = |\mathbf{a}| \times (\text{magnitude of projection of } \mathbf{b} \text{ on } \mathbf{a}).$$

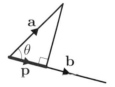

Figure 55 The projection **p**
of **a** on **b**

If θ is an obtuse angle, then the projection of **a** on **b** points in the opposite
direction to **b** (and similarly the projection of **b** on **a** points in the
opposite direction to **a**), and $\mathbf{a} \cdot \mathbf{b}$ is the negative of the quantity on the
right-hand side of each of the two equations above.

Activity 51 *Finding scalar products*

Suppose that **u**, **v** and **w** are two-dimensional vectors with magnitudes 4, 3
and 2, respectively, and directions as shown below.

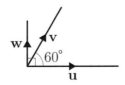

Use the definition of scalar product in the box above to find $\mathbf{u} \cdot \mathbf{v}$, $\mathbf{u} \cdot \mathbf{w}$
and $\mathbf{u} \cdot \mathbf{u}$.

Activity 51 illustrates two important properties of the scalar product.

First, if two non-zero vectors are perpendicular, then their scalar product is zero. This is because if $\mathbf{a}$ and $\mathbf{b}$ are perpendicular, then

$$\mathbf{a} \cdot \mathbf{b} = |\mathbf{a}|\,|\mathbf{b}| \cos 90° = |\mathbf{a}|\,|\mathbf{b}| \times 0 = 0.$$

It's also true that if the scalar product of two non-zero vectors is zero, then the vectors are perpendicular. This is because if $\mathbf{a}$ and $\mathbf{b}$ are non-zero vectors, then the only way that $\mathbf{a} \cdot \mathbf{b}$ can be equal to zero is if $\cos\theta = 0$, where θ is the angle between $\mathbf{a}$ and $\mathbf{b}$. This implies that $\theta = 90°$.

The second property illustrated by Activity 51 is that the scalar product of a vector with itself is equal to the square of the magnitude of the vector. This is obvious for the zero vector, and if $\mathbf{a}$ is any non-zero vector then the angle between $\mathbf{a}$ and itself is $0°$, so

$$\mathbf{a} \cdot \mathbf{a} = |\mathbf{a}|\,|\mathbf{a}| \cos 0° = |\mathbf{a}|\,|\mathbf{a}| \times 1 = |\mathbf{a}|^2.$$

These, and other, properties of the scalar product are summarised below. They can all be proved using the definition of the scalar product in the box above.

Properties of the scalar product

The following properties hold for all vectors $\mathbf{a}$, $\mathbf{b}$ and $\mathbf{c}$, and every scalar m.

1. Suppose that $\mathbf{a}$ and $\mathbf{b}$ are non-zero. If $\mathbf{a}$ and $\mathbf{b}$ are perpendicular, then $\mathbf{a} \cdot \mathbf{b} = 0$, and vice versa.
2. $\mathbf{a} \cdot \mathbf{a} = |\mathbf{a}|^2$
3. $\mathbf{a} \cdot \mathbf{b} = \mathbf{b} \cdot \mathbf{a}$
4. $\mathbf{a} \cdot (\mathbf{b} + \mathbf{c}) = \mathbf{a} \cdot \mathbf{b} + \mathbf{a} \cdot \mathbf{c}$
5. $(m\mathbf{a}) \cdot \mathbf{b} = m(\mathbf{a} \cdot \mathbf{b}) = \mathbf{a} \cdot (m\mathbf{b})$

Property 3 states that the operation of taking a scalar product is commutative. Property 4 states that the operation of taking a scalar product is distributive over vector addition. Property 5 states that multiplication by a scalar is distributive over the operation of taking a scalar product.

An alternative version of property 4 in which the vector $\mathbf{a}$ appears *after* the brackets also holds; that is,

$$(\mathbf{b} + \mathbf{c}) \cdot \mathbf{a} = \mathbf{b} \cdot \mathbf{a} + \mathbf{c} \cdot \mathbf{a}.$$

You can prove this property by combining property 4 with property 3.

The following example shows how you can use these properties to simplify expressions containing scalar products.

Example 21 *Simplifying an expression containing a scalar product*

Expand and simplify the expression $(\mathbf{a} + \mathbf{b}) \cdot (\mathbf{a} + \mathbf{b})$, where $\mathbf{a}$ and $\mathbf{b}$ are vectors.

Solution

Expand the brackets by using property 4 in the box above (and the alternative version).

$$(\mathbf{a} + \mathbf{b}) \cdot (\mathbf{a} + \mathbf{b}) = \mathbf{a} \cdot (\mathbf{a} + \mathbf{b}) + \mathbf{b} \cdot (\mathbf{a} + \mathbf{b})$$
$$= \mathbf{a} \cdot \mathbf{a} + \mathbf{a} \cdot \mathbf{b} + \mathbf{b} \cdot \mathbf{a} + \mathbf{b} \cdot \mathbf{b}$$

Simplify by using the fact that $\mathbf{a} \cdot \mathbf{b} = \mathbf{b} \cdot \mathbf{a}$ (by property 3).

$$= \mathbf{a} \cdot \mathbf{a} + 2\mathbf{a} \cdot \mathbf{b} + \mathbf{b} \cdot \mathbf{b}$$

Activity 52 *Simplifying expressions containing a scalar product*

Expand and simplify the expression $(\mathbf{a} + \mathbf{b}) \cdot (\mathbf{a} - \mathbf{b})$, where $\mathbf{a}$ and $\mathbf{b}$ are vectors.

Calculating scalar products from components

You can calculate the scalar product of two vectors directly from the components of the vectors.

Consider the two-dimensional vectors $\mathbf{a} = a_1\mathbf{i} + a_2\mathbf{j}$ and $\mathbf{b} = b_1\mathbf{i} + b_2\mathbf{j}$. Their scalar product is

$$\mathbf{a} \cdot \mathbf{b} = (a_1\mathbf{i} + a_2\mathbf{j}) \cdot (b_1\mathbf{i} + b_2\mathbf{j}).$$

Expanding the brackets and simplifying gives

$$\mathbf{a} \cdot \mathbf{b} = (a_1\mathbf{i}) \cdot (b_1\mathbf{i} + b_2\mathbf{j}) + (a_2\mathbf{j}) \cdot (b_1\mathbf{i} + b_2\mathbf{j})$$
$$= (a_1\mathbf{i}) \cdot (b_1\mathbf{i}) + (a_1\mathbf{i}) \cdot (b_2\mathbf{j}) + (a_2\mathbf{j}) \cdot (b_1\mathbf{i}) + (a_2\mathbf{j}) \cdot (b_2\mathbf{j})$$
$$= a_1b_1(\mathbf{i} \cdot \mathbf{i}) + a_1b_2(\mathbf{i} \cdot \mathbf{j}) + a_2b_1(\mathbf{j} \cdot \mathbf{i}) + a_2b_2(\mathbf{j} \cdot \mathbf{j}).$$

But the vectors $\mathbf{i}$ and $\mathbf{j}$ both have magnitude 1 and are perpendicular to each other, so

$$\mathbf{i} \cdot \mathbf{i} = |\mathbf{i}|^2 = 1, \quad \mathbf{j} \cdot \mathbf{j} = |\mathbf{j}|^2 = 1, \quad \mathbf{i} \cdot \mathbf{j} = 0 \quad \text{and} \quad \mathbf{j} \cdot \mathbf{i} = 0.$$

Substituting into the expression for $\mathbf{a} \cdot \mathbf{b}$ obtained above gives the following result.

Scalar product of two-dimensional vectors in terms of components

If $\mathbf{a} = a_1\mathbf{i} + a_2\mathbf{j}$ and $\mathbf{b} = b_1\mathbf{i} + b_2\mathbf{j}$, then

$$\mathbf{a} \cdot \mathbf{b} = a_1b_1 + a_2b_2.$$

In column notation,

$$\text{if } \mathbf{a} = \begin{pmatrix} a_1 \\ a_2 \end{pmatrix} \text{ and } \mathbf{b} = \begin{pmatrix} b_1 \\ b_2 \end{pmatrix}, \text{ then } \mathbf{a} \cdot \mathbf{b} = a_1b_1 + a_2b_2.$$

You can obtain a similar result for three-dimensional vectors, as follows.

Scalar product of three-dimensional vectors in terms of components

If $\mathbf{a} = a_1\mathbf{i} + a_2\mathbf{j} + a_3\mathbf{k}$ and $\mathbf{b} = b_1\mathbf{i} + b_2\mathbf{j} + b_3\mathbf{k}$, then

$$\mathbf{a} \cdot \mathbf{b} = a_1b_1 + a_2b_2 + a_3b_3.$$

In column notation,

$$\text{if } \mathbf{a} = \begin{pmatrix} a_1 \\ a_2 \\ a_3 \end{pmatrix} \text{ and } \mathbf{b} = \begin{pmatrix} b_1 \\ b_2 \\ b_3 \end{pmatrix}, \text{ then } \mathbf{a} \cdot \mathbf{b} = a_1b_1 + a_2b_2 + a_3b_3.$$

So, to calculate the scalar product of two vectors in component form, you multiply corresponding components and add the results.

Example 22   *Calculating a scalar product using components*

Suppose that $\mathbf{a} = 2\mathbf{i} + \mathbf{j} - 3\mathbf{k}$ and $\mathbf{b} = \mathbf{i} - 2\mathbf{j} + 2\mathbf{k}$. Find $\mathbf{a} \cdot \mathbf{b}$.

Solution

💭 Multiply corresponding components, and add the results. 💭

$$\mathbf{a} \cdot \mathbf{b} = (2 \times 1) + (1 \times (-2)) + ((-3) \times 2) = -6$$

Here is an example for you to try.

Activity 53   *Calculating scalar products using components*

Suppose that $\mathbf{u} = 3\mathbf{i} - 4\mathbf{j} + \mathbf{k}$, $\mathbf{v} = 2\mathbf{i} + 3\mathbf{j} - 2\mathbf{k}$ and $\mathbf{w} = -\mathbf{i} + \mathbf{j} + 3\mathbf{k}$. Find $\mathbf{u} \cdot \mathbf{v}$, $\mathbf{u} \cdot \mathbf{w}$ and $\mathbf{v} \cdot \mathbf{w}$.

7.2 Finding the angle between two vectors

The scalar product of two vectors has an important application in calculating the angle between two vectors.

Rearranging the definition of the scalar product gives the following fact.

Angle between two vectors

The angle θ between any two non-zero vectors $\mathbf{a}$ and $\mathbf{b}$ is given by

$$\cos \theta = \frac{\mathbf{a} \cdot \mathbf{b}}{|\mathbf{a}|\,|\mathbf{b}|},$$

where $0 \leq \theta \leq 180°$.

The next example demonstrates how to use this fact to find the angle between two vectors in component form.

Example 23 *Calculating the angle between two vectors in component form*

Find, to the nearest degree, the angle between the vectors $\mathbf{a} = 2\mathbf{i} + 2\mathbf{j} - \mathbf{k}$ and $\mathbf{b} = \mathbf{i} + 3\mathbf{j} + 2\mathbf{k}$.

Solution

🗨 Use the components of the vectors to find $\mathbf{a} \cdot \mathbf{b}$, $|\mathbf{a}|$ and $|\mathbf{b}|$. 🗨

We have

$$\begin{aligned}
\mathbf{a} \cdot \mathbf{b} &= (2\mathbf{i} + 2\mathbf{j} - \mathbf{k}) \cdot (\mathbf{i} + 3\mathbf{j} + 2\mathbf{k}) \\
&= 2 \times 1 + 2 \times 3 + (-1) \times 2 \\
&= 6,
\end{aligned}$$

$$|\mathbf{a}| = \sqrt{2^2 + 2^2 + (-1)^2} = \sqrt{9} = 3,$$

$$|\mathbf{b}| = \sqrt{1^2 + 3^2 + 2^2} = \sqrt{14}.$$

🗨 Apply the result in the box above. 🗨

Hence

$$\cos \theta = \frac{\mathbf{a} \cdot \mathbf{b}}{|\mathbf{a}|\,|\mathbf{b}|} = \frac{6}{3\sqrt{14}} = \frac{2}{\sqrt{14}},$$

so

$$\theta = \cos^{-1}\left(\frac{2}{\sqrt{14}}\right) = 57.68\ldots°.$$

That is, the angle between the vectors is $58°$, to the nearest degree.

Activity 54 *Calculating the angle between two vectors in component form*

Find, to the nearest degree, the angle between the vectors

$$\mathbf{a} = 2\mathbf{i} - 3\mathbf{j} + \mathbf{k} \quad \text{and} \quad \mathbf{b} = -\mathbf{i} + 2\mathbf{j} + 4\mathbf{k}.$$

The next activity is the final one in this unit. You'll need to apply many of the skills in working with vectors that you have learned.

Activity 55 *Calculating angles between velocities*

A yacht is sailing at $4.8\,\mathrm{m\,s^{-1}}$ on a course of $50°$, and a small rowing boat is travelling at $1.1\,\mathrm{m\,s^{-1}}$ on a course of $140°$.

(a) Write down the angle between the paths of the two boats.

(b) The wind suddenly changes, which results in each boat having an additional velocity imposed on it of $3.5\,\mathrm{m\,s^{-1}}$ with bearing $70°$. Calculate the new speed of each boat in $\mathrm{m\,s^{-1}}$ (to one decimal place) and the new angle between their paths (to the nearest degree).

Learning outcomes

After studying this unit, you should be able to:

- calculate the distance between two points in two and three dimensions
- find the midpoint and the perpendicular bisector of the line segment between two points
- recognise the equations of a circle and a sphere, and find the centre and radius of a circle or sphere from its equation
- find the equation of the circle through three points
- calculate the points of intersection of lines, circles and parabolas
- understand what a vector is, and understand the difference between vector and scalar quantities
- find the components of a two-dimensional vector from its magnitude and direction, and vice versa
- find the magnitude of a three-dimensional vector from its components
- add and subtract vectors, and multiply them by a scalar
- use vectors to solve some practical problems involving displacements and velocities
- calculate the scalar product of two vectors, and find the angle between two non-zero vectors.

Solutions to activities

Solution to Activity 1

(a) The distance between the points $(3, 2)$ and $(7, 5)$ is

$$\sqrt{(7-3)^2 + (5-2)^2} = \sqrt{4^2 + 3^2} = \sqrt{25} = 5.$$

(b) The distance between the points $(-1, 4)$ and $(3, -2)$ is

$$\sqrt{(3-(-1))^2 + (-2-4)^2} = \sqrt{4^2 + (-6)^2}$$
$$= \sqrt{52} = 2\sqrt{13}.$$

Solution to Activity 2

(The solution to this activity is discussed in the text after the activity.)

Solution to Activity 3

The midpoint of the line segment joining $(3, 4)$ and $(5, -3)$ is

$$\left(\frac{3+5}{2}, \frac{4-3}{2}\right) = (4, \tfrac{1}{2}).$$

Solution to Activity 4

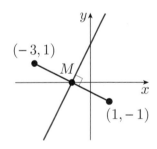

The midpoint of the line segment joining the points is

$$\left(\frac{-3+1}{2}, \frac{1-1}{2}\right) = (-1, 0).$$

The gradient of the line segment is

$$\frac{1-(-1)}{-3-1} = \frac{2}{-4} = -\frac{1}{2}.$$

So the gradient of the perpendicular bisector is 2.

Hence the equation of the perpendicular bisector is

$$y - 0 = 2(x - (-1)),$$

which simplifies to

$$y = 2x + 2.$$

Solution to Activity 5

(a) The equation of the circle with centre $(0, 0)$ and radius 3 is $x^2 + y^2 = 9$.

(b) The equation of the circle with centre $(5, 7)$ and radius $\sqrt{2}$ is

$$(x-5)^2 + (y-7)^2 = 2,$$

since $(\sqrt{2})^2 = 2$.

(c) The equation of the circle with centre $(-3, -1)$ and radius $\tfrac{1}{2}$ is

$$(x-(-3))^2 + (y-(-1))^2 = \left(\tfrac{1}{2}\right)^2;$$

that is,

$$(x+3)^2 + (y+1)^2 = \tfrac{1}{4}.$$

(d) The equation of the circle with centre $(3, -\sqrt{3})$ and radius $2/\sqrt{5}$ is

$$(x-3)^2 + (y-(-\sqrt{3}))^2 = \left(\frac{2}{\sqrt{5}}\right)^2;$$

that is,

$$(x-3)^2 + (y+\sqrt{3})^2 = \tfrac{4}{5}.$$

Solution to Activity 6

(a) The circle $(x-1)^2 + (y-2)^2 = 25$ has centre $(1, 2)$ and radius $\sqrt{25} = 5$.

(b) The circle $(x+1)^2 + (y+2)^2 = 49$ has centre $(-1, -2)$ and radius 7.

(c) The circle $(x-\pi)^2 + (y+\pi)^2 = \pi^2$ has centre $(\pi, -\pi)$ and radius π.

(d) The given equation is $4x^2 + 4(y-\sqrt{3})^2 = 7$. Dividing by 4, to express it in standard form, gives

$$x^2 + (y-\sqrt{3})^2 = \tfrac{7}{4},$$

so the centre is $(0, \sqrt{3})$ and the radius is $\sqrt{7/4} = \sqrt{7}/2$.

Solution to Activity 7

(a) The given equation is

$$x^2 + y^2 - 6x + 8y = 0.$$

Completing the squares gives

$$(x-3)^2 - 9 + (y+4)^2 - 16 = 0.$$

Simplifying gives

$$(x-3)^2 + (y+4)^2 = 25.$$

This equation is of the form
$(x - a)^2 + (y - b)^2 = r^2$, with $a = 3$, $b = -4$ and
$r^2 = 25$. So it represents a circle, with centre
$(3, -4)$ and radius 5.

(b) The given equation is
$$4x^2 + 4y^2 - 16x + 4y = 3.$$
Dividing through by 4 gives
$$x^2 + y^2 - 4x + y = \tfrac{3}{4}.$$
Completing the squares gives
$$(x - 2)^2 - 4 + (y + \tfrac{1}{2})^2 - \tfrac{1}{4} = \tfrac{3}{4}.$$
Simplifying gives
$$(x - 2)^2 + (y + \tfrac{1}{2})^2 = 5.$$
This equation is of the form
$(x - a)^2 + (y - b)^2 = r^2$, with $a = 2$, $b = -\tfrac{1}{2}$
and $r^2 = 5$. So it represents a circle, with centre
$(2, -\tfrac{1}{2})$ and radius $\sqrt{5}$.

Solution to Activity 8

(a) The equation $(x - 2)^2 - (y + 3)^2 = 4$ does not
represent a circle, because when the brackets
are expanded, the coefficient of x^2 is 1, but the
coefficient of y^2 is -1, which is different.

(b) The equation $(x + 1)^2 + (y - 2)^2 + 9 = 0$ does
not represent a circle. When it is written in
standard form, the term on the right-hand side
is -9, which is not the square of the radius of a
circle.

(c) The equation $(x + 1)^2 + (y - 3)^2 - 5 = 0$ can be
written as $(x + 1)^2 + (y - 3)^2 = 5$, which is the
equation of a circle with centre $(-1, 3)$ and
radius $\sqrt{5}$.

(d) The given equation is
$$2x^2 + 2y^2 - 20x + 16y + 90 = 0.$$
First simplify it by dividing by 2 to give
$$x^2 + y^2 - 10x + 8y + 45 = 0.$$
Then completing the squares gives
$$(x - 5)^2 - 25 + (y + 4)^2 - 16 + 45 = 0,$$
which simplifies to
$$(x - 5)^2 + (y + 4)^2 = -4.$$
This equation does not represent a circle, since
the number on the right-hand side is negative.

(e) The given equation is
$$x^2 + y^2 - 10x - 2y + 20 = 0.$$

Completing the squares gives
$$(x - 5)^2 - 25 + (y - 1)^2 - 1 + 20 = 0,$$
which simplifies to
$$(x - 5)^2 + (y - 1)^2 = 6.$$
This equation represents a circle with centre
$(5, 1)$ and radius $\sqrt{6}$.

(f) In the equation $2x^2 + 3y^2 - 5x + 4y - 8 = 0$,
the coefficients of x^2 and y^2 are different, so this
equation does not represent a circle.

Solution to Activity 9

(a) Substituting $y = 3$ into the equation of the
circle gives
$$(x - 1)^2 + (3 - 5)^2 = 9$$
$$(x - 1)^2 + 4 = 9$$
$$(x - 1)^2 = 5.$$
Taking the square root of both sides gives
$$x - 1 = \pm\sqrt{5}$$
$$x = 1 \pm \sqrt{5}$$
$$x = 1 + \sqrt{5} \quad \text{or} \quad x = 1 - \sqrt{5}.$$

So the points $(1 + \sqrt{5}, 3)$ and $(1 - \sqrt{5}, 3)$ lie on
the circle. (One lies on the right-hand part, and
one on the left-hand part.)

(b) Substituting $x = 4$ into the equation of the
circle gives
$$(4 - 1)^2 + (y - 5)^2 = 9$$
$$9 + (y - 5)^2 = 9$$
$$(y - 5)^2 = 0$$
$$y = 5.$$

So $(4, 5)$ is the only point on the circle with
x-coordinate 4. (It is the point at the extreme
right of the circle.)

Solution to Activity 10

Let the three points be $O(0,0)$, $A(-4,2)$ and $B(8,6)$.

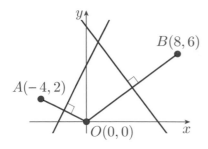

First, find the perpendicular bisector of OA. The midpoint of OA is

$$\left(\frac{0-4}{2}, \frac{0+2}{2}\right) = (-2, 1).$$

The gradient of OA is

$$\frac{2-0}{-4-0} = \frac{2}{-4} = -\frac{1}{2}.$$

So the gradient of the perpendicular bisector of OA is 2.

Hence its equation is

$$y - 1 = 2(x - (-2))$$
$$y - 1 = 2x + 4$$
$$y = 2x + 5.$$

Second, find the perpendicular bisector of OB. The midpoint of OB is

$$\left(\frac{0+8}{2}, \frac{0+6}{2}\right) = (4, 3).$$

The gradient of OB is

$$\frac{6-0}{8-0} = \frac{6}{8} = \frac{3}{4}.$$

So the gradient of the perpendicular bisector of OB is $-\frac{4}{3}$.

Hence its equation is

$$y - 3 = -\frac{4}{3}(x - 4)$$
$$y - 3 = -\frac{4}{3}x + \frac{16}{3}$$
$$y = -\frac{4}{3}x + \frac{25}{3}.$$

Now find the point of intersection of the perpendicular bisectors, by solving $y = 2x + 5$ and $y = -\frac{4}{3}x + \frac{25}{3}$ simultaneously.

Equating these expressions for y gives

$$2x + 5 = -\frac{4}{3}x + \frac{25}{3}$$
$$6x + 15 = -4x + 25$$
$$10x = 10$$
$$x = 1.$$

Using $y = 2x + 5$ gives $y = 2 \times 1 + 5 = 7$.

So the centre of the circle is $(1, 7)$.

The radius is the distance between the centre, $(1, 7)$, and one of the given points, say, $(0, 0)$. So it is

$$\sqrt{(1-0)^2 + (7-0)^2} = \sqrt{1 + 49} = \sqrt{50} = 5\sqrt{2}.$$

Hence the equation of the circle is

$$(x - 1)^2 + (y - 7)^2 = 50.$$

Solution to Activity 11

We need to find the centre of the circle passing through $(0, 0)$, $(6, 1)$ and $(9, \frac{5}{2})$.

To do this, first find the perpendicular bisector of the line segment that joins $(0, 0)$ and $(6, 1)$. The midpoint of this line segment is

$$\left(\frac{0+6}{2}, \frac{0+1}{2}\right) = \left(3, \tfrac{1}{2}\right).$$

Its gradient is

$$\frac{1-0}{6-0} = \frac{1}{6}.$$

So the gradient of the perpendicular bisector is -6, and hence its equation is

$$y - \frac{1}{2} = -6(x - 3)$$
$$y = -6x + 18 + \frac{1}{2}$$
$$y = -6x + \frac{37}{2}.$$

Next, find the perpendicular bisector of the line segment that joins $(6, 1)$ and $(9, \frac{5}{2})$. The midpoint of this line segment is

$$\left(\frac{6+9}{2}, \frac{1+5/2}{2}\right) = \left(\frac{15}{2}, \frac{7}{4}\right).$$

Its gradient is

$$\frac{5/2 - 1}{9 - 6} = \frac{3/2}{3} = \frac{1}{2}.$$

So the gradient of the perpendicular bisector is -2, and hence its equation is

$$y - \frac{7}{4} = -2\left(x - \frac{15}{2}\right)$$

$$y - \frac{7}{4} = -2x + 15$$

$$y = -2x + \frac{67}{4}.$$

Now find the point of intersection of the perpendicular bisectors by solving the equations

$$y = -6x + \frac{37}{2} \quad \text{and} \quad y = -2x + \frac{67}{4},$$

simultaneously.

Equating the expressions for y gives

$$-6x + \frac{37}{2} = -2x + \frac{67}{4}$$

$$-4x = -\frac{7}{4}$$

$$x = \frac{7}{16}.$$

Substituting into the equation $y = -2x + \frac{67}{4}$ gives

$$y = -2 \times \frac{7}{16} + \frac{67}{4} = -\frac{7}{8} + \frac{67}{4} = \frac{127}{8}.$$

So the centre of the circle is

$$\left(\frac{7}{16}, \frac{127}{8}\right) = (0.4375, 15.875).$$

The radius of the plate is the distance between the centre $(0.4375, 15.875)$ and one of the given points, say $(0, 0)$, which is

$$\sqrt{(0.4375 - 0)^2 + (15.875 - 0)^2} = 15.881\ldots.$$

So the radius of the plate is $15.9\,\text{cm}$, and its diameter is $31.8\,\text{cm}$, both to 1 d.p.

Solution to Activity 12

(a) Substituting the equation of the line, $y = 2x$, into the equation of the circle, $(x + 7)^2 + (y - 2)^2 = 80$, gives

$$(x + 7)^2 + (2x - 2)^2 = 80.$$

Expanding the brackets and simplifying gives

$$5x^2 + 6x - 27 = 0.$$

This factorises as $(x + 3)(5x - 9) = 0$.

So $x + 3 = 0$, that is, $x = -3$, or $5x - 9 = 0$, that is, $x = \frac{9}{5}$.

Substituting each of these values in turn into the equation of the line, we obtain, respectively,

$$y = 2 \times (-3) = -6 \text{ and } y = 2 \times \frac{9}{5} = \frac{18}{5}.$$

So the line intersects the circle at the two points $(-3, -6)$ and $\left(\frac{9}{5}, \frac{18}{5}\right)$.

(b) Substituting the equation of the line, $y = 2x - 6$, into the equation of the circle, $(x + 7)^2 + (y - 2)^2 = 80$, gives

$$(x + 7)^2 + (2x - 8)^2 = 80.$$

This equation simplifies to $5x^2 - 18x + 33 = 0$, which is a quadratic equation of the form $ax^2 + bx + c = 0$, with $a = 5$, $b = -18$ and $c = 33$. The discriminant of the quadratic expression is

$$b^2 - 4ac = (-18)^2 - 4 \times 5 \times 33 = -336.$$

Since this is negative, the quadratic equation has no real solutions.

So there are no points which lie on both the line and the circle: the line does not intersect the circle.

Solution to Activity 13

The two equations are $y = x + 11$ and $y = -x^2 - 2x + 15$. Their graphs intersect when

$$-x^2 - 2x + 15 = x + 11$$

$$x^2 + 3x - 4 = 0$$

$$(x + 4)(x - 1) = 0$$

$$x = -4 \quad \text{or} \quad x = 1.$$

We now substitute these solutions into the equation $y = x + 11$ to find the corresponding y-coordinates. Substituting $x = -4$ gives

$$y = -4 + 11 = 7.$$

Substituting $x = 1$ gives

$$y = 1 + 11 = 12.$$

So the points of intersection are $(-4, 7)$ and $(1, 12)$.

Solution to Activity 14

The equilibrium price is the value of p at the point (q, p) where the supply and demand curves intersect. At this point, we have

$$500 - 30q = \frac{q^2}{2} + \frac{q}{2}$$

$$1000 - 60q = q^2 + q$$

$$q^2 + 61q - 1000 = 0.$$

Using the quadratic formula with $a = 1$, $b = 61$ and $c = -1000$ gives

$$q = \frac{-61 \pm \sqrt{61^2 - 4 \times 1 \times (-1000)}}{2}$$

$$= \frac{-61 \pm \sqrt{7721}}{2}$$

$$= 13.434\ldots \quad \text{or} \quad -74.434\ldots.$$

Hence the amount of wheat expected to be produced in the next year is 13 million tonnes (to the nearest million tonnes). (We ignore the negative solution of the equation since the amount of wheat is positive.)

Substituting into the equation $p = 500 - 30q$ gives

$$p = 500 - 30 \times 13.434\ldots = 96.961\ldots.$$

So the trader expects that 13 million tonnes of wheat will be produced (to the nearest million tonnes), and that it will sell at £97 per tonne (to the nearest pound).

(The graphs of the functions are shown below.)

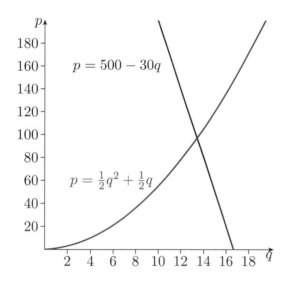

Solution to Activity 15

Expanding the equations and simplifying gives

$$x^2 + 2x + 1 + y^2 - 4y + 4 = 9$$

$$x^2 - 8x + 16 + y^2 + 6y + 9 = 36;$$

that is,

$$x^2 + y^2 + 2x - 4y - 4 = 0, \tag{7}$$

$$x^2 + y^2 - 8x + 6y - 11 = 0. \tag{8}$$

Subtracting equation (8) from equation (7) to eliminate the terms in x^2 and y^2 gives

$$10x - 10y + 7 = 0$$

$$10y = 10x + 7,$$

so $y = x + \frac{7}{10}$.

Using this equation to substitute for y in equation (7) gives

$$x^2 + \left(x + \frac{7}{10}\right)^2 + 2x - 4\left(x + \frac{7}{10}\right) - 4 = 0$$

$$x^2 + x^2 + \frac{7}{5}x + \frac{49}{100} + 2x - 4x - \frac{14}{5} - 4 = 0$$

$$2x^2 - \frac{3}{5}x - \frac{631}{100} = 0.$$

Using the quadratic formula, and writing the fractions as exact decimals, gives

$$x = \frac{0.6 \pm \sqrt{0.6^2 + 4 \times 2 \times 6.31}}{4}$$

$$x = 1.932\ldots \quad \text{or} \quad -1.632\ldots.$$

Substituting these values of x into the equation $y = x + \frac{7}{10}$ gives $y = 2.632\ldots$ and $y = -0.932\ldots$, respectively.

So the points of intersection are $(1.93, 2.63)$ and $(-1.63, -0.93)$ (to two decimal places).

Solution to Activity 17

(a) The curves are plotted below.

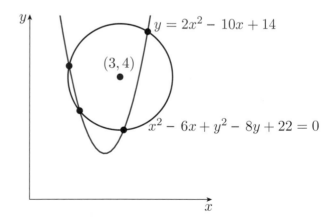

(b) The points of intersection are $(1.30, 4.36)$, $(1.66, 2.90)$, $(3.12, 2.27)$ and $(3.91, 5.47)$ (to 2 d.p.).

(c) The maximum number of points of intersection of a circle and a parabola is four. This fact can be justified by the geometric argument that each 'half' of the parabola (each part on one side of the vertex) can meet the circle at most twice.

Alternatively, if the equation of the parabola is used to substitute for y in the equation of the circle, then an equation for x containing terms in x^4, x^3, x^2, x and a constant term is obtained, and such an equation can have at most four solutions (by a result that you will meet in Unit 12).

(Details of how to use the CAS to find the points of intersection of two curves are given in the *Computer algebra guide*, in the 'Computer methods for the CAS Activities in Books A–D' section.)

Solution to Activity 18

The points are $A(2, 1, 0)$, $B(4, 4, 0)$, $C(4, 1, 4)$ and $D(2, 4, 4)$.

Solution to Activity 19

(a) The distance between the points $(1, 3, 5)$ and $(4, 1, 7)$ is
$$\sqrt{(4-1)^2 + (1-3)^2 + (7-5)^2}$$
$$= \sqrt{3^2 + (-2)^2 + 2^2}$$
$$= \sqrt{9 + 4 + 4} = \sqrt{17}.$$

(b) The distance between the points $(-1, 2, 5)$ and $(4, -1, 3)$ is
$$\sqrt{(4-(-1))^2 + (-1-2)^2 + (3-5)^2}$$
$$= \sqrt{5^2 + (-3)^2 + (-2)^2}$$
$$= \sqrt{25 + 9 + 4} = \sqrt{38}.$$

Solution to Activity 20

(a) The sphere with centre $(3, 5, 2)$ and radius 2 has equation $(x-3)^2 + (y-5)^2 + (z-2)^2 = 4$.

(b) The sphere with centre $(2, -1, -3)$ and radius $\sqrt{3}$ has equation
$$(x-2)^2 + (y-(-1))^2 + (z-(-3))^2 = 3;$$
that is,
$$(x-2)^2 + (y+1)^2 + (z+3)^2 = 3.$$

Solution to Activity 21

(a) The sphere $(x-2)^2 + (y-3)^2 + (z-5)^2 = 16$ has centre $(2, 3, 5)$ and radius 4.

(b) The sphere $(x+2)^2 + (y-4)^2 + (z+1)^2 = 7$ has centre $(-2, 4, -1)$ and radius $\sqrt{7}$.

Solution to Activity 22

(a) This equation can be written as
$$(x-4)^2 + (y-2)^2 + (z+5)^2 = 3,$$
so it is the equation of a sphere with centre $(4, 2, -5)$ and radius $\sqrt{3}$.

(b) This equation does not represent a sphere. It has all the terms involving x, y and z on the same side of the equation, but the coefficients of x^2, y^2 and z^2 are not the same.

(c) Dividing this equation through by 2 gives
$$x^2 + y^2 + z^2 + 2x - 6z + 6 = 0,$$
and completing the squares gives
$$(x+1)^2 + y^2 + (z-3)^2 = 4,$$
which is the equation of a sphere with centre $(-1, 0, 3)$ and radius 2.

(d) This equation does not represent a sphere. Dividing the equation through by 2 gives
$$x^2 + y^2 + z^2 + 4x - 2y + \tfrac{13}{2} = 0,$$
and completing the squares gives
$$(x+2)^2 + (y-1)^2 + z^2 = -\tfrac{3}{2}.$$
Since the constant term on the right-hand side is negative, this is not the equation of a sphere.

Solution to Activity 23

(a) The vector $\mathbf{f}$ is equal to the vector $\mathbf{a}$.

(b) The vector $\mathbf{d}$ is equal to the vector $\overrightarrow{PQ}$.

Solution to Activity 24

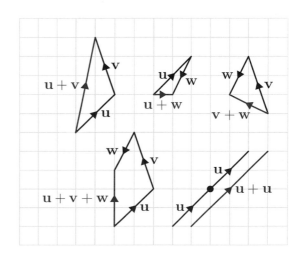

Solution to Activity 25

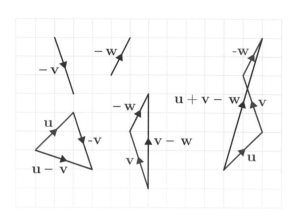

Solution to Activity 26

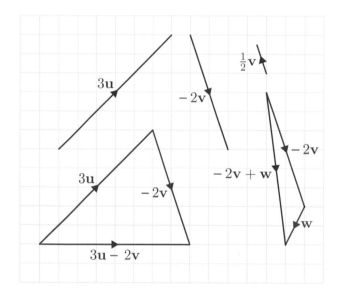

Solution to Activity 27

(a) The velocity of a wind of 70 knots blowing from the north-east is represented by $2\mathbf{v}$.

(b) The velocity of a wind of 35 knots blowing from the south-west is represented by $-\mathbf{v}$.

Solution to Activity 28

(a) $4(\mathbf{a} - \mathbf{c}) + 3(\mathbf{c} - \mathbf{b}) + 2(2\mathbf{a} - \mathbf{b} - 3\mathbf{c})$
$$= 4\mathbf{a} - 4\mathbf{c} + 3\mathbf{c} - 3\mathbf{b} + 4\mathbf{a} - 2\mathbf{b} - 6\mathbf{c}$$
$$= 8\mathbf{a} - 5\mathbf{b} - 7\mathbf{c}$$

(b) (i) $4\mathbf{x} = 7\mathbf{a} - 2\mathbf{b}$
$$\mathbf{x} = \tfrac{7}{4}\mathbf{a} - \tfrac{1}{2}\mathbf{b}$$

(ii) $5\mathbf{x} = 2(\mathbf{a} - \mathbf{b}) - 3(\mathbf{b} - \mathbf{a})$
$$= 2(\mathbf{a} - \mathbf{b}) + 3(\mathbf{a} - \mathbf{b})$$
$$= 5(\mathbf{a} - \mathbf{b})$$
$$\mathbf{x} = \mathbf{a} - \mathbf{b}$$

Solution to Activity 29

(a) The bearing of $\mathbf{a}$ is $45°$, the bearing of $\mathbf{b}$ is $315°$, and the bearing of $\mathbf{c}$ is $225°$, as shown below.

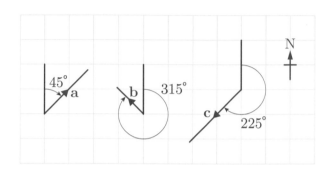

(b)

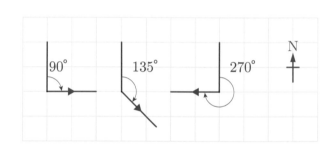

Solution to Activity 30

Represent the first part of the motion by the vector $\mathbf{a}$, and the second part by the vector $\mathbf{b}$. Then the resultant displacement is $\mathbf{a} + \mathbf{b}$.

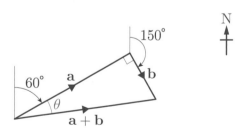

Since **a** and **b** are perpendicular, and $|\mathbf{a}| = 5.3\,\text{km}$ and $|\mathbf{b}| = 2.1\,\text{km}$,

$$|\mathbf{a} + \mathbf{b}| = \sqrt{|\mathbf{a}|^2 + |\mathbf{b}|^2}$$
$$= \sqrt{5.3^2 + 2.1^2} = \sqrt{32.5}$$
$$= 5.70\ldots \text{km}.$$

The angle marked θ is given by

$$\tan\theta = \frac{|\mathbf{b}|}{|\mathbf{a}|} = \frac{2.1}{5.3},$$

so

$$\theta = \tan^{-1}\left(\frac{2.1}{5.3}\right) = 22° \text{ (to the nearest degree).}$$

So the bearing of $\mathbf{a} + \mathbf{b}$ is $60° + 22° = 82°$ (to the nearest degree).

The resultant displacement of the yacht has magnitude $5.7\,\text{km}$ (to 1 d.p.) and bearing $82°$ (to the nearest degree).

Solution to Activity 31

Represent the first part of the motion by the vector **a**, and the second part by the vector **b**. Then the resultant displacement is $\mathbf{a} + \mathbf{b}$.

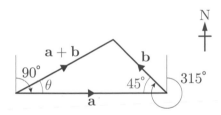

The angle at the tip of **a** in the triangle above is $315° - 270° = 45°$, as shown.

We know that $|\mathbf{a}| = 40\,\text{cm}$ and $|\mathbf{b}| = 20\,\text{cm}$.

The magnitude of the resultant $\mathbf{a} + \mathbf{b}$ can be found by using the cosine rule:

$$|\mathbf{a} + \mathbf{b}|^2 = |\mathbf{a}|^2 + |\mathbf{b}|^2 - 2 \times |\mathbf{a}| \times |\mathbf{b}| \times \cos 45°,$$

which gives

$$|\mathbf{a} + \mathbf{b}| = \sqrt{|\mathbf{a}|^2 + |\mathbf{b}|^2 - 2 \times |\mathbf{a}| \times |\mathbf{b}| \times \cos 45°}$$
$$= \sqrt{40^2 + 20^2 - 2 \times 40 \times 20 \times \cos 45°}$$
$$= 29.472\ldots \text{cm}.$$

The angle marked θ can be found by using the sine rule:

$$\frac{|\mathbf{b}|}{\sin\theta} = \frac{|\mathbf{a} + \mathbf{b}|}{\sin 45°}$$

$$\frac{20}{\sin\theta} = \frac{29.472\ldots}{\sin 45°}$$

$$\sin\theta = \frac{20\sin 45°}{29.472\ldots}.$$

Now,

$$\sin^{-1}\left(\frac{20\sin 45°}{29.472\ldots}\right) = 28.67\ldots°,$$

so

$$\theta = 28.67\ldots°$$

or

$$\theta = 180° - 28.67\ldots° = 151.32\ldots°.$$

Since $|\mathbf{b}| < |\mathbf{a} + \mathbf{b}|$, we expect $\theta < 45°$, so the required solution is $\theta = 29°$ (to the nearest degree).

The bearing of $|\mathbf{a} + \mathbf{b}|$ is $90° - 29° = 61°$ (to the nearest degree).

So the resultant displacement of the grab has magnitude $29\,\text{cm}$ (to the nearest cm) and bearing $61°$ (to the nearest degree).

Solution to Activity 32

Let **s** be the velocity of the ship, and let **b** be the velocity of the boy relative to the ship. Then the resultant velocity of the boy is $\mathbf{s} + \mathbf{b}$, as shown below.

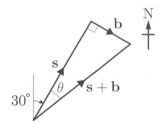

We know that $|\mathbf{s}| = 10.0\,\text{m s}^{-1}$ and $|\mathbf{b}| = 4.0\,\text{m s}^{-1}$. Since the triangle is right-angled,

$$|\mathbf{s} + \mathbf{b}| = \sqrt{|\mathbf{s}|^2 + |\mathbf{b}|^2}$$
$$= \sqrt{10^2 + 4^2}$$
$$= \sqrt{116}$$
$$= 10.77\ldots \text{m s}^{-1}.$$

The angle θ is given by

$$\tan\theta = \frac{|\mathbf{b}|}{|\mathbf{s}|} = \frac{4}{10} = \frac{2}{5}.$$

So

$$\theta = \tan^{-1}\tfrac{2}{5} = 21.8\ldots°.$$

The bearing of $\mathbf{s} + \mathbf{b}$ is $30° + 21.8\ldots° = 51.8\ldots°.$

So the resultant velocity of the boy is $10.8\,\text{m s}^{-1}$ (to 1 d.p.) on a bearing of $52°$ (to the nearest degree).

Solution to Activity 33

Let **s** be the velocity of the ship in still water, and let **c** be the velocity of the current. The resultant velocity of the ship is **s** + **c**, as shown below.

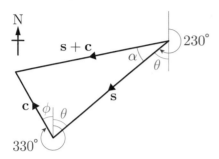

We know that $|\mathbf{s}| = 5.7\,\mathrm{m\,s^{-1}}$ and $|\mathbf{c}| = 2.5\,\mathrm{m\,s^{-1}}$.

The angle marked θ at the tail of **s** is given by $\theta = 230° - 180° = 50°$. Since alternate angles are equal, the angle θ marked at the tip of **s** has the same size.

The angle ϕ marked at the tail of **c** is given by $\phi = 360° - 330° = 30°$.

So the bottom angle of the triangle is $\theta + \phi = 50° + 30° = 80°$.

Applying the cosine rule gives

$$|\mathbf{s}+\mathbf{c}|^2 = |\mathbf{s}|^2 + |\mathbf{c}|^2 - 2|\mathbf{s}||\mathbf{c}|\cos(\theta+\phi),$$

so

$$|\mathbf{s}+\mathbf{c}| = \sqrt{5.7^2 + 2.5^2 - 2 \times 5.7 \times 2.5 \times \cos 80°}$$
$$= 5.813\ldots\mathrm{m\,s^{-1}}.$$

The angle α can be found by using the sine rule:

$$\frac{|\mathbf{c}|}{\sin\alpha} = \frac{|\mathbf{s}+\mathbf{c}|}{\sin(\theta+\phi)}$$

$$\sin\alpha = \frac{|\mathbf{c}|\sin(\theta+\phi)}{|\mathbf{s}+\mathbf{c}|} = \frac{2.5\sin 80°}{5.813\ldots}.$$

Now,

$$\sin^{-1}\left(\frac{2.5\sin 80°}{5.813\ldots}\right) = 25.058\ldots°.$$

So $\alpha = 25.058\ldots°$ or $\alpha = 180° - 25.058\ldots° = 154.941\ldots°$.

But $|\mathbf{c}| < |\mathbf{s}+\mathbf{c}|$, so we expect $\alpha < \theta+\phi$; that is, $\alpha < 80°$. So $\alpha = 25.058\ldots°$, and hence the bearing of **s** + **c** is $230° + 25.058\ldots° = 255.058\ldots°$.

The resultant velocity of the ship is $5.8\,\mathrm{m\,s^{-1}}$ (to 1 d.p.) on a bearing of 255° (to the nearest degree).

Solution to Activity 34

The component forms are $\mathbf{p} = 0\mathbf{i} + 3\mathbf{j} = 3\mathbf{j}$, $\mathbf{q} = 3\mathbf{i} + 4\mathbf{j}$ and $\mathbf{r} = 2\mathbf{i} - 3\mathbf{j}$.

Solution to Activity 35

The column forms of these vectors are

$$\mathbf{p} = 0\mathbf{i} + 3\mathbf{j} = \begin{pmatrix} 0 \\ 3 \end{pmatrix}, \quad \mathbf{q} = 3\mathbf{i} + 4\mathbf{j} = \begin{pmatrix} 3 \\ 4 \end{pmatrix} \text{ and}$$

$$\mathbf{r} = 2\mathbf{i} - 3\mathbf{j} = \begin{pmatrix} 2 \\ -3 \end{pmatrix}.$$

Solution to Activity 36

(a) $(4\mathbf{i} - 2\mathbf{j}) + (-3\mathbf{i} + \mathbf{j}) = 4\mathbf{i} - 3\mathbf{i} - 2\mathbf{j} + \mathbf{j} = \mathbf{i} - \mathbf{j}$

(b) $\begin{pmatrix} 5 \\ 3 \end{pmatrix} + \begin{pmatrix} -4 \\ -3 \end{pmatrix} = \begin{pmatrix} 5-4 \\ 3-3 \end{pmatrix} = \begin{pmatrix} 1 \\ 0 \end{pmatrix}$

(c) $\begin{pmatrix} -7 \\ -4 \\ 1 \end{pmatrix} + \begin{pmatrix} 2 \\ 7 \\ -3 \end{pmatrix} + \begin{pmatrix} 5 \\ 1 \\ 4 \end{pmatrix}$
$= \begin{pmatrix} -7+2+5 \\ -4+7+1 \\ 1-3+4 \end{pmatrix} = \begin{pmatrix} 0 \\ 4 \\ 2 \end{pmatrix}$

Solution to Activity 37

(a) $(2\mathbf{i} + \mathbf{j}) - (3\mathbf{i} + 2\mathbf{j})$
$= 2\mathbf{i} + \mathbf{j} - 3\mathbf{i} - 2\mathbf{j} = -\mathbf{i} - \mathbf{j}$

(b) $(3\mathbf{i} + 2\mathbf{j} - 4\mathbf{k}) - (-2\mathbf{i} + 4\mathbf{j} + 2\mathbf{k})$
$= 3\mathbf{i} + 2\mathbf{j} - 4\mathbf{k} + 2\mathbf{i} - 4\mathbf{j} - 2\mathbf{k} = 5\mathbf{i} - 2\mathbf{j} - 6\mathbf{k}$

(c) $\begin{pmatrix} 3 \\ 4 \\ -1 \end{pmatrix} - \begin{pmatrix} 2 \\ -1 \\ 3 \end{pmatrix} = \begin{pmatrix} 3-2 \\ 4-(-1) \\ -1-3 \end{pmatrix} = \begin{pmatrix} 1 \\ 5 \\ -4 \end{pmatrix}$

Solution to Activity 38

(a) $4\mathbf{a} = 4\begin{pmatrix} 2 \\ -1 \end{pmatrix} = \begin{pmatrix} 8 \\ -4 \end{pmatrix}$

(b) $-2\mathbf{a} = -2\begin{pmatrix} 2 \\ -1 \end{pmatrix} = \begin{pmatrix} -4 \\ 2 \end{pmatrix}$

(c) $\frac{1}{2}\mathbf{a} = \frac{1}{2}\begin{pmatrix} 2 \\ -1 \end{pmatrix} = \begin{pmatrix} 1 \\ -\frac{1}{2} \end{pmatrix}$

(d) $3\mathbf{b} = 3(\mathbf{i} + 3\mathbf{j} - 6\mathbf{k}) = 3\mathbf{i} + 9\mathbf{j} - 18\mathbf{k}$

(e) $-4\mathbf{b} = -4(\mathbf{i} + 3\mathbf{j} - 6\mathbf{k}) = -4\mathbf{i} - 12\mathbf{j} + 24\mathbf{k}$

(f) $\frac{1}{3}\mathbf{b} = \frac{1}{3}(\mathbf{i} + 3\mathbf{j} - 6\mathbf{k}) = \frac{1}{3}\mathbf{i} + \mathbf{j} - 2\mathbf{k}$

Solution to Activity 39

(a) $-2\mathbf{a} + 3\mathbf{b} + 4\mathbf{c}$

$= -2(2\mathbf{i} + 3\mathbf{j}) + 3(\mathbf{i} - 4\mathbf{j}) + 4(-5\mathbf{i} + 7\mathbf{j})$

$= -4\mathbf{i} - 6\mathbf{j} + 3\mathbf{i} - 12\mathbf{j} - 20\mathbf{i} + 28\mathbf{j}$

$= -21\mathbf{i} + 10\mathbf{j}$

(b) $2\begin{pmatrix} 6 \\ -3 \end{pmatrix} - 7\begin{pmatrix} 1 \\ 2 \end{pmatrix} + 5\begin{pmatrix} -1 \\ 4 \end{pmatrix}$

$= \begin{pmatrix} 2 \times 6 - 7 \times 1 + 5 \times (-1) \\ 2 \times (-3) - 7 \times 2 + 5 \times 4 \end{pmatrix} = \begin{pmatrix} 0 \\ 0 \end{pmatrix}$

(c) $a_1 \begin{pmatrix} 1 \\ 0 \end{pmatrix} + a_2 \begin{pmatrix} 0 \\ 1 \end{pmatrix}$

$= \begin{pmatrix} a_1 \times 1 + a_2 \times 0 \\ a_1 \times 0 + a_2 \times 1 \end{pmatrix} = \begin{pmatrix} a_1 \\ a_2 \end{pmatrix}$

(d) $2\begin{pmatrix} 1 \\ 3 \\ 4 \end{pmatrix} + 3\begin{pmatrix} 0 \\ 3 \\ 1 \end{pmatrix} - 2\begin{pmatrix} 1 \\ 4 \\ 2 \end{pmatrix}$

$= \begin{pmatrix} 2 \times 1 + 3 \times 0 - 2 \times 1 \\ 2 \times 3 + 3 \times 3 - 2 \times 4 \\ 2 \times 4 + 3 \times 1 - 2 \times 2 \end{pmatrix} = \begin{pmatrix} 0 \\ 7 \\ 7 \end{pmatrix}$

Solution to Activity 40

In component form, $\overrightarrow{OA} = 5\mathbf{i} + 3\mathbf{j}$ and $\overrightarrow{OB} = -2\mathbf{i} + 4\mathbf{j}$, so

$\overrightarrow{AB} = \overrightarrow{OB} - \overrightarrow{OA}$

$= -2\mathbf{i} + 4\mathbf{j} - (5\mathbf{i} + 3\mathbf{j})$

$= -7\mathbf{i} + \mathbf{j}.$

Solution to Activity 41

(a) $\overrightarrow{AB} = \overrightarrow{OB} - \overrightarrow{OA} = \mathbf{b} - \mathbf{a}.$

(b) Since both OAB and OBC are equilateral triangles, $\angle ABO = \angle BOC = 60°$. So OC is parallel to AB, and $\overrightarrow{OC} = \overrightarrow{AB} = \mathbf{b} - \mathbf{a}.$

(c) $\overrightarrow{BC} = \overrightarrow{OC} - \overrightarrow{OB} = (\mathbf{b} - \mathbf{a}) - \mathbf{b} = -\mathbf{a}.$
Alternatively, notice that BC is parallel to OA, so $\overrightarrow{BC} = -\overrightarrow{OA} = -\mathbf{a}.$

(d) OD is parallel to OA and of equal length, so $\overrightarrow{AD} = -2\overrightarrow{OA} = -2\mathbf{a}.$

(e) $\overrightarrow{AE} = \overrightarrow{AO} + \overrightarrow{OE} = -\mathbf{a} - \mathbf{b}.$

Solution to Activity 42

(a) The point C is the midpoint of OB, so its position vector is $\frac{1}{2}\mathbf{b}$. Hence $\overrightarrow{AC} = \frac{1}{2}\mathbf{b} - \mathbf{a}.$

The point D is the midpoint of OA, so its position vector is $\frac{1}{2}\mathbf{a}$. Hence $\overrightarrow{BD} = \frac{1}{2}\mathbf{a} - \mathbf{b}.$

(b) The point E is the midpoint of AB, so its position vector is $\frac{1}{2}(\mathbf{a} + \mathbf{b})$. Hence the position vector of the point $\frac{2}{3}$ of the way along OE from O is

$$\tfrac{2}{3} \times \tfrac{1}{2}(\mathbf{a} + \mathbf{b}) = \tfrac{1}{3}(\mathbf{a} + \mathbf{b}).$$

The position vector of the point $\frac{2}{3}$ of the way along AC from A is

$\overrightarrow{OA} + \tfrac{2}{3}\overrightarrow{AC} = \mathbf{a} + \tfrac{2}{3} \times (\tfrac{1}{2}\mathbf{b} - \mathbf{a})$

$= \mathbf{a} + \tfrac{1}{3}\mathbf{b} - \tfrac{2}{3}\mathbf{a}$

$= \tfrac{1}{3}(\mathbf{a} + \mathbf{b}).$

The position vector of the point $\frac{2}{3}$ of the way along BD from B is

$\overrightarrow{OB} + \tfrac{2}{3}\overrightarrow{BD} = \mathbf{b} + \tfrac{2}{3} \times (\tfrac{1}{2}\mathbf{a} - \mathbf{b})$

$= \mathbf{b} + \tfrac{1}{3}\mathbf{a} - \tfrac{2}{3}\mathbf{b}$

$= \tfrac{1}{3}(\mathbf{a} + \mathbf{b}).$

(c) The three points in part (b) all have the same position vector, so they are all the same point. Hence the lines OE, AC and BD are concurrent.

Solution to Activity 43

(a) $|-3\mathbf{i} + \mathbf{j}| = \sqrt{(-3)^2 + 1^2} = \sqrt{10}$

(b) $|2\mathbf{i} + 4\mathbf{j} - 3\mathbf{k}| = \sqrt{2^2 + 4^2 + (-3)^2} = \sqrt{29}$

(c) $\left|\begin{pmatrix} -2 \\ 0 \end{pmatrix}\right| = \sqrt{(-2)^2 + 0^2} = 2$

(d) $\left|\begin{pmatrix} 3 \\ -1 \\ 3 \end{pmatrix}\right| = \sqrt{3^2 + (-1)^2 + 3^2} = \sqrt{19}$

Solution to Activity 44

(a) The magnitude of the vector $\mathbf{a} = -2\mathbf{i} + 3\mathbf{j}$ is

$$|\mathbf{a}| = \sqrt{(-2)^2 + 3^2} = \sqrt{13}.$$

The vector **a** is shown below.

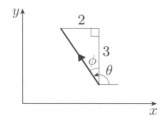

The angle ϕ is given by

$$\phi = \tan^{-1}\frac{2}{3} = 34° \text{ (to the nearest degree).}$$

So the angle θ that **a** makes with the positive x-direction is $34° + 90° = 124°$ (to the nearest degree).

(b) The magnitude of the vector $\mathbf{b} = \begin{pmatrix} 0 \\ -3.5 \end{pmatrix}$ is

$$|\mathbf{b}| = \sqrt{0^2 + (-3.5)^2} = 3.5.$$

The vector **b** has **i**-component 0, so it is parallel to the y-axis. Its **j**-component is negative, so it points in the negative y-direction. Hence the angle that it makes with the positive x-direction is $270°$.

Solution to Activity 45

(a) The magnitude of the vector $\mathbf{u} = 4\mathbf{i} - 2\mathbf{j}$ is

$$|\mathbf{u}| = \sqrt{4^2 + (-2)^2}$$
$$= \sqrt{20} = 4.5\,\mathrm{m\,s^{-1}} \text{ (to 1 d.p.).}$$

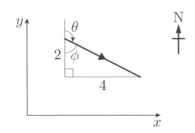

The angle ϕ is given by

$$\phi = \tan^{-1}\left(\frac{4}{2}\right) = \tan^{-1} 2 = 63.43\ldots°.$$

So the bearing of **u** is
$\theta = 180° - 63.43\ldots° = 117°$ (to the nearest degree).

(b) The magnitude of the vector $\mathbf{v} = \begin{pmatrix} -1 \\ -4 \end{pmatrix}$ is

$$|\mathbf{v}| = \sqrt{(-1)^2 + (-4)^2}$$
$$= \sqrt{17} = 4.1\,\mathrm{m\,s^{-1}} \text{ (to 1 d.p.).}$$

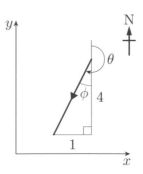

The angle ϕ is given by

$$\phi = \tan^{-1}\frac{1}{4} = 14.03\ldots°.$$

So the bearing of **v** is
$\theta = 180° + 14.03\ldots° = 194°$ (to the nearest degree).

Solution to Activity 46

In each case, we draw a diagram and calculate the lengths of the shorter sides of the right-angled triangle whose hypotenuse is the vector, and whose shorter sides are parallel to the axes.

(a)

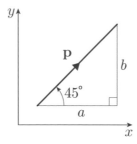

The side lengths a and b are given by

$$a = |\mathbf{p}| \cos 45° = 1 \times \cos 45° = 0.7 \text{ (to 1 d.p)}$$
$$b = |\mathbf{p}| \sin 45° = 1 \times \sin 45° = 0.7 \text{ (to 1 d.p).}$$

The diagram shows that both components of **p** are positive, so
$$\mathbf{p} = 0.7\mathbf{i} + 0.7\mathbf{j} \text{ (to 1 d.p).}$$

(b)

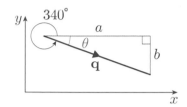

The acute angle marked θ in the diagram is given by $\theta = 360° - 340° = 20°$. Hence the side lengths a and b are given by

$$a = |\mathbf{q}| \cos \theta = 2.5 \cos 20° = 2.3 \text{ (to 1 d.p)}$$

$$b = |\mathbf{q}| \sin \theta = 2.5 \sin 20° = 0.9 \text{ (to 1 d.p)}.$$

The diagram shows that the $\mathbf{i}$-component is positive and the $\mathbf{j}$-component is negative, so

$$\mathbf{q} = 2.3\mathbf{i} - 0.9\mathbf{j} \text{ (to 1 d.p)}.$$

Solution to Activity 47

In each case, we draw a diagram of the right-angled triangle whose hypotenuse is the vector, and whose shorter sides are parallel to the axes. The required components are equal to the lengths of the shorter sides, with their signs deduced from the diagram.

(a)

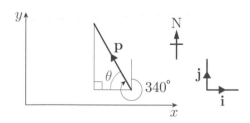

The angle θ is given by $\theta = 340° - 270° = 70°$. Hence the $\mathbf{i}$- and $\mathbf{j}$-components of $\mathbf{p}$ are

$$-|\mathbf{p}| \cos \theta = -3.5 \cos 70° = -1.2 \text{ (to 1 d.p.)}$$

and

$$|\mathbf{p}| \sin \theta = 3.5 \sin 70° = 3.3 \text{ (to 1 d.p.)},$$

respectively. Hence

$$\mathbf{p} = -1.2\mathbf{i} + 3.3\mathbf{j} \text{ (in m, to 1 d.p.)}.$$

(b)

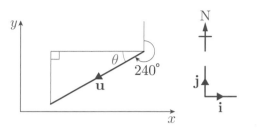

The angle θ is given by $\theta = 270° - 240° = 30°$. Hence the $\mathbf{i}$- and $\mathbf{j}$-components of $\mathbf{u}$ are

$$-|\mathbf{u}| \cos \theta = -5.2 \cos 30° = -4.5 \text{ (to 1 d.p.)}$$

and

$$-|\mathbf{u}| \sin \theta = -5.2 \sin 30° = -2.6,$$

respectively. Hence

$$\mathbf{u} = -4.5\mathbf{i} - 2.6\mathbf{j} \text{ (in m s}^{-1}\text{, to 1 d.p.)}.$$

Solution to Activity 48

(a) By the formula for the components in the box before the activity,

$$\begin{aligned}\mathbf{a} &= 78 \cos 216°\mathbf{i} + 78 \sin 216°\mathbf{j} \\ &= -63.103\ldots\mathbf{i} - 45.847\ldots\mathbf{j} \\ &= -63\mathbf{i} - 46\mathbf{j} \text{ (to 2 s.f.)}.\end{aligned}$$

(b) The vector $\mathbf{w}$ has bearing $119°$, so it makes an angle of $-(119° - 90°) = -29°$ with the positive x-direction, as shown below.

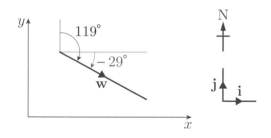

Hence, by the formula for components,

$$\begin{aligned}\mathbf{w} &= 4.4 \cos(-29°)\mathbf{i} + 4.4 \sin(-29°)\mathbf{j} \\ &= 3.848\ldots\mathbf{i} - 2.133\ldots\mathbf{j} \\ &= 3.8\mathbf{i} - 2.1\mathbf{j} \text{ (in m s}^{-1}\text{, to 2 s.f.)}.\end{aligned}$$

Solution to Activity 49

Denote Exeter by E, Belfast by B, and Glasgow by G.

We know that $EB = 460\,\text{km}$ and $BG = 173\,\text{km}$.

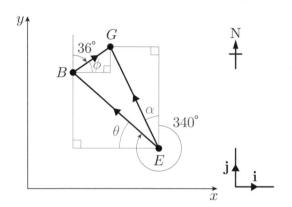

Choose a coordinate system as shown.

The angle θ at E is given by $\theta = 340° - 270° = 70°$, so

$$\overrightarrow{EB} = -|\overrightarrow{EB}|\cos\theta\,\mathbf{i} + |\overrightarrow{EB}|\sin\theta\,\mathbf{j}$$
$$= -460\cos 70°\mathbf{i} + 460\sin 70°\mathbf{j}$$
$$= -157.329\ldots\mathbf{i} + 432.258\ldots\mathbf{j}.$$

The angle ϕ at B is given by $\phi = 90° - 36° = 54°$, so

$$\overrightarrow{BG} = |\overrightarrow{BG}|\cos\phi\,\mathbf{i} + |\overrightarrow{BG}|\sin\phi\,\mathbf{j}$$
$$= 173\cos 54°\mathbf{i} + 173\sin 54°\mathbf{j}$$
$$= 101.686\ldots\mathbf{i} + 139.959\ldots\mathbf{j}.$$

Hence

$$\overrightarrow{EG} = \overrightarrow{EB} + \overrightarrow{BG}$$
$$= -157.329\ldots\mathbf{i} + 432.258\ldots\mathbf{j}$$
$$\quad + 101.686\ldots\mathbf{i} + 139.959\ldots\mathbf{j}$$
$$= -55.642\ldots\mathbf{i} + 572.218\ldots\mathbf{j}.$$

The magnitude of $\overrightarrow{EG}$ is

$$|\overrightarrow{EG}| = \sqrt{(-55.642\ldots)^2 + (572.218\ldots)^2} = 575\,\text{km}$$

(to the nearest km).

The direction of $\overrightarrow{EG}$ can be found from the angle α in the diagram. We have

$$\alpha = \tan^{-1}\left(\frac{55.642\ldots}{572.218\ldots}\right) = 5.55\ldots° = 6°$$

(to the nearest degree). Hence the bearing of $\overrightarrow{EG}$ is $360° - 6° = 354°$ (to the nearest degree).

So the magnitude of the displacement of Glasgow from Exeter is $575\,\text{km}$ (to the nearest km) and the bearing is $354°$ (to the nearest degree).

Solution to Activity 50

(a) Let the horizontal ground velocity of the aircraft be the vector $\mathbf{g}$. A sketch of $\mathbf{g}$ is shown below.

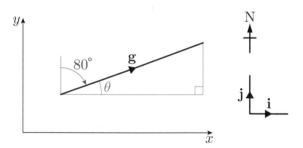

The angle θ in the diagram is given by $\theta = 90° - 80° = 10°$.

The magnitude of $\mathbf{g}$ is $600\,\text{mph}$, so

$$\mathbf{g} = |\mathbf{g}|\cos\theta\,\mathbf{i} + |\mathbf{g}|\sin\theta\,\mathbf{j}$$
$$= 600\cos 10°\mathbf{i} + 600\sin 10°\mathbf{j}$$
$$= 590.88\ldots\mathbf{i} + 104.18\ldots\mathbf{j}$$
$$= 591\mathbf{i} + 104\mathbf{j} \text{ (to the nearest mph)}.$$

(b) Let the resultant velocity of the aircraft be the vector $\mathbf{t}$. The vertical component of $\mathbf{t}$ is $30\mathbf{k}$, so

$$\mathbf{t} = \mathbf{g} + 30\mathbf{k}$$
$$= 590.88\ldots\mathbf{i} + 104.18\ldots\mathbf{j} + 30\mathbf{k}$$
$$= 591\mathbf{i} + 104\mathbf{j} + 30\mathbf{k} \text{ (to the nearest mph)}.$$

Hence the magnitude of the resultant velocity is

$$|\mathbf{t}| = \sqrt{(590.88\ldots)^2 + (104.18\ldots)^2 + 30^2}$$
$$= 600.74\ldots = 601\,\text{mph (to the nearest mph)}.$$

(c) Let the air velocity of the aircraft be $\mathbf{a}$, and the wind velocity be $\mathbf{w}$. Then $\mathbf{t} = \mathbf{a} + \mathbf{w}$, so
$$\mathbf{a} = \mathbf{t} - \mathbf{w}.$$

We express $\mathbf{w}$ in component form, by first drawing a diagram. The wind is blowing *from* the direction with a bearing of $290°$, so it is blowing *towards* the direction with a bearing of $290° - 180° = 110°$, as shown in the following diagram.

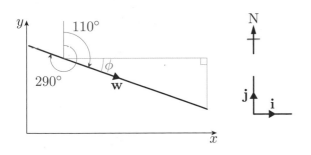

The angle ϕ is given by $\phi = 110° - 90° = 20°$.

The magnitude of $\mathbf{w}$ is $100\,\text{mph}$, so
$$\mathbf{w} = |\mathbf{w}| \cos\phi\,\mathbf{i} - |\mathbf{w}| \sin\phi\,\mathbf{j}$$
$$= 100\cos 20°\mathbf{i} - 100\sin 20°\mathbf{j}$$
$$= 93.96\ldots\mathbf{i} - 34.20\ldots\mathbf{j}.$$

Hence
$$\mathbf{a} = \mathbf{t} - \mathbf{w}$$
$$= 590.88\ldots\mathbf{i} + 104.18\ldots\mathbf{j} + 30\mathbf{k}$$
$$- (93.96\ldots\mathbf{i} - 34.20\ldots\mathbf{j})$$
$$= 496.91\ldots\mathbf{i} + 138.39\ldots\mathbf{j} + 30\mathbf{k}$$
$$= 497\mathbf{i} + 138\mathbf{j} + 30\mathbf{k} \text{ (to the nearest mph)}.$$

The magnitude of the air velocity is
$$|\mathbf{a}| = \sqrt{(496.91\ldots)^2 + (138.39\ldots)^2 + 30^2}$$
$$= 516.69\ldots = 517\,\text{mph (to the nearest mph)}.$$

Solution to Activity 51

These scalar products are
$$\mathbf{u} \cdot \mathbf{v} = |\mathbf{u}|\,|\mathbf{v}| \cos\theta = 4 \times 3 \times \cos 60° = 6$$
$$\mathbf{u} \cdot \mathbf{w} = |\mathbf{u}|\,|\mathbf{w}| \cos\theta = 4 \times 2 \times \cos 90° = 0$$
$$\mathbf{u} \cdot \mathbf{u} = |\mathbf{u}|\,|\mathbf{u}| \cos\theta = 4 \times 4 \times \cos 0 = 16.$$

Solution to Activity 52
$$(\mathbf{a} + \mathbf{b}) \cdot (\mathbf{a} - \mathbf{b}) = \mathbf{a} \cdot (\mathbf{a} - \mathbf{b}) + \mathbf{b} \cdot (\mathbf{a} - \mathbf{b})$$
$$= \mathbf{a} \cdot \mathbf{a} - \mathbf{a} \cdot \mathbf{b} + \mathbf{b} \cdot \mathbf{a} - \mathbf{b} \cdot \mathbf{b}$$
$$= \mathbf{a} \cdot \mathbf{a} - \mathbf{a} \cdot \mathbf{b} + \mathbf{a} \cdot \mathbf{b} - \mathbf{b} \cdot \mathbf{b}$$
$$= \mathbf{a} \cdot \mathbf{a} - \mathbf{b} \cdot \mathbf{b}$$

Solution to Activity 53
$$\mathbf{u} \cdot \mathbf{v} = (3\mathbf{i} - 4\mathbf{j} + \mathbf{k}) \cdot (2\mathbf{i} + 3\mathbf{j} - 2\mathbf{k})$$
$$= 3 \times 2 + (-4) \times 3 + 1 \times (-2)$$
$$= 6 - 12 - 2 = -8$$

$$\mathbf{u} \cdot \mathbf{w} = (3\mathbf{i} - 4\mathbf{j} + \mathbf{k}) \cdot (-\mathbf{i} + \mathbf{j} + 3\mathbf{k})$$
$$= 3 \times (-1) + (-4) \times 1 + 1 \times 3$$
$$= -3 - 4 + 3 = -4$$
$$\mathbf{v} \cdot \mathbf{w} = (2\mathbf{i} + 3\mathbf{j} - 2\mathbf{k}) \cdot (-\mathbf{i} + \mathbf{j} + 3\mathbf{k})$$
$$= 2 \times (-1) + 3 \times 1 + (-2) \times 3$$
$$= -2 + 3 - 6 = -5$$

Solution to Activity 54

We have
$$\mathbf{a} \cdot \mathbf{b} = 2 \times (-1) + (-3) \times 2 + 1 \times 4 = -4,$$
$$|\mathbf{a}| = \sqrt{2^2 + (-3)^2 + 1^2} = \sqrt{14},$$
$$|\mathbf{b}| = \sqrt{(-1)^2 + 2^2 + 4^2} = \sqrt{21}.$$

So, if θ is the angle between $\mathbf{a}$ and $\mathbf{b}$, then
$$\cos\theta = \frac{\mathbf{a} \cdot \mathbf{b}}{|\mathbf{a}|\,|\mathbf{b}|} = \frac{-4}{\sqrt{14} \times \sqrt{21}} = -\frac{4}{7\sqrt{6}}$$
and hence
$$\theta = \cos^{-1}\left(-\frac{4}{7\sqrt{6}}\right) = 103.49\ldots°.$$

So the angle between the vectors is $103°$ (to the nearest degree).

Solution to Activity 55

(a) The initial angle between the paths of the boats is the difference between their courses, $140° - 50° = 90°$.

(b) Let $\mathbf{s}$ be the initial velocity of the yacht, let $\mathbf{r}$ be the initial velocity of the rowing boat, and let $\mathbf{w}$ be the velocity imposed by the wind. These vectors are shown below. A coordinate system with $\mathbf{i}$ pointing east and $\mathbf{j}$ pointing north has been chosen, as shown.

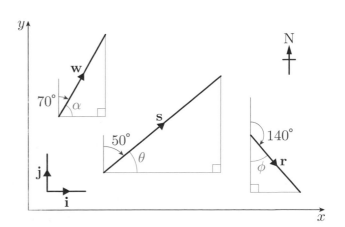

We express the three vectors $\mathbf{s}$, $\mathbf{r}$ and $\mathbf{w}$ in component form.

The angle θ is given by $\theta = 90° - 50° = 40°$, so
$$\mathbf{s} = |\mathbf{s}| \cos\theta\,\mathbf{i} + |\mathbf{s}| \sin\theta\,\mathbf{j}$$
$$= 4.8 \cos 40°\,\mathbf{i} + 4.8 \sin 40°\,\mathbf{j}$$
$$= 3.677\ldots\mathbf{i} + 3.085\ldots\mathbf{j}.$$

The angle ϕ is given by $\phi = 180° - 140° = 40°$, so
$$\mathbf{r} = |\mathbf{r}| \sin\phi\,\mathbf{i} - |\mathbf{r}| \cos\phi\,\mathbf{j}$$
$$= 1.1 \sin 40°\,\mathbf{i} - 1.1 \cos 40°\,\mathbf{j}$$
$$= 0.707\ldots\mathbf{i} - 0.842\ldots\mathbf{j}.$$

The angle α is given by $\alpha = 90° - 70° = 20°$, so
$$\mathbf{w} = |\mathbf{w}| \cos\alpha\,\mathbf{i} + |\mathbf{w}| \sin\alpha\,\mathbf{j}$$
$$= 3.5 \cos 20°\,\mathbf{i} + 3.5 \sin 20°\,\mathbf{j}$$
$$= 3.288\ldots\mathbf{i} + 1.197\ldots\mathbf{j}.$$

The new velocity of the yacht is
$$\mathbf{s} + \mathbf{w} = (3.677\ldots\mathbf{i} + 3.085\ldots\mathbf{j}) + (3.288\ldots\mathbf{i} + 1.197\ldots\mathbf{j})$$
$$= 6.965\ldots\mathbf{i} + 4.282\ldots\mathbf{j}.$$
Hence its speed is
$$\sqrt{(6.965\ldots)^2 + (4.282\ldots)^2} = 8.177\ldots = 8.2\,\text{m}\,\text{s}^{-1} \text{ (to 1 d.p.)}.$$

The new velocity of the rowing boat is
$$\mathbf{r} + \mathbf{w} = (0.707\ldots\mathbf{i} - 0.842\ldots\mathbf{j}) + (3.288\ldots\mathbf{i} + 1.197\ldots\mathbf{j})$$
$$= 3.995\ldots\mathbf{i} + 0.354\ldots\mathbf{j}.$$
Hence its speed is
$$\sqrt{(3.995\ldots)^2 + (0.354\ldots)^2} = 4.011\ldots = 4.0\,\text{m}\,\text{s}^{-1} \text{ (to 1 d.p.)}.$$

Let β be the angle between the new velocities, $\mathbf{s} + \mathbf{w}$ and $\mathbf{r} + \mathbf{w}$. Then
$$\cos\beta = \frac{(\mathbf{s} + \mathbf{w}) \cdot (\mathbf{r} + \mathbf{w})}{|\mathbf{s} + \mathbf{w}|\,|\mathbf{r} + \mathbf{w}|}.$$
We have
$$(\mathbf{s} + \mathbf{w}) \cdot (\mathbf{r} + \mathbf{w})$$
$$= (6.965\ldots\mathbf{i} + 4.282\ldots\mathbf{j}) \cdot (3.995\ldots\mathbf{i} + 0.354\ldots\mathbf{j})$$
$$= (6.965\ldots) \times (3.995\ldots) + (4.282\ldots) \times (0.354\ldots)$$
$$= 29.353\ldots.$$
So
$$\beta = \cos^{-1}\left(\frac{(\mathbf{s} + \mathbf{w}) \cdot (\mathbf{r} + \mathbf{w})}{|\mathbf{s} + \mathbf{w}|\,|\mathbf{r} + \mathbf{w}|}\right)$$
$$= \cos^{-1}\left(\frac{29.353\ldots}{(8.177\ldots) \times (4.011\ldots)}\right)$$
$$= 26.5\ldots° = 27° \text{ (to the nearest degree)}.$$

So the new angle between the paths of the boats is 27° (to the nearest degree).

So, in summary, the new speeds of the yacht and the rowing boat are $8.2\,\text{m}^{-1}$ and $4.0\,\text{m}^{-1}$, respectively (both to one decimal place), and the new angle between their paths is 27° (to the nearest degree).

Unit 6

Differentiation

Introduction

This unit is the first of three that together introduce the fundamentally important topic of *calculus*. Calculus provides a way of solving many mathematical problems that can't be solved using algebra alone. It's the basis of essential mathematical models in areas such as science, engineering, economics and medicine, and is a fascinating topic in its own right.

In essence, calculus allows you to work with situations where a quantity is continuously changing and its rate of change isn't necessarily constant. As a simple example, imagine a man walking along a straight path, as shown in Figure 1. His displacement from his starting point changes continuously as he walks. As you've seen, the rate of change of displacement is called *velocity*.

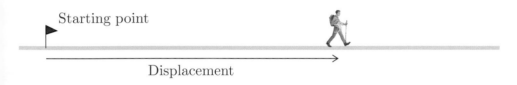

Figure 1 A man's displacement along a path

Since the man's displacement and velocity are along a straight line, they are one-dimensional vectors, and hence can be represented by scalars, with direction along the line indicated by the signs (plus or minus) of the scalars, as in Subsection 2.4 of Unit 2, and as mentioned near the start of Subsection 5.1 of Unit 5. In the calculus units in this module, we'll work with displacement and velocity only along straight lines, and hence we'll always represent these quantities by scalars.

If the man's velocity is constant, then it's straightforward to work with the relationship between the time that he's been walking and his displacement from his starting point. As you saw in Unit 2, you just use the equation

displacement = constant velocity × time.

For example, if the man walks at a constant velocity of 6 kilometres per hour, then after two hours his displacement is

$(6 \times 2)\,\text{km} = 12\,\text{km}.$

However, suppose that the man doesn't walk at a constant velocity. For example, he might become more tired as he walks, and hence gradually slow down. Then the relationship between the time that he's been walking and his displacement is more complicated. Calculus allows you to deal with relationships like this.

Calculus applies to all situations where one quantity changes smoothly with respect to another quantity. In the example above, the displacement of the walking man changes with respect to the time that he's been walking. Similarly, the temperature in a metal rod with one end near a heat source changes with respect to the distance along the rod. Similarly again, the air pressure at a point in the Earth's atmosphere changes with respect to the height of the point above the Earth's surface, the concentration of a prescription drug in a patient's bloodstream changes with respect to the time since the drug was administered, and the total cost of manufacturing many copies of a product changes with respect to the quantity of the product manufactured. You can see from the diversity of these examples just how widely applicable calculus is.

Basic calculus splits into two halves, known as **differential calculus** and **integral calculus**. (In this context 'integral' is pronounced with the emphasis on the 'int' rather than on the 'eg'.) Roughly speaking, in differential calculus, you start off knowing the values taken by a changing quantity throughout a period of change, and you use this information to find the values taken by the rate of change of the quantity throughout the same period. For example, suppose that you're interested in modelling the man's walk as he gradually slows down. You might have worked out a formula that expresses his displacement at any moment during his walk in terms of the time that he's been walking. Differential calculus allows you to use this information to deduce his *velocity* (his rate of change of displacement) at any moment during his walk.

In integral calculus, you carry out the opposite process to differential calculus. For example, suppose that you've modelled the man's walk by finding a formula that expresses his velocity at any moment during his walk in terms of the time that he's been walking. Integral calculus allows you to use this information to deduce his displacement at any moment during his walk.

Surprisingly, you can also use integral calculus to solve some types of problem that at first sight seem to have little connection with rates of change. For example, you can use it to find the exact area of a shape whose boundary is a curve or is made up of several curves.

This unit, together with the first half of Unit 7, introduces differential calculus, while the second half of Unit 7, together with Unit 8, introduces integral calculus. You'll also use calculus in Unit 11, *Taylor polynomials*.

The name 'calculus' is actually a shortened version of the historical name given to the subject, which is 'the calculus of infinitesimals'. The word 'calculus' just means a system of calculation. The word comes from Latin, in which 'calculus' means 'stone' – the link is in the use of stones for counting.

The calculus of infinitesimals became so overwhelmingly important compared to other types of calculus that the word 'calculus', used alone, is now always understood to refer to it.

An 'infinitesimal' was regarded as an infinitely small part of something. When you consider an object's velocity, for example, in the calculus of infinitesimals, you don't consider its *average velocity* over some period of time, but rather its 'instantaneous velocity' – the velocity that it has during an infinitely small interval of time.

Although the ideas behind calculus are explained in quite a lot of detail in this unit, and in the later calculus units in the module, many of the explanations aren't as mathematically precise and rigorous as it's possible to make them, and the proofs of some results and formulas aren't given at all. For example, the idea of a *limit* of an expression is introduced, but this idea is described in an intuitive way: the unit doesn't give a precise mathematical definition.

The reason for this is that it's quite complicated to make the ideas of calculus absolutely precise. At this stage in your studies it's not appropriate for you to learn about how this can be done, because the necessary profusion of small details would make it harder for you to understand the main ideas. Instead, the precise mathematical ideas behind calculus are covered in the subject area known as *real analysis*. You might study this subject at Level 2, depending on your chosen study programme.

The fundamental ideas of calculus were developed in the 1600s, independently by Isaac Newton in England and Gottfried Wilhelm Leibniz in Germany. ('Leibniz' is pronounced as 'Libe-nits'.) Neither Newton nor Leibniz made their ideas rigorous – this work was done later by other mathematicians. There's more about Newton and Leibniz later in the unit.

1 What is differentiation?

This first section introduces you to the fundamental ideas of differential calculus.

1.1 Graphs of relationships

Throughout Units 6, 7 and 8, you'll learn the ideas of basic calculus by thinking in terms of graphs. As you've seen, the relationship between two quantities, such as the time that a man has been walking and his displacement, can be represented by a graph. For example, the two displacement–time graphs in Figure 2 represent a man's walk along a straight path, on two different occasions.

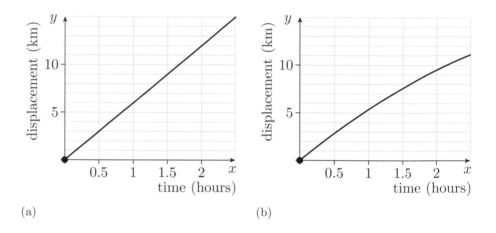

(a)   (b)

Figure 2 Displacement–time graphs for a man walking along a straight path (a) with constant velocity (b) with decreasing velocity

As you can see, the first graph is a straight line. You saw in Unit 2 that if a graph representing the relationship between two quantities is a straight line, then the quantity on the vertical axis is changing at a constant rate with respect to the quantity on the horizontal axis, and the gradient of the graph is this constant rate of change. So the first graph represents a walk in which the man's rate of change of displacement with respect to time, that is, his velocity, is constant. The gradient of the graph is his constant velocity – you can see that it is about $6 \, \mathrm{km \, h^{-1}}$.

The second graph is curved. This graph represents a walk in which the man gradually slows down as time goes on – you can see that the longer he's been walking, the less his displacement changes in a given period of time.

Activity 1   *Working with a curved displacement–time graph*

Estimate from the graph in Figure 2(b) roughly how far the man walks in the first half-hour and in the final half-hour of his walk.

If a graph that represents the relationship between two quantities is curved, then there's no single gradient value that applies to the whole graph. However, the graph has a gradient at *each point* on the graph – you'll learn in the next subsection how this is defined. As with a straight-line graph, the gradient at each point is the rate of change of the quantity on the vertical axis with respect to the quantity on the horizontal axis; the only difference is that it takes different values at different points. For example, in Figure 2(b), the gradient of the graph at each point is the man's velocity at a moment in time, and it gradually decreases as time goes on.

So in this unit you'll begin your study of calculus by looking at how the idea of gradient applies to curved graphs.

All the relationships between two variables that you'll consider in the calculus units in this module are those in which one variable is a *function* of the other. (For instance, in the example of the man's walk, his displacement is a function of the time that he's been walking.) So, in every graph in these units, every value on the horizontal axis corresponds to at most one value on the vertical axis. As in Unit 3, we'll use the word 'function' to mean 'real function'; that is, a function whose input and output values are real numbers. This is the only type of function that we'll deal with in the calculus units in this module.

1.2 Gradients of curved graphs

As mentioned above, in this section you'll learn about gradients of curved graphs. We'll begin with a quick reminder about gradients of straight lines, as these ideas will be crucial in what follows.

As you saw in Unit 2, the gradient of a straight line is a measure of how steep it is. To calculate the gradient of a straight line, you choose any two points on it and find the *run* and the *rise* from the first point to the second point. The *run* is the change in the x-coordinates, and the *rise* is the change in the y-coordinates, as illustrated in Figure 3. Then

$$\text{gradient} = \frac{\text{rise}}{\text{run}}.$$

The run and the rise from one point to another on a straight line can be positive, negative or zero, depending on whether the relevant coordinates increase, decrease or stay the same from the first point to the second point. If the *run* is zero, which happens when the line is vertical, then the gradient of the line is undefined, since division by zero isn't possible. Vertical lines are the only straight lines that don't have gradients.

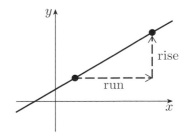

Figure 3   The run and the rise between two points on a straight-line graph

If the two points that you choose to calculate the gradient of a line are (x_1, y_1) and (x_2, y_2), as illustrated in Figure 4, then

$$\text{run} = x_2 - x_1 \quad \text{and} \quad \text{rise} = y_2 - y_1.$$

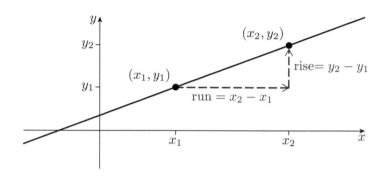

Figure 4   The run and the rise in terms of the coordinates of the two points

These equations give the formula below.

Gradient of a straight line

The gradient of the straight line through the points (x_1, y_1) and (x_2, y_2), where $x_1 \neq x_2$, is given by

$$\text{gradient} = \frac{\text{rise}}{\text{run}} = \frac{y_2 - y_1}{x_2 - x_1}.$$

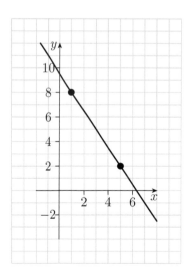

Figure 5   The straight line through the points $(1, 8)$ and $(5, 2)$

Remember that when you use this formula to calculate the gradient of a straight line, it doesn't matter which point you take to be the first point, (x_1, y_1), and which you take to be the second point, (x_2, y_2), as you get the same result either way. For example, using the formula to calculate the gradient of the line through the points $(1, 8)$ and $(5, 2)$, which is shown in Figure 5, gives either

$$\text{gradient} = \frac{\text{rise}}{\text{run}} = \frac{2 - 8}{5 - 1} = \frac{-6}{4} = -\frac{3}{2}$$

or

$$\text{gradient} = \frac{\text{rise}}{\text{run}} = \frac{8 - 2}{1 - 5} = \frac{6}{-4} = -\frac{3}{2}.$$

You saw the following facts in Unit 2. A straight-line graph that slopes *down* from left to right has a *negative* gradient, one that's *horizontal* has a gradient of *zero*, and one that slopes *up* from left to right has a *positive* gradient. The steeper the graph, the larger the magnitude of the gradient.

Activity 2   *Relating gradients to graphs*

Match each of the following descriptions to the appropriate graph.

(a) Large negative gradient   (b) Small negative gradient

(c) Zero gradient   (d) Small positive gradient

(e) Large positive gradient

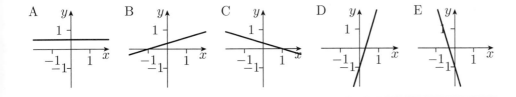

Now let's look at how the idea of gradient applies to curved graphs. For example, consider the graph of the equation $y = x^2$, which is shown in Figure 6.

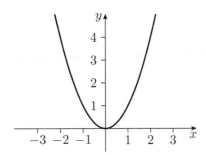

Figure 6   The graph of $y = x^2$

This graph has no single gradient value, since it's not a straight line, but if you choose any particular point on it, then it has a gradient at that point.

To understand what's meant by the gradient of a curved graph at a particular point, consider the point on the graph of $y = x^2$ marked in Figure 7(a). Imagine that you're tracing your pen tip along the graph, but when it reaches the marked point you just carry on moving it in the direction in which it's been moving, instead of following the graph. Then it will move along the straight line drawn in Figure 7(b). No matter whether you trace your pen tip along the graph towards the point from the left or the right, you'll end up moving it along the same straight line, just in different directions. This straight line 'just touches' the graph at the marked point, and is called the **tangent** to the graph at that point.

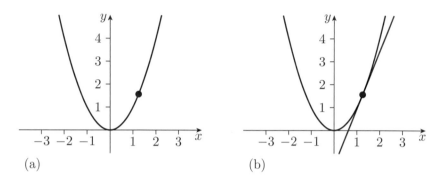

(a)   (b)

Figure 7   (a) A particular point on the graph of $y = x^2$ (b) the tangent to the graph of $y = x^2$ at that point

The word 'tangent' comes from the Latin word 'tangere', which means 'to touch'. The English word 'tangible', which means 'capable of being touched', comes from the same Latin word. You might remember from Unit 1 that the word 'integer' also comes from this Latin word (an integer is a whole, or 'untouched', number).

The tangent to any curved graph at a particular point can be defined in a similar way. Because the tangent to a graph at a point has the same steepness as the graph at that point, we make the following definition.

The **gradient** of a graph at a particular point is the gradient of the tangent to the graph at that point.

Although this definition is made with curved graphs in mind, it also applies to straight-line graphs. To see this, consider a point on a straight-line graph, as illustrated in Figure 8. If you trace your pen tip along the graph towards the point and continue moving it in the same direction when you get to the point, then it will just continue moving along the graph. So the tangent to the graph at that point is just the

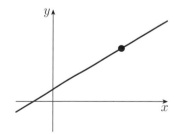

Figure 8   A point on a straight-line graph

straight-line graph itself, and hence the gradient of the graph at the point is just the gradient of the whole straight line, as you'd expect.

It's possible for a graph to have no gradient at a particular point. For example, consider the graph of $y = |x|$, which is shown in Figure 9(a). Imagine tracing your pen tip along this graph towards the origin, and continuing to move it in the same direction when you get to the origin. If you trace it along the graph towards the origin from the left, then you'll end up moving it along a *different* straight line than if you trace it along the graph towards the origin from the right. So there's no tangent to the graph at the origin, and hence the graph doesn't have a gradient at this point. In general, if a graph has a 'sharp corner' at a point, then it has no gradient at that point.

As another example, consider the graph in Figure 9(b). You can trace your pen tip along the graph to the origin from the left, but you can't do the same from the right, because you can't reach the origin that way. So this graph has no tangent at the origin, and hence has no gradient at the origin. In general, if a graph has a 'break' (known as a **discontinuity**) at a particular point, then the graph has no tangent, and hence no gradient, at this point.

As a third example, consider the graph in Figure 9(b). It has a tangent at the origin, but the tangent is vertical, and hence itself has no gradient. So this graph has no gradient at the origin. In general, if a graph has a vertical tangent at a point, then the graph has no gradient at that point.

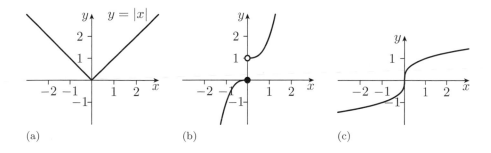

(a)   (b)   (c)

Figure 9   Graphs with points at which there is no gradient

Now let's think about how you could find the gradient of a curved graph at a particular point at which it *does* have a gradient. An obvious thing to do would be to draw the tangent at that point, choose two points on it and use them to calculate the gradient in the usual way, but this wouldn't be a very accurate method, as it's difficult to draw a tangent accurately by eye.

The next subsection shows you a better method. It considers the particular example of the graph of $y = x^2$.

1.3   Gradients of the graph of $y = x^2$

The graph of $y = x^2$ has a gradient at *every* point, because it has a tangent, which is not vertical, at every point.

Let's try to find the gradient of this graph at the point $(1, 1)$, which is shown in Figure 10. That is, we want to find the gradient of the tangent to the graph at this point, which is also shown in Figure 10.

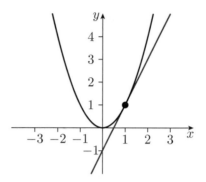

Figure 10   The point $(1, 1)$ on the graph of $y = x^2$ and the tangent at this point

The way to find the gradient at $(1, 1)$ is to begin by thinking about how you could find an *approximate* value for this gradient. Here's how you can do that. You choose a second point on the graph of $y = x^2$, fairly close to $(1, 1)$, as illustrated in blue in Figure 11. The straight line that passes through both $(1, 1)$ and the second point is an approximation for the tangent to the graph at $(1, 1)$. So the gradient of this line, which you can calculate using the two points on the line in the usual way, is an approximation for the gradient of the graph at $(1, 1)$.

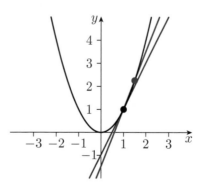

Figure 11   An approximation to the tangent to the graph of $y = x^2$ at $(1, 1)$

The closer to $(1, 1)$ you choose the second point to be, the better the approximation will be. For example, the second point in Figure 12 will give a better approximation than the second point in Figure 11.

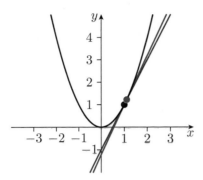

Figure 12   Another approximation to the tangent to the graph of $y = x^2$ at $(1, 1)$

As an example, let's calculate the approximation to the gradient at $(1, 1)$ that you get by choosing the second point to be the point with x-coordinate 1.1, which is the point shown in blue in Figure 12. Since the equation of the graph is $y = x^2$, the y-coordinate of this second point is $1.1^2 = 1.21$. So the second point is $(1.1, 1.21)$. The gradient of the line through $(1, 1)$ and $(1.1, 1.21)$ is

$$\frac{\text{rise}}{\text{run}} = \frac{1.21 - 1}{1.1 - 1} = \frac{0.21}{0.1} = 2.1.$$

So an approximate value for the gradient of the graph at $(1, 1)$ is 2.1.

The second point that you choose on the graph can lie either to the left or to the right of $(1, 1)$. In the next activity, you're asked to calculate the approximation to the gradient that you get by choosing a second point on the graph that lies to the left of $(1, 1)$, as illustrated in Figure 13.

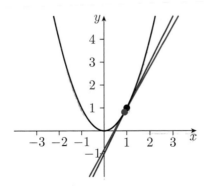

Figure 13   Yet another approximation to the tangent to the graph of $y = x^2$ at $(1, 1)$

Activity 3   *Calculating an approximation to the gradient at a point*

Calculate the approximation to the gradient of the graph of $y = x^2$ at the point with x-coordinate 1 that you get by taking the second point on the graph to be the point with x-coordinate 0.9.

Notice that although you can take the second point to be as close to $(1, 1)$ as you like, either on the left or on the right, you can't take it to be *actually equal* to $(1, 1)$. This is because you can't apply the formula for gradient to the points $(1, 1)$ and $(1, 1)$, since that would involve division by zero, which is meaningless.

In the next activity, you can use a computer to see the gradients of some more lines that pass through $(1, 1)$ and a second point on the graph close to $(1, 1)$, calculated by using the coordinates of the two points.

Activity 4   *Calculating more approximations to the gradient at a point*

Open the applet *Approximations to the gradient at a point*. Make sure that the function is set to $f(x) = x^2$ and that the original point on its graph is set to the point with x-coordinate 1. Move the second point closer and closer to the original point, and observe the gradients of the resulting lines, which are calculated by the computer using the coordinates of the two points. What do you think is the gradient of the tangent at $(1, 1)$?

Table 1 gives the gradients of some of the lines that you might have seen in Activity 4.

Table 1   The gradients of lines through $(1, 1)$ and a second point close to $(1, 1)$ on the graph of $y = x^2$

x-coordinate of second point	0.8	0.9	0.99	0.999	1.001	1.01	1.1	1.2
Gradient of line	1.8	1.9	1.99	1.999	2.001	2.01	2.1	2.2

From Activity 4 and Table 1, it looks as if the closer the second point on the graph is to $(1, 1)$, the closer the gradient of the line through $(1, 1)$ and the second point is to 2. So it looks as if the gradient of the graph at $(1, 1)$ might be exactly 2.

Neither Activity 4 nor Table 1 shows this for certain, however. For example, Table 1 doesn't rule out the possibility that the gradient at $(1, 1)$ might be some other number between 1.999 and 2.001. However, you can confirm that the gradient is *exactly* 2 by using an algebraic version of the method above.

Let's use the variable h to denote the increase in the x-coordinate from the original point $(1,1)$ to the second point. The value of h can be either positive or negative, but not zero, since the second point can be either to the right or to the left of $(1,1)$, but can't be $(1,1)$ itself. The x-coordinate of the second point is $1 + h$, so, since the equation of the graph is $y = x^2$, the y-coordinate of the second point is $(1 + h)^2$. These coordinates are shown in Figure 14.

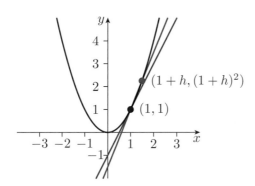

Figure 14   The points $(1,1)$ and $(1+h, (1+h)^2)$ on the graph of $y = x^2$, and the line through them

The gradient of the line that passes through the two points is

$$\frac{\text{rise}}{\text{run}} = \frac{(1+h)^2 - 1}{(1+h) - 1}.$$

This expression can be simplified as follows:

$$\begin{aligned}
\text{gradient} &= \frac{(1+h)^2 - 1}{(1+h) - 1} \\
&= \frac{1 + 2h + h^2 - 1}{1 + h - 1} \\
&= \frac{2h + h^2}{h} \\
&= \frac{h(2 + h)}{h} \\
&= 2 + h.
\end{aligned}$$

So the gradient of the line that passes through $(1,1)$ and $(1+h, (1+h)^2)$ is given by the expression $2 + h$. (You can see examples of this in Table 1.)

Now think about what happens to this gradient as the second point gets closer and closer to $(1,1)$. That is, think about what happens as the value of h gets closer and closer to zero.

As the value of h gets closer and closer to zero, the gradient of the line, $2 + h$, gets closer and closer to 2. So the gradient of the graph at $(1,1)$ must indeed be exactly 2, as we expected.

The fact that, as h gets closer and closer to zero, the value of the expression $2 + h$ gets closer and closer to 2 is expressed mathematically by saying that

$2 + h$ **tends** to 2 as h **tends** to 0,

or

the **limit** of $2 + h$ as h **tends** to zero is 2.

So we've now succeeded in finding the gradient of the graph of $y = x^2$ at the point $(1, 1)$. You could use the same algebraic method to find the gradient of the graph at any other point.

A cleverer thing to do, however, is to use the same method to find the gradient of the graph of $y = x^2$ at a *general point* on the graph, whose x-coordinate is denoted by x. This will give you a formula for the gradient of the graph *at any point*, in terms of the x-coordinate of the point. You can then find the gradient of the graph at any particular point by just substituting into the formula, instead of having to go through the algebraic method again.

So let's now apply the algebraic method to find the gradient of the graph of $y = x^2$ at the general point whose x-coordinate is denoted by x. The situation is shown in Figure 15. The point at which we want to find the gradient is (x, x^2). The second point on the graph is $(x + h, (x + h)^2)$, where h is a positive or negative number, but not zero.

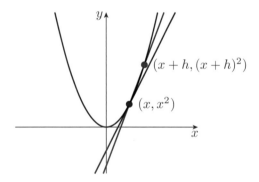

Figure 15   The points (x, x^2) and $(x + h, (x + h)^2)$ on the graph of $y = x^2$, and the line through them

The gradient of the line that passes through the two points is

$$\frac{\text{rise}}{\text{run}} = \frac{(x + h)^2 - x^2}{(x + h) - x}.$$

This expression can be simplified as follows:

$$\begin{aligned}
\text{gradient} &= \frac{(x+h)^2 - x^2}{(x+h) - x} \\
&= \frac{x^2 + 2xh + h^2 - x^2}{x + h - x} \\
&= \frac{2xh + h^2}{h} \\
&= \frac{h(2x + h)}{h} \\
&= 2x + h.
\end{aligned}$$

As the second point gets closer and closer to the original point, the value of h gets closer and closer to 0, and the gradient of the line, $2x + h$, gets closer and closer to $2x$. So the gradient of the graph of $y = x^2$ at the point whose x-coordinate is denoted by x is given by the formula

$$\text{gradient} = 2x. \tag{1}$$

For example, this formula tells you that at the point with x-coordinate 1,

$$\text{gradient} = 2 \times 1 = 2,$$

as we found earlier.

In the next activity you're asked to use formula (1) to find the gradient of the graph of $y = x^2$ at two more points.

Activity 5   *Finding the gradients of the graph of $y = x^2$ at particular points*

Use formula (1) to find the gradient of the graph of $y = x^2$ at the point with x-coordinate 3, and at the point with x-coordinate -1.5.

Figure 16 shows the tangents to the graph of $y = x^2$ at the points with x-coordinates 3 and -1.5. You can see, by estimating the rise and run between two points on each tangent, that the gradients of these tangents do seem to be at least roughly the values calculated in the solution to Activity 5.

In general, if you have the equation of a graph, then it's often possible to use an algebraic method similar to the one that you've seen in this subsection to find a formula for the gradient of the graph. You'll see some more examples in the next subsection.

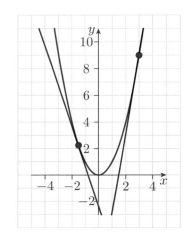

Figure 16   Two tangents to the graph of $y = x^2$

1.4 Derivatives

In Subsection 1.3 you saw how to find a formula for the gradients of the graph of $y = x^2$. In this subsection you'll see how you can use the same method to find formulas for the gradients of some other graphs. Before you do that, it's useful for you to learn some terminology and notation that are used when working with such formulas.

Consider a function f and a particular input value x. The point on the graph of f that corresponds to the input value x is $(x, f(x))$. If the graph of f has a gradient at the point $(x, f(x))$, then we say that f is **differentiable** at x. For example, you've seen that the function $f(x) = x^2$ is differentiable at every value of x. If the graph of f doesn't have a gradient at the point $(x, f(x))$ (because the graph has no tangent at that point, or because the tangent is vertical), then f isn't differentiable at x. For example, you've seen that the function $f(x) = |x|$ isn't differentiable at 0. Similarly, if a function f isn't even defined at a particular input value x, then it's not differentiable at x.

You've seen that, usually, the gradient of the graph of a function f varies depending on which value of x you're considering. It's convenient to think of these gradients as defining a new function, related to f. The rule of the new function is:

if the input value is x, then the output value is
the gradient of the graph of f at the point $(x, f(x))$.

This new function is called the **derivative** (or **derived function**) of the function f, and is denoted by f' (which is read as 'f prime' or 'f dash' or 'f dashed'). The domain of the derivative consists of all the values at which f is differentiable. The process of finding the derivative of a given function f is called **differentiation**, and when we carry out this process, we say that we're **differentiating** the function f.

For example, in the previous subsection we *differentiated* the function $f(x) = x^2$, and we found that its *derivative* has the rule $f'(x) = 2x$.

The word 'derivative' can be applied to expressions, as well as to functions. For example, rather than saying that

the derivative of $f(x) = x^2$ is $f'(x) = 2x$,

you can simply say that

the derivative of x^2 is $2x$.

The word 'derivative' is also used with a slightly different meaning. The *value* of the derivative of a function f at a particular input value x is called the **derivative of f at x**. For example, you saw in the last subsection that the derivative of the function $f(x) = x^2$ at 1 is $f'(1) = 2$.

The notation for derivatives can of course be used with letters other than the standard ones, f for the function and x for the input variable. For example, if the function g is given by $g(t) = t^2$, then the gradient of the graph of g at the point $(t, g(t))$ is given by the formula $2t$, and we express this by writing

$$g'(t) = 2t.$$

You should now be ready to see some more examples of finding formulas for the gradients of graphs – that is, formulas for derivatives. We'll begin by setting out the general method that can be used to find such formulas. This is just the algebraic method that you saw in Subsection 1.3, where the formula for the derivative of the function $f(x) = x^2$ was found. It's known as **differentiation from first principles**.

Differentiation from first principles

Suppose that f is any function. Let x denote any value in the domain of f such that f is differentiable at x (that is, such that the graph of f has a gradient at the point $(x, f(x))$, as illustrated in Figure 17. Now consider a second point on the graph, with coordinates $(x + h, f(x + h))$, where h is a positive or negative number, but not zero.

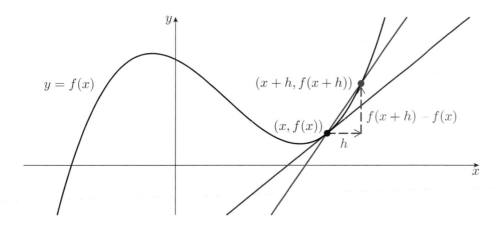

Figure 17   The points $(x, f(x))$ and $(x + h, f(x + h))$ on the graph of $y = f(x)$, and the line through them

The gradient of the line that passes through the two points is

$$\frac{\text{rise}}{\text{run}} = \frac{f(x + h) - f(x)}{(x + h) - x},$$

and this expression can be simplified slightly to give

$$\frac{f(x + h) - f(x)}{h}. \tag{2}$$

This expression is known as the **difference quotient** for the function f at the value x. As the second point $(x + h, f(x + h))$ gets closer and closer to the first point $(x, f(x))$, that is, as the value of h gets closer and closer to zero, the value of the difference quotient gets closer and closer to the gradient of the graph at the point $(x, f(x))$. That is, it gets closer and closer to $f'(x)$. (Remember that the value of h can never actually be 0.)

So, to find a formula for $f'(x)$, you need to consider what happens to the difference quotient for f at x, as h gets closer and closer to zero, taking either positive or negative values as it does so. In other words, you need to find, in terms of x, the *limit* of the difference quotient as h tends to zero. You saw this procedure carried out for the function $f(x) = x^2$ in the last subsection, and in the next example you'll see it carried out for the function $f(x) = x^3$.

Example 1   *Differentiating from first principles*

Differentiate from first principles the function $f(x) = x^3$.

Solution

🔍 Write down the difference quotient and use the fact that $f(x) = x^3$. 💬

The difference quotient for the function $f(x) = x^3$ at x is
$$\frac{f(x+h) - f(x)}{h} = \frac{(x+h)^3 - x^3}{h}.$$

🔍 Simplify the difference quotient. Start by multiplying out the term $(x+h)^3$ in the numerator. 💬

Multiplying out $(x+h)^3$ gives
$$\begin{aligned}
(x+h)^3 &= (x+h)(x+h)^2 \\
&= (x+h)(x^2 + 2xh + h^2) \\
&= x(x^2 + 2xh + h^2) + h(x^2 + 2xh + h^2) \\
&= x^3 + 2x^2h + xh^2 + x^2h + 2xh^2 + h^3 \\
&= x^3 + 3x^2h + 3xh^2 + h^3.
\end{aligned}$$

So
$$\begin{aligned}
\frac{f(x+h) - f(x)}{h} &= \frac{x^3 + 3x^2h + 3xh^2 + h^3 - x^3}{h} \\
&= \frac{3x^2h + 3xh^2 + h^3}{h} \\
&= \frac{h(3x^2 + 3xh + h^2)}{h} \\
&= 3x^2 + 3xh + h^2.
\end{aligned}$$

🗨 Work out what happens to the value of the difference quotient as h gets closer and closer to zero. 🗨

The second term in the final expression above contains the factor h, and the third term is h^2, so as h gets closer and closer to zero, both of these terms get closer and closer to zero. So the value of the whole expression gets closer and closer to the value of the first term, $3x^2$. That is, the formula for the derivative of the function $f(x) = x^3$ is

$$f'(x) = 3x^2.$$

The formula for the derivative of $f(x) = x^3$ found in Example 1 tells you that, for example, the gradient of the graph of $y = x^3$ at the point with x-coordinate 1 is

$$f'(1) = 3 \times 1^2 = 3,$$

and the gradient of this graph at the point with x-coordinate $\frac{1}{2}$ is

$$f'(\tfrac{1}{2}) = 3 \times \left(\tfrac{1}{2}\right)^2 = \tfrac{3}{4}.$$

You can see from Figure 18 that the gradients of the tangents to the graph at these two points do seem to be the numbers calculated using the formula.

In the next activity, you're asked to use differentiation from first principles to find the derivative of the function $f(x) = x^4$.

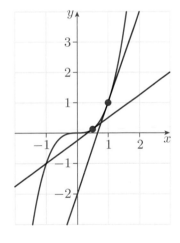

Figure 18   Two tangents to the graph of $f(x) = x^3$

Activity 6   *Differentiating from first principles*

(a) Multiply out the expression $(x + h)^4$. To do this, start by writing $(x + h)^4 = (x + h)(x + h)^3$. Then replace the expression $(x + h)^3$ by the expansion of $(x + h)^3$ that was found in the solution to Example 1, remembering to enclose it in brackets. Finally, multiply out the brackets and collect like terms.

(b) Hence differentiate from first principles the function $f(x) = x^4$.

(c) What is the gradient of the graph of the function $f(x) = x^4$ at the point with x-coordinate $\frac{1}{4}$?

In each of the three examples of differentiation from first principles that you've seen so far, the function was differentiable at *every* value of x. If a function isn't differentiable at some values of x, then you can still differentiate it from first principles, but the process won't work for the values of x at which it's not differentiable. For these values of x the value of the difference quotient won't get closer and closer to a particular number as h gets closer and closer to zero (where h can be either positive or negative).

For example, if the graph of a function f has a sharp corner at $(x, f(x))$, then the difference quotient for f at x will get closer and closer to a particular value when h is *positive*, but will get closer and closer to a *different* value when h is *negative*. As another example, if the graph of the function has a vertical tangent at $(x, f(x))$, then the magnitude of the difference quotient for f at x will just keep getting larger and larger, without getting closer and closer to any particular value.

In general, saying that a function f is differentiable at a particular value of x is the same as saying that the difference quotient for f at x tends to a limit as h tends to zero. It must tend to the same limit for positive values of h as for negative values.

The method of differentiation from first principles is summarised in the box below. The notation '$\lim_{h\to 0}$' means 'the limit as h tends to zero of'.

Differentiation from first principles

For any function f, the derivative f' of f is given by the equation

$$f'(x) = \lim_{h\to 0} \frac{f(x+h) - f(x)}{h}$$

for each value of x in the domain of f for which this limit exists.

Differentiation from first principles can be used to find formulas for the derivatives of many of the functions that you'll need to work with. However, it's a laborious process, so usually we don't do it! Instead, in this unit and in the first half of Unit 7 you'll get to know the formulas for the derivatives of a range of standard functions, such as $f(x) = x^2$, $f(x) = x^3$, $f(x) = \sin x$, $f(x) = e^x$, and so on. You'll also learn about ways in which you can combine these formulas to obtain formulas for the derivatives of other, related functions. For example, if you know the formulas for the derivatives of $f(x) = x^2$ and $f(x) = x^3$, then you can combine them to obtain a formula for the derivative of $f(x) = x^2 + x^3$. In these ways you'll be able to find formulas for the derivatives of most of the functions that you'll need to work with.

Of course, the idea of differentiation from first principles is still needed, to find the derivatives of the standard functions, to check that the rules for combining them are valid, and to differentiate functions that aren't standard functions or combinations of standard functions.

Formulas for derivatives are powerful mathematical tools in many different situations, in both pure and applied mathematics. In this module, not only will you learn how to find such formulas, but you'll also be introduced to a few of the ways in which they can be used. You'll see many more uses of them if you go on to study further modules in mathematics, or some modules in areas such as science and economics.

The invention of calculus

The history of calculus goes back to the second half of the seventeenth century, when Isaac Newton in England and Gottfried Wilhelm Leibniz in what is now Germany both independently developed the basic ideas. Newton's ideas were rooted in the applications of mathematics, while Leibniz's were rooted in pure mathematics.

Newton developed the ideas of calculus starting in about 1665. He called his ideas the 'method of fluxions' and wrote a treatise about them in 1671, which was not published in his lifetime, although its contents circulated in manuscript form, and a publication containing the method appeared in 1704. Leibniz then independently developed similar ideas, starting in about 1674. A manuscript that he wrote in 1675 includes the notation used in integral calculus to this day, as well as a standard rule for combining derivatives, the *product rule*, which you'll meet in Unit 7. Leibniz's notation for differential calculus is also still used today, as you'll see shortly. Leibniz first published work on calculus in 1684.

The two men continued to develop their ideas for the next few years. However by the early 1700s Leibniz was being accused by Newton's associates of having plagiarised Newton's work. The allegation was that Leibniz had seen some of Newton's unpublished papers and had merely invented a new notation for Newton's ideas. The ensuing bitter argument led to a Royal Society investigation, which upheld the charge. However, the investigation was largely carried out by Newton's friends, and Newton, who was President of the Royal Society, secretly guided its report. Investigations by modern historians have shown that the accusation against Leibniz was unjust. Newton and Leibniz arrived at equivalent results following different paths of discovery.

Isaac Newton (1642–1727)

Gottfried Wilhelm Leibniz (1646–1716)

Isaac Newton

Isaac Newton was born in Lincolnshire, and studied and worked at the University of Cambridge. He was one of the world's greatest physicists, mathematicians and astronomers, and is remembered in particular for his work on classical mechanics. He did much of his initial work on calculus at his family home in Lincolnshire, while Cambridge University was closed due to an outbreak of plague. In his later life Newton largely abandoned physics and mathematics, and wrote theological tracts before becoming Master of the Mint, a highly-paid government official, in London. He also worked on alchemy throughout his life. He was knighted in 1705, but for political reasons rather than for his scientific work or public service.

Gottfried Wilhelm Leibniz

Gottfried Wilhelm Leibniz was born in Leipzig, and attended university there and in Altdorf. He was a universal thinker who graduated in philosophy and law, and was self-taught in mathematics. He went on to work intensively on mathematics in Paris, before accepting the position of Counsellor and librarian at the court in Hanover, where he remained for the rest of his life. While there, he worked on many different projects, making important contributions to mathematics, philosophy, theology and history. Some of Leibniz's projects were related to his salaried position, but his employers also allowed him to work on other projects of his choosing. He was interested in formalising calculations, and constructed the first mechanical calculator that could add, subtract, multiply and divide.

Before we begin the process of building up a collection of formulas for the derivatives of standard functions, and techniques for combining them, it's useful for you to learn an alternative notation for derivatives.

Leibniz notation

The notation that we've been using so far, in which the derivative of a function f is denoted by f', is called **Lagrange notation** or **prime notation**. ('Lagrange' is pronounced as a French word: 'La-grawnge'.) It was invented by Joseph-Louis Lagrange, about a century after calculus was discovered. The term 'prime notation' arises from the fact that the symbol $'$ in the notation f' is often called 'prime'.

However, there's another notation, called **Leibniz notation**, invented by Gottfried Wilhelm Leibniz. (Remember that 'Leibniz' is pronounced as a German word: 'Libe-nits'.) You'll need to become familiar with both notations, as they're both used throughout this module, and throughout mathematics generally.

Each type of notation has different advantages in different situations. Generally, Lagrange notation is used when you're thinking in terms of a variable, and a function of this variable. On the other hand, Leibniz notation is often used when you're thinking more of the relationship between two variables. The distinction will become clearer as you become used to working with the two notations.

Joseph-Louis Lagrange

Joseph-Louis Lagrange was an Italian-French mathematician who made important contributions in many areas, including calculus, mechanics, astronomy, probability and number theory. He was appointed as a professor of mathematics at the Royal Artillery School in Turin at the age of only 19, and was a dedicated and prolific mathematician for the rest of his life, working mainly in Turin and Berlin.

Joseph-Louis Lagrange
(1736–1813)

To see how derivatives are written in Leibniz notation, consider the equation $y = x^2$, which expresses a relationship between the variables x and y. You've seen that the formula for the gradient of the graph of the equation $y = x^2$ is

gradient $= 2x$.

In Leibniz notation this equation is written as

$$\frac{\mathrm{d}y}{\mathrm{d}x} = 2x.$$

So the notation $\frac{\mathrm{d}y}{\mathrm{d}x}$ means the same as $f'(x)$, where $y = f(x)$. It's read as 'd y by d x'. When Leibniz notation is being used, $\frac{\mathrm{d}y}{\mathrm{d}x}$ is often referred to as the **derivative of y with respect to** x.

If you want to write the notation $\frac{\mathrm{d}y}{\mathrm{d}x}$ in a line of text, then you can write it as $\mathrm{d}y/\mathrm{d}x$, just as you would do for a fraction. However, although the notation looks like a fraction, it's important to remember that it isn't a fraction!

Also, you should be aware that the 'd' that's part of Leibniz notation has no meaning outside of it. In particular, although $\mathrm{d}y$ and $\mathrm{d}x$ look like $\mathrm{d} \times y$ and $\mathrm{d} \times x$, respectively, the 'd' is certainly not a factor and must not be cancelled! In many mathematical texts, including this one, the 'd' in Leibniz notation appears in upright type, rather than the italic type used for variables, to emphasise this fact. (You don't need to do anything special when you handwrite Leibniz notation – you should just write the 'd' in the normal way.)

To understand the thinking behind Leibniz notation, consider Figure 19. It's exactly the same as Figure 17 on page 223, which illustrates differentiation from first principles, except that some things are labelled differently. For example, the point at which we want to find the gradient is labelled (x, y) instead of $(x, f(x))$. This is because the emphasis here is on the relationship between the variables x and y, rather than on the idea of f as a function of x. Another difference is that the change in the x-coordinate from the point at which we want to find the gradient to the second point is denoted by δx instead of h, so the x-coordinate of the second point is written as $x + \delta x$ instead of $x + h$.

The symbol δ is the lower-case Greek letter delta, and is read as 'delta'. By convention, when the symbol δ is used as a prefix it indicates 'a small change in', so δx denotes a small change in x. The change in the y-coordinate from the point at which we want to find the gradient to the second point is denoted in a similar way, as δy, which means that the y-coordinate of the second point is $y + \delta y$.

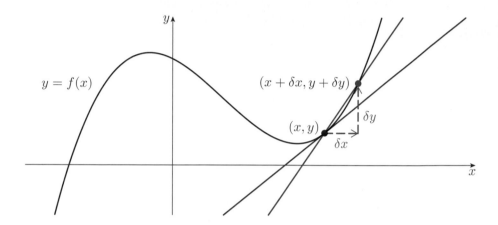

Figure 19   The points (x, y) and $(x + \delta x, y + \delta y)$ on the graph of $y = f(x)$, and the line through them

The gradient of the line that passes through the two points is then

$$\frac{\text{rise}}{\text{run}} = \frac{\delta y}{\delta x}.$$

As the second point gets closer and closer to the first point, the value of $\delta y / \delta x$ gets closer and closer to the gradient of the curve at the point (x, y). In other words, the gradient is the limit of $\delta y / \delta x$ as the second point gets closer and closer to the first point (and so as δx and δy get smaller and smaller). This is why the notation dy/dx, which looks similar to $\delta y / \delta x$, was chosen to represent the gradient.

The expression $\delta y / \delta x$ can be used instead of expression (2) on page 223 to carry out differentiation from first principles, and you might see this done in some other texts on calculus. The process is exactly the same, just with h replaced by δx, but it can look a bit more complicated at first sight.

Leibniz notation can be used in a variety of ways. For example, the symbol

$$\frac{d}{dx}$$

means 'the derivative with respect to x of'. So, for example, a concise way to express the fact that the gradient of the graph of the equation $y = x^2$ is given by the formula $2x$ is to write

$$\frac{d}{dx}(x^2) = 2x.$$

As with Lagrange notation, Leibniz notation can be used with variable names other than the standard ones, x and y. For example,

if $s = t^2$, then $\dfrac{\mathrm{d}s}{\mathrm{d}t} = 2t$,

and

if $p = q^3$, then (by Example 1) $\dfrac{\mathrm{d}p}{\mathrm{d}q} = 3q^2$.

Similarly (by Activity 6),

$$\frac{\mathrm{d}}{\mathrm{d}w}(w^4) = 4w^3.$$

Sometimes, particularly on a computer algebra system, you might see $\mathrm{d}y/\mathrm{d}x$ written as

$$\frac{\mathrm{d}}{\mathrm{d}x}y.$$

Usually, if a function is specified using function notation, then you use Lagrange notation for its derivative, whereas if it's specified using an equation that expresses one variable in terms of another, then you use Leibniz notation. For example, if you know that $f(x) = x^2$, then you write $f'(x) = 2x$, whereas if you know that $y = x^2$, then you write $\mathrm{d}y/\mathrm{d}x = 2x$. However, there are no absolute rules about this, and in fact it's often helpful to mix the two notations. In particular, it's often convenient to use the symbol $\mathrm{d}/\mathrm{d}x$, even when you're mostly using Lagrange notation, as you'll see.

Lagrange notation and Leibniz notation are the two most common notations for derivatives, but there are other useful notations, including one invented by Isaac Newton. You'll meet some of these notations if you go on to study calculus beyond this module, particularly in the area of applied mathematics.

Herr Leibniz, what are the three most important things about a theory of calculus?

Notation, notation, notation!

Functions whose domains include endpoints

It's often useful to find the derivative of a function whose domain includes an endpoint. For example, the function $f(x) = x^{3/2}$, whose graph is shown in Figure 20, has domain $[0, \infty)$, which includes 0 as an endpoint.

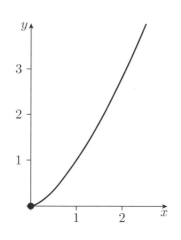

Any function whose domain includes an endpoint isn't differentiable at this endpoint. For example, consider the function $f(x) = x^{3/2}$. The point on its graph that corresponds to the endpoint 0 of its domain is the origin. You can trace your pen tip along the graph to the origin from the right, but you can't do the same from the left, so the graph doesn't have a tangent at the origin. Hence it doesn't have a gradient at the origin; that is, it's not differentiable at $x = 0$.

However, the graph of $f(x) = x^{3/2}$ does have a 'tangent on the right' at the origin, in the sense that you can trace your pen tip along the graph towards the origin from the right, and continue moving it in the direction in which it's been moving when it reaches the origin. It will then move along a straight line, namely the x-axis, in this case. So the graph has a 'gradient on the right' at the origin, namely 0, the gradient of the x-axis.

Figure 20 The graph of $f(x) = x^{3/2}$

Because of this, we say that the function $f(x) = x^{3/2}$ is **right-differentiable** at $x = 0$, and that its **right derivative** at 0 is 0. Similarly, a function can be **left-differentiable** at a particular x-value, and it will then have a **left derivative** at that x-value.

The left or right derivative of a function at a particular x-value can be found by using differentiation from first principles in much the same way as the usual, two-sided derivatives. The only difference is that instead of the increase in the x-coordinates, h, taking either positive or negative values as it gets closer and closer to zero, for a right-sided derivative h takes just positive values, and for a left-sided derivative h takes just negative values.

Saying that a function is differentiable at a particular x-value is the same as saying that it has both a left and a right derivative at that x-value, and the left and right derivatives are equal.

If f is a function whose domain includes one or more endpoints, then we adjust the definition of its derivative f' slightly to allow for these, as follows. We include in the domain of f' not just the values of x at which f is differentiable, but also the values of x that are endpoints of the domain of f and at which f is left- or right-differentiable. The value of f' at each of these endpoints is the appropriate left or right derivative.

All the results about derivatives that you'll meet in this module apply, with the appropriate adjustments, to left and right derivatives as well as to the usual, two-sided derivatives. For simplicity, this isn't stated explicitly for each individual result. For example, in the next subsection you'll learn how to find a formula for the derivative of the function $f(x) = x^{3/2}$. This formula is valid for all values of x in the domain $[0, \infty)$ of this function f, but the value that it gives for $x = 0$ is the right derivative of f at 0, rather than the derivative of f at 0, which doesn't exist.

Summary of important ideas

To finish this section, here's a summary of some of the important ideas that you've met.

Derivatives

The **derivative** (or **derived function**) of a function f is the function f' such that

$$f'(x) = \text{gradient of the graph of } f \text{ at the point } (x, f(x)).$$

The domain of f' consists of the values in the domain of f at which f is **differentiable** (that is, the x-values that give points at which the gradient exists).

If $y = f(x)$, then $f'(x)$ is also denoted by $\dfrac{dy}{dx}$.

The derivative f' is given by the equation

$$f'(x) = \lim_{h \to 0} \frac{f(x+h) - f(x)}{h}.$$

The procedure of using this equation to find a formula for the derivative f' is called **differentiation from first principles**.

2 Finding derivatives of simple functions

In this section you'll meet the formulas for the derivatives of standard functions of a particular type, and you'll also meet two rules for combining formulas for derivatives.

2.1 Derivatives of power functions

In the previous section you saw formulas for the derivatives of the functions

$$f(x) = x^2, \quad f(x) = x^3 \quad \text{and} \quad f(x) = x^4.$$

Any function of the form

$$f(x) = x^n,$$

where n is a real number, is called a **power function**. In this subsection you'll see how to find the formula for the derivative of any power function, without having to use differentiation from first principles.

The formulas that you saw for the derivatives of the three power functions above can be stated as follows, using Leibniz notation:

$$\frac{d}{dx}(x^2) = 2x, \quad \frac{d}{dx}(x^3) = 3x^2, \quad \frac{d}{dx}(x^4) = 4x^3.$$

Notice that they all follow the same pattern. In each case, to obtain the derivative, you multiply by the power, then reduce the power by 1, as shown below.

$$
\begin{array}{ccccc}
 & \text{multiply by} & & \text{reduce the} & \\
 & \text{the power} & & \text{power by 1} & \\
x^2 & \xrightarrow{\hspace{2cm}} & 2x^2 & \xrightarrow{\hspace{2cm}} & 2x \\
x^3 & \xrightarrow{\hspace{2cm}} & 3x^3 & \xrightarrow{\hspace{2cm}} & 3x^2 \\
x^4 & \xrightarrow{\hspace{2cm}} & 4x^4 & \xrightarrow{\hspace{2cm}} & 4x^3
\end{array}
$$

It turns out that the derivative of every power function follows the same pattern. This fact can be stated algebraically as follows.

Derivative of a power function

For any number n,

$$\frac{d}{dx}(x^n) = nx^{n-1}.$$

You can confirm this formula for any particular value of n that's a *positive integer* by differentiating from first principles. You saw this process carried out for the particular power functions $f(x) = x^2$, $f(x) = x^3$ and $f(x) = x^4$ in the last subsection. In general, for the power function $f(x) = x^n$, the process involves multiplying out the expression $(x+h)^n$. (In Unit 10 you'll meet a quick way to multiply out expressions like this, namely by using the *binomial theorem*.)

However, the formula holds not just for values of n that are positive integers, but for *all* values of n, including negative and fractional values. You'll see a proof of this fact in Unit 7.

As you'd expect, for any particular value of n, the formula holds for all values of x for which the function $f(x) = x^n$ is differentiable. For example, if $n = 2$, then the formula holds for *all* values of x. On the other hand, if $n = \frac{1}{2}$, then the formula holds only for *positive* values of x. The function $f(x) = x^{1/2}$, that is, $f(x) = \sqrt{x}$, whose graph is shown in Figure 21, isn't defined for negative values of x, and isn't differentiable (or even right-differentiable) at $x = 0$.

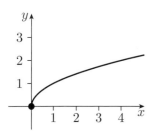

Figure 21 The graph of $f(x) = \sqrt{x}$

More generally, whenever you see a formula for the derivative of a function, such as

$$\frac{d}{dx}(x^2) = 2x \quad \text{or} \quad f'(x) = 2x,$$

you can assume that the formula holds for all values of the variable (usually x) for which the function is differentiable, unless it's stated otherwise. You can follow the same convention when you write such formulas yourself. Remember in particular that for a function to be *differentiable* at a particular value of x, it must also be *defined* there. For example, the function $f(x) = \sqrt{x}$ isn't differentiable at $x = -3$, since it isn't even defined there.

The next example shows you how to use the general formula for the derivative of a power function. In parts (b) and (c), the expression on the right-hand side of the rule of the function isn't given in the form x^n, but you can use some of the index laws that you met in Unit 1 to rewrite it in this form. The two index laws that are the most useful for this sort of situation are repeated in the box below.

Two index laws

$$a^{-n} = \frac{1}{a^n} \qquad a^{1/n} = \sqrt[n]{a}$$

For example, using these laws you can write $1/x^3$ as x^{-3}, and $\sqrt[3]{x}$ as $x^{1/3}$.

In the solution to the example, Lagrange notation is used where the function is specified using function notation, and Leibniz notation is used where it is specified by an equation expressing one variable in terms of another. You should do likewise in the activity that follows the example.

Example 2   *Differentiating power functions*

Differentiate the following functions.

(a) $f(x) = x^{10}$ (b) $f(x) = \dfrac{1}{x^5}$ (c) $y = \sqrt{x}$

Solution

(a) 🔍 Multiply by the power, then reduce the power by 1. 💬

$f'(x) = 10x^9$.

(b) 🔍 First write the function in the form $f(x) = x^n$. 💬

The function is $f(x) = x^{-5}$.

🔍 Multiply by the power, then reduce the power by 1. 💬

So $f'(x) = -5x^{-6}$

🔍 Simplify the answer. 💬

$$= -\frac{5}{x^6}.$$

(c) 🔍 First write the function in the form $y = x^n$. 💭

The function is $y = x^{1/2}$.

🔍 Multiply by the power, then reduce the power by 1. 💭

So $\dfrac{dy}{dx} = \dfrac{1}{2}x^{-1/2}$

🔍 Simplify the answer. 💭

$$= \frac{1}{2} \times \frac{1}{x^{1/2}} = \frac{1}{2} \times \frac{1}{\sqrt{x}} = \frac{1}{2\sqrt{x}}.$$

As illustrated in Example 2, whenever you find the derivative of a function, you should simplify your answer, if possible. As is often the case with algebraic simplifications, there may be no 'right answer' for the simplest form, as any of several different possibilities might do. The derivatives of the functions in Example 2 and the next activity contain indices – you saw some general guidelines for simplifying expressions that contain indices in Subsection 4.3 of Unit 1.

Activity 7   Differentiating power functions

Differentiate the following functions.

(a) $f(x) = x^8$ (b) $f(x) = x^5$ (c) $f(x) = \dfrac{1}{x^3}$ (d) $f(x) = x^{3/2}$

(e) $f(x) = \dfrac{1}{x}$ (f) $f(x) = x^{5/2}$ (g) $f(x) = x^{4/3}$ (h) $f(x) = \dfrac{1}{x^8}$

(i) $y = \dfrac{1}{x^{1/4}}$ (j) $y = x^{1/3}$ (k) $y = \dfrac{1}{\sqrt{x}}$ (l) $y = \sqrt[3]{x^5}$

(m) $y = x^{2/7}$ (n) $f(x) = x^{-2}$ (o) $f(x) = \dfrac{1}{x^{1/3}}$ (p) $f(x) = \dfrac{1}{x^4}$

Activity 8   Finding the gradient at a point on the graph of a power function

Use the solution to Example 2(c) to find the gradient of the graph of $y = \sqrt{x}$ at the point with x-coordinate 4. (The tangent to the graph at this point is shown in Figure 22.)

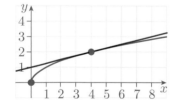

Figure 22   The graph of $y = \sqrt{x}$, and its tangent at the point with x-coordinate 4

Notice that the formula for the derivative of a power function tells you that the function

$$f(x) = x \quad \text{(which is the same as } f(x) = x^1 \text{)}$$

has derivative

$$f'(x) = 1 \times x^0; \quad \text{that is,} \quad f'(x) = 1.$$

This is as you'd expect, because the graph of the function $f(x) = x$ (shown in Figure 23(a)) is a straight line with gradient 1, which means that the gradient at every point on the graph is 1.

Another simple power function is the constant function

$$f(x) = 1 \quad \text{(which is the same as } f(x) = x^0 \text{)}.$$

Its graph (shown in Figure 23(b)) is a straight line with gradient 0, so the gradient at every point on its graph is 0. So its derivative is simply

$$f'(x) = 0.$$

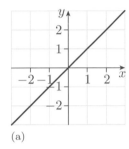

(a)

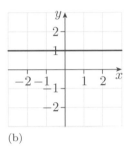

(b)

Figure 23 The graphs of (a) $f(x) = x$ (b) $f(x) = 1$

Note that to make the general formula work for the functions $f(x) = x$ and $f(x) = 1$ when $x = 0$, we have to assume that $0^0 = 1$. The value of 0^0 was discussed in Unit 1.

2.2 Constant multiple rule

In this subsection and the next, you'll see two ways in which you can use formulas that you know for the derivatives of functions to find formulas for the derivatives of other, related functions.

First, suppose that you know the formula for the derivative of a particular function, and you want to know the formula for the derivative of a constant multiple of the function. For example, you already know the formula for the derivative of the function $f(x) = x^2$, but suppose that you want to know the formula for the derivative of the function $g(x) = 3x^2$. Let's think about how the formula for the derivative of the second function can be worked out from the formula for the derivative of the first function.

When you multiply a function by a constant, the effect on its graph is that, for each x-value, the corresponding y-value is multiplied by the constant. So the graph is stretched or squashed vertically, and, if the constant is negative, then it's also reflected in the x-axis. As you saw in Unit 3, these effects are called *vertical scalings*. For example, Figure 24 shows the graphs of $y = x^2$, $y = 3x^2$, $y = \frac{1}{2}x^2$ and $y = -x^2$, and the point with x-coordinate 1 on each of these graphs.

You can see the following effects.

- Multiplying the function $f(x) = x^2$ by the constant 3 scales its graph vertically by a factor of 3 (which stretches it).

- Multiplying the function $f(x) = x^2$ by the constant $\frac{1}{2}$ scales its graph vertically by a factor of $\frac{1}{2}$ (which squashes it).

- Multiplying the function $f(x) = x^2$ by the constant -1 scales its graph vertically by a factor of -1 (which reflects it in the x-axis).

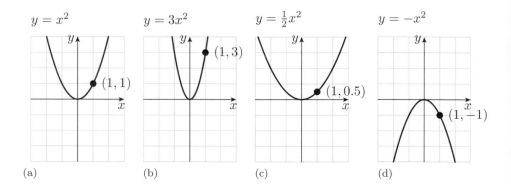

Figure 24   The graphs of (a) $y = x^2$ (b) $y = 3x^2$ (c) $y = \frac{1}{2}x^2$ (d) $y = -x^2$

The stretching or squashing, and possible reflection, of the graph causes the gradient at each x-value to change. For example, you can see that, at the point with x-coordinate 1, the graph of $y = 3x^2$ is steeper than the graph of $y = x^2$.

To see exactly how the gradients change, first consider what happens to the gradient of a straight line when you scale it vertically by a particular factor, say a. The scaled line will go up by a times as many units for every one unit that it goes along, compared to the unscaled line. In other words, its gradient is multiplied by the factor a. For example, Figure 25(a) illustrates what happens when you take a straight line with gradient 1 and scale it vertically by a factor of 3.

The same thing happens for any graph: if you scale it vertically by a particular factor, then its gradient at any particular x-value is multiplied by this factor. For example, Figure 25(b) illustrates that if you take a curve that has gradient 1 at a particular x-value, and scale it vertically by a factor of 3, then the new curve has gradient 3 at that x-value.

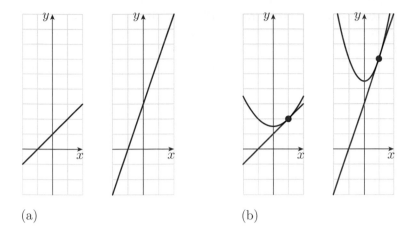

(a)   (b)

Figure 25   (a) A straight line with gradient 1, and the result of scaling it vertically by a factor of 3 (b) a curve that has gradient 1 at a particular x-value, and the result of scaling it vertically by a factor of 3

So, if you multiply a function by a constant, then its derivative is multiplied by the same constant. This fact can be stated as in the box below.

> **Constant multiple rule (Lagrange notation)**
>
> If the function k is given by $k(x) = af(x)$, where f is a function and a is a constant, then
>
> $$k'(x) = af'(x),$$
>
> for all values of x at which f is differentiable.

For example, since the derivative of $f(x) = x^2$ is $f'(x) = 2x$, it follows by the constant multiple rule that

- the derivative of $g(x) = 3x^2$ is $g'(x) = 3 \times 2x = 6x$
- the derivative of $h(x) = \frac{1}{2}x^2$ is $h'(x) = \frac{1}{2} \times 2x = x$
- the derivative of $p(x) = -x^2$ is $p'(x) = -2x$.

The third of these follows because taking a negative is the same as multiplying by -1. It's useful to remember in general that if f and k are functions such that $k(x) = -f(x)$, then, by the constant multiple rule,

$$k'(x) = -f'(x),$$

for all values of x at which f is differentiable.

Like everything involving derivatives, the constant multiple rule can also be stated in Leibniz notation, as follows.

> **Constant multiple rule (Leibniz notation)**
>
> If $y = au$, where u is a function of x and a is a constant, then
>
> $$\frac{dy}{dx} = a\frac{du}{dx},$$
>
> for all values of x at which u is differentiable.

(The phrase 'u is differentiable' in the box above is a condensed way of saying that if we write $u = f(x)$ then f is differentiable at x.)

The constant multiple rule can be proved formally by using the idea of differentiation from first principles, and you'll see this done at the end of this subsection. First, however, you should concentrate on learning to use it. Here's an example.

Example 3   *Using the constant multiple rule*

Differentiate the following functions.

(a) $f(x) = 8x^4$ (b) $f(x) = -\sqrt{x}$ (c) $y = \dfrac{3}{x}$

Solution

(a) 🔍 The derivative is 8 times the derivative of x^4. 💭

$$f'(x) = 8 \times 4x^3 = 32x^3$$

(b) 🔍 The derivative is the negative of the derivative of $\sqrt{x}$. 💭

$f(x) = -x^{1/2}$, so

$$f'(x) = -\frac{1}{2}x^{-1/2} = -\frac{1}{2} \times \frac{1}{x^{1/2}} = -\frac{1}{2x^{1/2}} = -\frac{1}{2\sqrt{x}}$$

(c) 🔍 The derivative is 3 times the derivative of $1/x$. 💭

$y = 3x^{-1}$, so

$$\frac{dy}{dx} = 3 \times (-1)x^{-2} = -\frac{3}{x^2}$$

Here are some examples for you to try. Notice that in some of them the letters used are not the standard ones, x, y and f.

Activity 9   *Using the constant multiple rule*

Differentiate the following functions.

(a) $f(x) = 5x^3$ (b) $f(x) = -x^7$ (c) $f(x) = 2\sqrt{x}$

(d) $f(x) = 6x$ (e) $f(x) = \dfrac{x}{4}$ (f) $f(t) = \dfrac{2}{t}$ (g) $g(u) = -7u$

(h) $y = \dfrac{\sqrt{x}}{3}$ (i) $y = \dfrac{8}{x^2}$ (j) $y = -\dfrac{5}{x}$ (k) $y = \dfrac{4}{\sqrt{x}}$

(l) $y = 4x^{3/2}$ (m) $p = \dfrac{1}{3\sqrt{u}}$ (n) $q = -12r^{1/3}$

Activity 10   *Using the constant multiple rule to find a gradient*

Find the gradient of the graph of the function $f(x) = 3x^2$ at the point with x-coordinate 2.

You saw in the previous subsection that the function

$$f(x) = 1$$

has derivative

$$f'(x) = 0.$$

This fact, together with the constant multiple rule, tells you that if a is any constant, then the function

$$f(x) = a \quad \text{(which is the same as } f(x) = a \times 1\text{)}$$

has derivative

$$f'(x) = a \times 0 = 0.$$

For example, the function $f(x) = 3$ has derivative $f'(x) = 0$.

This is as you would expect, because the graph of the function $f(x) = a$ (which is illustrated in Figure 26, in the case where a is positive) is a straight line with gradient 0, which means that the gradient at every point on the graph is 0.

This fact about the derivative of a constant function can be stated as follows.

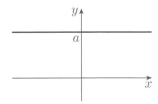

Figure 26   The graph of $f(x) = a$

> **Derivative of a constant function**
>
> If a is a constant, then
>
> $$\frac{\mathrm{d}}{\mathrm{d}x}(a) = 0.$$

To finish this subsection, here's a formal proof of the constant multiple rule, using differentiation from first principles. It uses the Lagrange notation form of the constant multiple rule, which is repeated below.

Constant multiple rule (Lagrange notation)

If the function k is given by $k(x) = af(x)$, where f is a function and a is a constant, then

$$k'(x) = af'(x),$$

for all values of x at which f is differentiable.

A proof of the constant multiple rule

Suppose that f is a function and a is a constant. Consider the function k given by $k(x) = af(x)$. Let x be any value at which f is differentiable. To find $k'(x)$, you have to consider what happens to the difference quotient for k at x, which is

$$\frac{k(x + h) - k(x)}{h}$$

(where h can be positive or negative but not zero), as h gets closer and closer to zero. Since $k(x) = af(x)$, the difference quotient for k at x is equal to

$$\frac{af(x + h) - af(x)}{h},$$

which is equal to

$$a\left(\frac{f(x + h) - f(x)}{h}\right).$$

The expression in the large brackets is the difference quotient for f at x, so, as h gets closer and closer to zero, it gets closer and closer to $f'(x)$. Hence the whole expression gets closer and closer to $af'(x)$. In other words,

$$k'(x) = af'(x),$$

which is the constant multiple rule.

2.3 Sum rule

Now suppose that you know the formulas for the derivatives of two functions, and you want to know the formula for the derivative of their sum. For example, you already know the formulas for the derivatives of the functions $f(x) = x^2$ and $g(x) = x^3$, but suppose that you want to know the formula for the derivative of the function $k(x) = x^2 + x^3$.

When you add two functions, the y-coordinates of the points on the two graphs are added. For example, Figure 27 shows the graphs of $f(x) = x^2$, $g(x) = x^3$ and $k(x) = x^2 + x^3$, and the point with x-coordinate 1 on each of the three graphs.

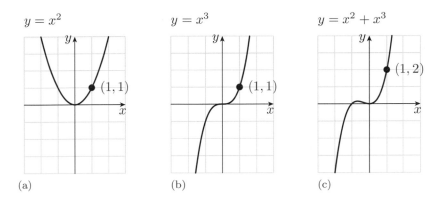

(a) (b) (c)

Figure 27 The graphs of two functions, and the graph of the sum of these functions

The effect that adding the functions has on the gradients is quite complicated to think about, but in fact it's just what you might expect: if you add two functions, then the gradient of the sum function at any particular x-value is the sum of the gradients of the two original functions at that x-value.

For example, Figure 28 shows the tangents at the three points marked in Figure 27. You can see that they have gradients 2, 3 and 5 (the sum of 2 and 3), respectively.

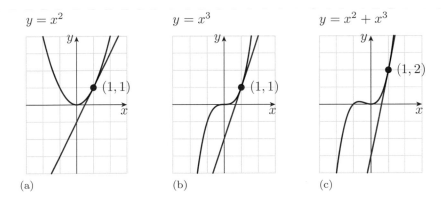

(a) (b) (c)

Figure 28 Tangents to the graphs in Figure 27

The general rule can be stated as follows.

> ### Sum rule (Lagrange notation)
>
> If $k(x) = f(x) + g(x)$, where f and g are functions, then
> $$k'(x) = f'(x) + g'(x),$$
> for all values of x at which both f and g are differentiable.

For example, since the derivative of $f(x) = x^2$ is $f'(x) = 2x$, and the derivative of $g(x) = x^3$ is $g'(x) = 3x^2$, it follows from the sum rule that the derivative of $k(x) = x^2 + x^3$ is

$$k'(x) = 2x + 3x^2.$$

The sum rule extends to sums of larger numbers of functions. For example, if $k(x) = f(x) + g(x) + h(x)$, then

$$k'(x) = f'(x) + g'(x) + h'(x),$$

for all values of x at which all of f, g and h are differentiable.

It also follows from the sum rule, together with the constant multiple rule, that if $k(x) = f(x) - g(x)$, then

$$k'(x) = f'(x) - g'(x),$$

for all values of x at which both f and g are differentiable. You can see this by writing the equation $k(x) = f(x) - g(x)$ as

$$k(x) = f(x) + (-g(x)).$$

Then, since the derivative of $-g(x)$ is $-g'(x)$ by the constant multiple rule, it follows by the sum rule that

$$
\begin{aligned}
k'(x) &= f'(x) + (-g'(x)) \\
&= f'(x) - g'(x),
\end{aligned}
$$

as claimed. Again, this fact extends to sums and differences of larger numbers of functions. For example, if $k(x) = f(x) + g(x) - h(x)$, then $k'(x) = f'(x) + g'(x) - h'(x)$ for all values of x at which all of f, g and h are differentiable.

Here is the sum rule expressed in Leibniz notation.

> ### Sum rule (Leibniz notation)
>
> If $y = u + v$, where u and v are functions of x, then
> $$\frac{dy}{dx} = \frac{du}{dx} + \frac{dv}{dx},$$
> for all values of x at which both u and v are differentiable.

Like the constant multiple rule, the sum rule can be formally proved by using the idea of differentiation from first principles, and you'll see this done at the end of this subsection. First, however, you need to practise using it.

The next example shows you how to do this. In particular, it illustrates that you can sometimes differentiate a function that isn't expressed as a sum of functions by first rearranging its formula so that it is. It also illustrates how you can use the sum rule together with the constant multiple rule.

Example 4 *Using the sum rule*

Differentiate the following functions.

(a) $f(x) = x + 2x^{1/3}$ (b) $f(x) = (x + 2)(x - 5)$

(c) $y = \dfrac{2x - 1}{x}$ (d) $y = 5(x^2 - 2x + 1)$

Solution

(a) 🔍 By the sum rule, you can differentiate each term individually (and add the results). 💬

   $f(x) = x + 2x^{1/3}$, so

   $$f'(x) = 1 + 2 \times \frac{1}{3}x^{-2/3}$$

   $$= 1 + \frac{2}{3x^{2/3}}.$$

(b) 🔍 First write the function as a sum of functions, by multiplying out. 💬

   $f(x) = (x + 2)(x - 5) = x^2 - 3x - 10$, so

   🔍 Differentiate each term individually. 💬

   $$f'(x) = 2x - 3 - 0$$

   $$= 2x - 3.$$

(c) 🔍 First write the function as a sum of functions, by expanding the fraction. 💬

   $$y = \frac{2x - 1}{x} = \frac{2x}{x} - \frac{1}{x} = 2 - \frac{1}{x} = 2 - x^{-1}, \text{ so}$$

   🔍 Differentiate each term individually. Simplify your answer. 💬

   $$\frac{dy}{dx} = 0 - (-1)x^{-2}$$

   $$= x^{-2} = \frac{1}{x^2}.$$

(d) 🔍 By the constant multiple rule, the derivative of $5(x^2 - 2x + 1)$ is 5 times the derivative of $x^2 - 2x + 1$. To differentiate $x^2 - 2x + 1$, differentiate each term individually. 💬

$y = 5(x^2 - 2x + 1)$, so

$$\frac{dy}{dx} = 5(2x - 2 + 0) = 10(x - 1).$$

🔍 Alternatively, multiply out the brackets and then differentiate each term individually. 💬

$y = 5(x^2 - 2x + 1) = 5x^2 - 10x + 5$, so

$$\frac{dy}{dx} = 5 \times 2x - 10 \times 1 + 0 = 10x - 10.$$

Activity 11   *Using the sum rule*

Differentiate the following functions.

(a) $f(x) = 6x^2 - 2x + 1$ (b) $f(x) = \frac{2}{3}x^3 + 2x^2 + x - \frac{1}{2}$

(c) $f(x) = 5x + 1$ (d) $g(t) = \frac{1}{2}t + \sqrt{t}$ (e) $f(x) = (1 + x^2)(1 + 3x)$

(f) $k(u) = (u + 3)^2$ (g) $f(x) = 30(x^{3/2} - x)$

(h) $f(x) = x(x^{3/2} - x)$ (i) $v = \dfrac{(t - 2)(t + 5)}{t}$

(j) $y = \dfrac{x + \sqrt{x}}{x^2}$ (k) $y = (x^{1/3} + 1)(x^{1/3} + 5x)$

In this section you've seen how to differentiate any power function, and you've met the constant multiple rule and the sum rule. So, in particular, you can now differentiate any polynomial function, that is, any function of the form

$f(x) = $ a sum of terms, each of the form ax^n,
      where a is a number and n is a non-negative integer.

Of course, you can also differentiate many other functions too, such as some functions involving negative or fractional powers of x.

You've seen that every function of the form $f(x) = x^n$, where n is a positive integer, is differentiable at every value of x, and that so is every constant function. These facts, together with the constant multiple rule and the sum rule, give the following useful fact.

Every polynomial function (with domain $\mathbb{R}$) is differentiable at *every* value of x.

To finish this subsection, here's a proof of the sum rule, using differentiation from first principles. It uses the Lagrange notation form of the sum rule, which is repeated below.

Sum rule (Lagrange notation)

If $k(x) = f(x) + g(x)$, where f and g are functions, then

$$k'(x) = f'(x) + g'(x),$$

for all values of x at which both f and g are differentiable.

A proof of the sum rule

Suppose that f and g are functions, and that the function k is given by $k(x) = f(x) + g(x)$. Let x denote any value at which both f and g are differentiable. To find $k'(x)$, you have to consider what happens to the difference quotient for k at x, which is

$$\frac{k(x + h) - k(x)}{h}$$

(where h can be either positive or negative, but not zero), as h gets closer and closer to zero. Since $k(x) = f(x) + g(x)$, this expression is equal to

$$\frac{(f(x + h) + g(x + h)) - (f(x) + g(x))}{h},$$

that is,

$$\frac{f(x + h) + g(x + h) - f(x) - g(x)}{h},$$

which is equal to

$$\left(\frac{f(x + h) - f(x)}{h} \right) + \left(\frac{g(x + h) - g(x)}{h} \right).$$

The expression in the first pair of large brackets is the difference quotient for f at x, and the expression in the second pair of large brackets is the difference quotient for g at x. So as h gets closer and closer to zero, the values of these two expressions get closer and closer to $f'(x)$ and $g'(x)$, respectively. Hence the whole expression gets closer and closer to $f'(x) + g'(x)$. So

$$k'(x) = f'(x) + g'(x),$$

which is the sum rule.

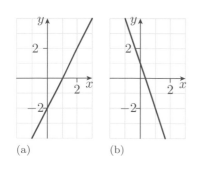

Figure 29 The lines
(a) $y = 2x - 2$
(b) $y = -3x + 1$

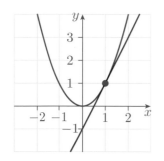

Figure 30 The tangent to
the graph of $y = x^2$ at the
point with x-coordinate 1

3 Rates of change

You saw in Unit 2 that the gradient of a straight-line graph is the rate of change of the variable on the vertical axis with respect to the variable on the horizontal axis. For example, if the relationship between the variables x and y is represented by a straight line with gradient 2, then y is increasing at the rate of 2 units for every unit that x increases, as illustrated in Figure 29(a). Similarly, if the relationship between x and y is represented by a straight line with gradient -3, then y is *decreasing* at the rate of 3 units for every unit that x increases, as illustrated in Figure 29(b).

As mentioned in Subsection 1.1, the idea of a gradient as a rate of change also applies to curved graphs. For example, you've seen that the graph of the equation $y = x^2$ has gradient 2 at the point with x-coordinate 1. This means that, when $x = 1$, the variable y is increasing at the rate of 2 units for every unit that x increases, as illustrated in Figure 30.

Of course, unlike in Figure 29(a), in Figure 30 the variable y doesn't *actually* increase by two units for every unit that x increases. This rate of change is an 'instantaneous' value, valid only for the x-value 1. For other values of x, the rate of change of y with respect to x (the gradient of the graph) is different.

Since the gradient of any graph of the variable y against the variable x is given by the derivative dy/dx, another way to think about the derivative dy/dx is that it is the rate of change of y with respect to x.

As you've seen, it's particularly helpful to think of a gradient as a rate of change when you're working with a graph that models a real-life situation. In this section you'll look at two types of real-life situation involving rates of change.

3.1 Displacement and velocity

Remember from Subsection 2.4 of Unit 2 that when you model the motion of an object along a straight line, you choose some point on the line to be the reference point, and one of the two directions along the line to be the positive direction. Then the object's **displacement** at any particular time is its distance from the reference point, with a plus or minus sign to indicate its direction from this point. For example, in Figure 31 an object at position A has a displacement of $12\,\text{m}$, and an object at position B has a displacement of $-7\,\text{m}$.

Figure 31   Positions along a straight line

You saw that if the displacement of an object along a straight line is plotted against time, then the gradient of the resulting graph is the rate of change of the object's displacement with respect to time, which is called its **velocity**. (Remember that, in the calculus units in this module, displacement and velocity are always one-dimensional, and hence are represented by scalars, with direction indicated by the signs of the scalars.)

For example, Figure 32 shows the two displacement–time graphs for a man walking along a straight path that you saw in Subsection 1.1. The reference point on the straight path has been chosen to be the point where the man begins his walk, and the positive direction has been chosen to be the direction in which he walks. Time is measured from the moment when the man begins his walk.

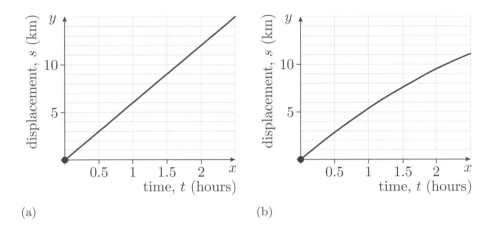

(a)   (b)

Figure 32   Two displacement–time graphs for a man walking along a straight path

In each of the two graphs in Figure 32, the quantity on the horizontal axis (time) is measured in hours, and the quantity on the vertical axis (distance) is measured in kilometres, so the gradient is measured in kilometres per hour. The graph in Figure 32(a) is a straight line with gradient $6\,\mathrm{km\,h^{-1}}$, which means that the man is walking at a constant velocity of $6\,\mathrm{km\,h^{-1}}$. In the graph in Figure 32(b), the man seems to start off walking at a velocity of about $6\,\mathrm{km\,h^{-1}}$, but his velocity continuously decreases as he walks.

In general, since the gradient of the displacement–time graph of any object that moves along a straight line is the velocity of the object, we have the following important fact.

Relationship between displacement and velocity

Suppose that an object is moving along a straight line. If t is the time that has elapsed since some chosen point in time, s is the displacement of the object from some chosen reference point, and v is the velocity of the object, then

$$v = \frac{\mathrm{d}s}{\mathrm{d}t}.$$

(Time, displacement and velocity can be measured in any suitable units, as long as they're consistent.)

An example of a set of consistent units is seconds for time, metres for displacement, and metres per second for velocity. These units are consistent because the units for time and displacement are the same as the units for time and displacement within the derived units for velocity.

Notice that displacement is denoted by the letter s in the box above and in Figure 32. This is the usual choice of letter for this quantity. The more natural choice of d is usually avoided, because it might cause confusion with the d used in Leibniz notation. Velocity is usually denoted by the letter v, and time by the letter t, as you'd expect.

One explanation of the fact that displacement (or distance) is usually denoted by the letter s is that it is the initial letter of the Latin word for distance, which is 'spatium'.

The fact in the box headed 'Relationship between displacement and velocity' above tells you that if you have a formula for the displacement of an object moving along a straight line, in terms of time, then you can use differentiation to obtain a formula for the object's velocity in terms of time.

This fact is used in the next example. Here the equation of the displacement–time graph in Figure 32(b), which is

$$s = 6t - \tfrac{5}{8}t^2,$$

is used to obtain an equation for the man's velocity in terms of time.

Example 5   *Using differentiation to find a velocity*

Suppose that a man walks along a straight path, and his displacement s (in kilometres) at time t (in hours) after he begins his walk is given by

$$s = 6t - \tfrac{5}{8}t^2.$$

Let the man's velocity at time t be v (in kilometres per hour).

(a) Find an equation expressing v in terms of t.

(b) Hence find the man's velocity one hour into his walk.

Solution

(a) The man's displacement s at time t is given by

$$s = 6t - \tfrac{5}{8}t^2.$$

Hence his velocity v at time t is given by

$$\begin{aligned}
v &= \frac{\mathrm{d}s}{\mathrm{d}t} \\
&= 6 - \tfrac{5}{8} \times 2t \\
&= 6 - \tfrac{5}{4}t.
\end{aligned}$$

That is, the required equation is $v = 6 - \tfrac{5}{4}t$.

(b) When $t = 1$,

$$v = 6 - \tfrac{5}{4} \times 1 = 4.75.$$

So the man's velocity after one hour is 4.75 km h^{-1}.

Figure 33 shows the tangent to the graph in Figure 32(b) at the point one hour after the man begins his walk. You can see that the gradient of the tangent – that is, the man's velocity – does indeed seem to be roughly 4.75 km h^{-1}, as calculated in the example above.

Notice that in Example 5 we started off knowing how the man's displacement changed with time – the relationship between these two quantities is given by the equation $s = 6t - \tfrac{5}{8}t^2$. We used this information to find how the man's velocity (his rate of change of displacement) changed with time – we found that this relationship is given by the equation $v = 6 - \tfrac{5}{4}t$. This is the sort of calculation that differential calculus allows you to carry out: if you know the values taken by a changing quantity throughout a period of change, then you can use differentiation to find the values taken by the rate of change of the quantity throughout the same period.

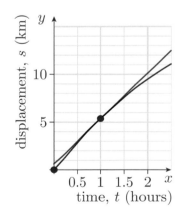

Figure 33   The tangent to the graph of $s = 6t - \tfrac{5}{8}t^2$ at the point with t-coordinate 1

You might find it enlightening to think about what the process of differentiation from first principles means when it is applied to a displacement–time graph. In this case the difference quotient at a particular time value represents the *average velocity* over a time interval starting or ending at that time value. As the time interval gets smaller and smaller, the average velocity gets closer and closer to the instantaneous velocity at that time value.

The next activity is about a particular type of motion in a straight line: that of an object falling vertically from rest, near the surface of the Earth. The phrase 'from rest' here means that the object has no initial velocity when it begins falling. If the effect of air resistance is negligible (which it is if the object is fairly compact and the fall is fairly short), then the distance fallen by the object isn't affected by how heavy it is, for example, but depends only on the time that it has been falling. In fact, the total distance fallen is proportional to the square of the time that it has been falling. If time is measured in seconds and distance is measured in metres, then the constant of proportionality is about 4.9, so at time t (in seconds) after the object began falling it will have fallen a total distance of about $4.9t^2$ (in metres).

When we model the motion of a falling object using displacement rather than distance, we often take the positive direction along the line of motion to be upwards. So, if we also take the reference point to be the point from which the object starts to fall, then the displacement s (in metres) of the object at time t (in seconds) after it starts to fall is given by the equation

$$s = -4.9t^2.$$

The graph of this equation is shown in Figure 34.

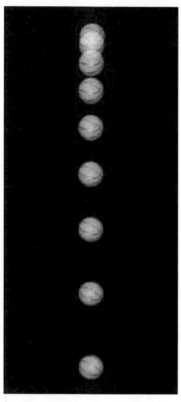

A falling ball, photographed at equal time intervals

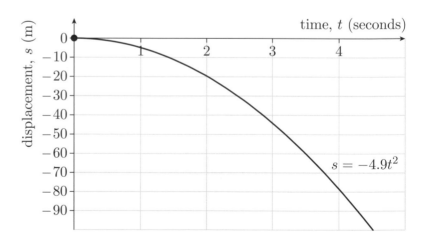

Figure 34   The displacement–time graph for an object falling from rest

In the next activity, remember that, just as distance is the magnitude of displacement, so speed is the magnitude of velocity. So, for example, an object with a velocity of $-3\,\mathrm{m\,s^{-1}}$ has a speed of $3\,\mathrm{m\,s^{-1}}$.

Activity 12 *Finding the velocity of a falling object*

(a) You saw above that the displacement s (in metres) of an object falling from rest, at time t (in seconds) since it began falling, is given by the equation $s = -4.9t^2$. Use this equation to find an equation for the velocity v (in $\mathrm{m\,s^{-1}}$) of the object at time t.

(b) Hence find the velocity of such an object three seconds into its fall. Give your answer in metres per second, to one decimal place.

(c) If an object is dropped from the top of a tower, how long does it take to reach a speed of $15\,\mathrm{m\,s^{-1}}$? Give your answer in seconds, to one decimal place.

The fact that the distance travelled by a falling object is proportional to the square of the time that it has been falling was determined by the Italian physicist Galileo Galilei in the sixteenth century, using experiments that he carried out in his workshop. At the time, there were no clocks that could measure intervals of time short enough to allow him to determine the motion of a falling object, but instead he rolled balls down a sloping groove, and reasoned that their motion would be similar to that of a falling object, but slower.

3.2 Total cost and marginal cost

Galileo Galilei (1564–1642)

Here's another example of a situation where it's useful to think of the gradient of a graph (and hence the derivative of a function) as a rate of change. This example shows you one way in which the idea of differentiation can be used in economics.

Suppose that a small confectionery company has found that the weekly cost of making its milk chocolate consists of a fixed cost of £3000 (to pay for the rent and maintenance of its premises and equipment, for example), plus £8 per kilogram of chocolate made (to pay for the ingredients and staff time, for example). In other words, the weekly cost, c (in £), is modelled by the equation

$$c = 3000 + 8q, \tag{3}$$

where q is the amount of chocolate made in the week, in kilograms. The graph of this equation is shown in Figure 35.

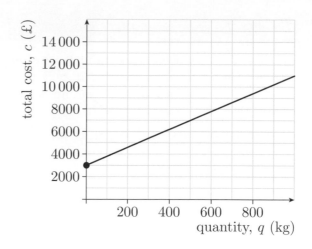

Figure 35   The graph of the equation $c = 3000 + 8q$, a model for the total weekly cost c (in £) of making milk chocolate in terms of the quantity q (in kg) of chocolate made

On average, each person in the UK consumes about $10\,\mathrm{kg}$ of chocolate per year

Suppose that the company is currently making a particular quantity of milk chocolate per week, but is thinking of increasing its production. Then the additional weekly cost of making the extra chocolate will, of course, be £8 per extra kilogram made. This is known as the **marginal cost** per kilogram of making the extra chocolate. It's different from the real cost per kilogram of making the chocolate (usually called the **unit cost** or **average cost**), which is equal to the total cost, $3000 + 8q$ (in £), divided by the quantity in kilograms of chocolate made, q.

In fact, the marginal cost of making the extra chocolate is the gradient of the graph in Figure 35. This is because the gradient of the graph is the rate at which the quantity on the vertical axis (the total cost, in £) increases as the quantity on the horizontal axis (the quantity of chocolate made, in kg) increases. The fact that the gradient is 8 pounds per kilogram, which is normally written as £8 per kilogram, tells you that the total cost is increasing at a rate of £8 for every kilogram by which the quantity of chocolate increases.

Often an equation that models the total cost of making a quantity of a product doesn't have a straight-line graph. For example, suppose that the confectionery company has found that a better model for the total weekly cost c (in £) of making a quantity q (in kg) of milk chocolate is

$$c = 3000 + 4q + \tfrac{1}{125}q^2.$$

The graph of this equation is shown in Figure 36.

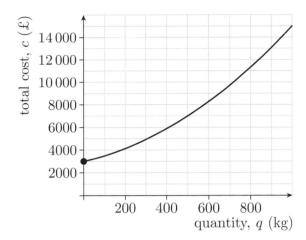

Figure 36 The graph of the equation $c = 3000 + 4q + \frac{1}{125}q^2$, an alternative model for the total weekly cost c (in £) of making milk chocolate in terms of the quantity q (in kg) of chocolate made

As before, the gradient of the graph tells you the rate at which the total weekly cost increases as the amount of chocolate made increases. In other words, the gradient of the graph is the marginal cost per kilogram of making extra chocolate. You can see that the gradient of the graph – the marginal cost per kilogram – *increases* as the quantity of chocolate made increases. This tells you that the more chocolate the company makes, the larger is the cost of making an extra kilogram of chocolate.

There are various reasons why this might be the case. For example, to increase its production of chocolate the company might have to pay its staff at higher rates, for overtime or non-standard hours.

For any particular quantity q (in kg) of chocolate being made, the marginal cost per kilogram of making any extra chocolate is the gradient of the graph at that value of q, which as you know is given by dc/dq. Of course, this is an 'instantaneous' value, valid only for that value of q.

Activity 13   *Working with marginal cost*

Suppose that the confectionery company discussed above has decided that the second equation above, namely

$$c = 3000 + 4q + \tfrac{1}{125}q^2,$$

is an appropriate model for the total weekly cost of making its milk chocolate. Here q is the quantity of chocolate made (in kg), and c is the total cost (in £). Let the marginal cost per kilogram of making any extra chocolate be m (in £).

(a) Use differentiation to find an equation for the marginal cost m in terms of the quantity q.

(b) What is the marginal cost per kilogram of making extra chocolate when the amount of chocolate already being made is 300 kilograms?

(c) The company sells all the chocolate that it makes at a price of £16 per kilogram. It decides to keep increasing its weekly production of chocolate until the marginal cost is equal to the price at which it sells the chocolate. (This is because if it increases its production any further, then it will cost more money to make the extra chocolate than the company will obtain by selling it.) By writing down and solving a suitable equation, find the weekly quantity of chocolate that the company should make.

The fact that marginal cost is the derivative of total cost is used in many economic models.

4 Finding where functions are increasing, decreasing or stationary

Because the derivative of a function tells you the gradient at each point on the graph of the function, it gives you information about the shape of the graph. In this section, you'll see how you can use the derivative of a function to deduce useful facts about its graph.

4.1 Increasing/decreasing criterion

You saw the following definitions in Unit 3.

Functions increasing or decreasing on an interval

A function f is **increasing on the interval** I if for all values x_1 and x_2 in I such that $x_1 < x_2$,

$$f(x_1) < f(x_2).$$

A function f is **decreasing on the interval** I if for all values x_1 and x_2 in I such that $x_1 < x_2$,

$$f(x_1) > f(x_2).$$

(The interval I must be part of the domain of f.)

Informally, a function is increasing on an interval if its graph slopes up on that interval, and is decreasing on an interval if its graph slopes down on the interval. For example, the function $f(x) = 2x^3 - 3x^2 - 36x$ is increasing on the interval $(-\infty, -2)$, decreasing on the interval $(-2, 3)$, and increasing on the interval $(3, \infty)$, as illustrated in Figure 37.

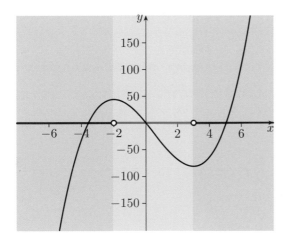

Figure 37 The graph of the function $f(x) = 2x^3 - 3x^2 - 36x$

Of course, you can't tell from the graph alone that this function stops increasing and starts decreasing when x is *exactly* -2, or that it stops decreasing and starts increasing when x is *exactly* 3. You'll see shortly how to confirm that the function is increasing and decreasing on the intervals mentioned above, exactly.

You could also say that the function in Figure 37 is increasing on the interval $(-\infty, -2]$, decreasing on the interval $[-2, 3]$, and increasing on the interval $[3, \infty)$. However, when we discuss intervals on which a function is increasing or decreasing, it's often helpful to consider intervals that don't overlap, so we usually consider *open* intervals.

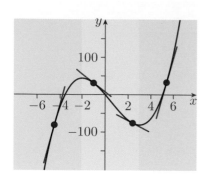

Figure 38 Some tangents to the graph of
$f(x) = 2x^3 - 3x^2 - 36x$

Since positive gradients correspond to a graph sloping up, while negative gradients correspond to a graph sloping down, the derivative of a function tells you the intervals on which the function is increasing or decreasing, as set out below.

> ### Increasing/decreasing criterion
>
> If $f'(x)$ is positive for all x in an interval I, then f is increasing on I.
>
> If $f'(x)$ is negative for all x in an interval I, then f is decreasing on I.

For example, Figure 38 shows parts of the tangents to some points on the graph of the function $f(x) = 2x^3 - 3x^2 - 36x$. It illustrates that positive gradients correspond to intervals on which the graph is increasing, and negative gradients correspond to intervals on which the graph is decreasing.

It's sometimes useful to determine whether a particular function that you're working with is increasing on a particular interval, or decreasing on a particular interval. (For example, this can help you sketch its graph.) You can often use the increasing/decreasing criterion to do this, as illustrated in the next example. This example confirms that the function in Figure 37 is increasing and decreasing on the intervals mentioned earlier.

Example 6   *Using the increasing/decreasing criterion*

Show that the function $f(x) = 2x^3 - 3x^2 - 36x$ is increasing on each of the intervals $(-\infty, -2)$ and $(3, \infty)$, and decreasing on the interval $(-2, 3)$.

Solution

🔍 Find the derivative. 💭

The derivative is

$$f'(x) = 6x^2 - 6x - 36.$$

🔍 Show that the derivative is always positive when x is in the interval $(-\infty, -2)$ or in the interval $(3, \infty)$, and always negative when x is in the interval $(-2, 3)$. Try factorising to help you do this. 💭

Factorising gives

$$f'(x) = 6(x^2 - x - 6) = 6(x + 2)(x - 3).$$

When x is less than -2, the values of $x + 2$ and $x - 3$ are both negative, and hence the value of $f'(x) = 6(x + 2)(x - 3)$ is positive.

Similarly, when x is greater than 3, the values of $x + 2$ and $x - 3$ are both positive, and hence the value of $f'(x) = 6(x + 2)(x - 3)$ is also positive.

When x is in the interval $(-2, 3)$, the value of $x + 2$ is positive and the value of $x - 3$ is negative, and hence the value of $f'(x) = 6(x + 2)(x - 3)$ is negative.

Therefore, by the increasing/decreasing criterion, the function f is increasing on each of the intervals $(-\infty, -2)$ and $(3, \infty)$, and decreasing on the interval $(-2, 3)$.

Activity 14   *Using the increasing/decreasing criterion*

Consider the function $f(x) = \frac{2}{3}x^3 - 8x^2 + 30x - 36$.

(a) Find the derivative $f'(x)$, and factorise it.

(b) Show that f is increasing on each of the intervals $(-\infty, 3)$ and $(5, \infty)$.

(c) Show that f is decreasing on the interval $(3, 5)$.

An alternative way to set out working of the type in Example 6 and in the solution to Activity 14 is to use a table of signs, in the way that you saw in Section 5.4 of Unit 3. You'll see examples of this in the next subsection.

Activity 15   *Using the increasing/decreasing criterion again*

Consider the function $f(x) = x^3 - 3x^2 + 4x + 3$.

(a) Find the derivative $f'(x)$, and complete the square on this expression. (You saw how to complete the square in Unit 2.)

(b) Hence show that f is increasing on the interval $(-\infty, \infty)$ (that is, on the whole of its domain).

If you look back to the statement of the increasing/decreasing criterion on page 258, you'll see that the first part begins

    If $f'(x)$ is positive for all x in an interval I ....

A slightly more concise way to express the same thing is to say

    If f' is positive *on* an interval I ....

Similarly, the beginning of the second part of the increasing/decreasing criterion,

    If $f'(x)$ is negative for all x in an interval I ...,

can be expressed as

    If f' is negative *on* an interval I ....

These more concise forms are used in the next subsection.

4.2 Stationary points

Consider again the function

$$f(x) = 2x^3 - 3x^2 - 36x,$$

which was discussed in the previous subsection. Its graph is shown again in Figure 39. As you saw earlier, the gradient of the graph is positive on the interval $(-\infty, -2)$, negative on the interval $(-2, 3)$ and positive again on the interval $(3, \infty)$.

Between these open intervals, there are points at which the gradient of the graph is zero, as shown in Figure 39. A point at which the gradient of a graph is zero is called a **stationary point**. So the graph in Figure 39 has stationary points at the points with x-coordinates -2 and 3. If you work out the corresponding y-coordinates (by substituting the x-coordinates into the rule of f in the usual way), then you find that the stationary points are $(-2, 44)$ and $(3, -81)$.

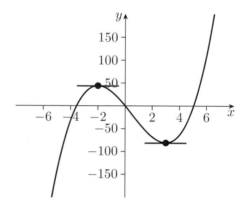

Figure 39   The stationary points on the graph of $f(x) = 2x^3 - 3x^2 - 36x$

The term 'stationary point' is used to refer to the x-coordinate of a stationary point, as well as to the point itself. This is because real numbers are sometimes called *points* – you can think of them as points on the number line. (You've already seen that a real number at one end of an interval is known as an *endpoint*.) So, for example, we can say that the stationary points of the function $f(x) = 2x^3 - 3x^2 - 36x$ are -2 and 3.

At the left-hand stationary point in Figure 39, the value taken by the function is larger than at any other point nearby, so we say that the function has a **local maximum** at this point. Similarly, at the right-hand stationary point, the value taken by the function is smaller than at any other point nearby, so we say that the function has a **local minimum** at this point.

Notice that the value taken by a function at a local maximum or local minimum isn't necessarily the greatest or least value that the function takes overall. For example, you can see from Figure 39 that the function $f(x) = 2x^3 - 3x^2 - 36x$ takes a larger value when $x = 6$, say, than it does at its local maximum, at $x = -2$. This is why the word 'local' is used.

A point where a function has a local maximum or local minimum is called a **turning point**, because if you imagine tracing your pen tip along the graph of the function from left to right, then at a local maximum or minimum it stops going up or down, and turns to go the other way.

Notice that at a local maximum the graph of a function is increasing on the left and decreasing on the right, and at a local minimum it is decreasing on the left and increasing on the right.

There are other types of stationary points, apart from turning points. For example, Figure 40(a) shows the graph of the function $f(x) = x^3$. The derivative of this function is $f'(x) = 3x^2$, so the gradient of the graph when $x = 0$ is

$$f'(0) = 3 \times 0^2 = 0.$$

So the function $f(x) = x^3$ has a stationary point at $x = 0$. However, this stationary point isn't a turning point. The graph of the function $f(x) = x^3$ is increasing on *both* sides of the stationary point, and just levels off momentarily at the stationary point itself.

Similarly, the graph of the function $g(x) = -x^3$ is *decreasing* on both sides of its stationary point, as illustrated in Figure 40(b).

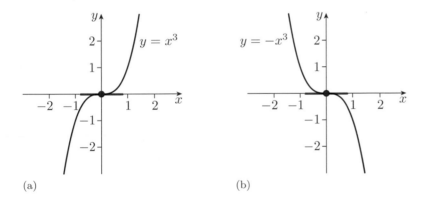

(a)   (b)

Figure 40   The graphs of (a) $f(x) = x^3$ (b) $g(x) = -x^3$

A stationary point of either of the types shown in Figure 40 is called a **horizontal point of inflection**. You'll see the reason for this term later in the unit. Notice that the tangent to a curve at a horizontal point of inflection crosses the curve at that point.

Some stationary points are neither turning points nor horizontal points of inflection. For example, every point on the graph of the equation $y = 1$ (see Figure 41), or on any horizontal line, is a stationary point that is neither a turning point nor a horizontal point of inflection.

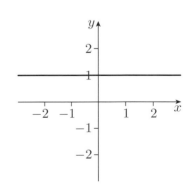

Figure 41   The graph of $y = 1$

When you're working with a function, it's sometimes useful to find its stationary points, and, if possible, determine the nature of each stationary point – that is, determine whether it is a local maximum, a local minimum or a horizontal point of inflection. In the rest of this subsection you'll learn

261

how to do this, and in the next subsection you'll see some examples of why it can be a useful thing to do.

You've seen that the stationary points of a function are the values of x at which the gradient of its graph is zero. So the method for finding the stationary points of a function is as follows.

> **Strategy:**
> **To find the stationary points of a function f**
>
> Solve the equation $f'(x) = 0$.

In the next example, this strategy is used to confirm that the function

$$f(x) = 2x^3 - 3x^2 - 36x,$$

which we considered at the beginning of this subsection and in the last subsection, has stationary points at $x = -2$ and $x = 3$.

Example 7   *Finding the stationary points of a function*

Find the stationary points of the function

$$f(x) = 2x^3 - 3x^2 - 36x.$$

Solution

🗪 Find the derivative $f'(x)$. Factorise it if possible. 🗪

The derivative is

$$\begin{aligned} f'(x) &= 6x^2 - 6x - 36 \\ &= 6(x^2 - x - 6) \\ &= 6(x+2)(x-3). \end{aligned}$$

🗪 Solve the equation $f'(x) = 0$. 🗪

Solving the equation $f'(x) = 0$ gives

$$6(x+2)(x-3) = 0;$$

that is,

$$x = -2 \quad \text{or} \quad x = 3.$$

Hence the stationary points are -2 and 3.

Activity 16   *Finding the stationary points of a function*

Find the approximate values, to two decimal places, of the stationary points of the function

$$f(x) = x^3 - x^2 - 2x.$$

To determine whether a stationary point of a function f is a local maximum, local minimum or horizontal point of inflection, you can use the following facts. If there's an open interval immediately to the left of the stationary point, and an open interval immediately to the right of the stationary point, such that

- f is increasing on the left interval and decreasing on the right interval, then the stationary point is a local maximum

- f is decreasing on the left interval and increasing on the right interval, then the stationary point is a local minimum

- f is increasing on both intervals or decreasing on both intervals, then the stationary point is a horizontal point of inflection.

For example, Figure 42 shows the graph of a function with a local maximum, and open intervals immediately to the left and right of the local maximum. The function is increasing on the left interval, and decreasing on the right interval.

Combining the facts above with the increasing/decreasing criterion (stated on page 258) gives the following useful test for determining the nature of a stationary point. It's known as the *first derivative test* – the reason for the word 'first' is explained in Section 5.

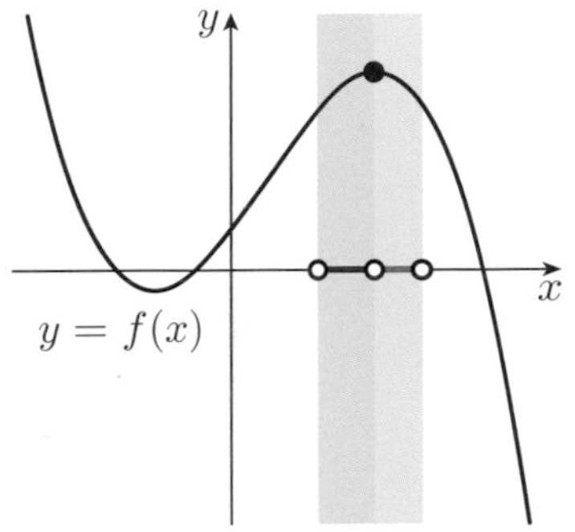

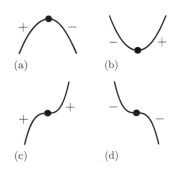

Figure 42   Open intervals immediately to the left and right of a local maximum

---

First derivative test (for determining the nature of a stationary point of a function f)

If there are open intervals immediately to the left and right of a stationary point such that

- $f'(x)$ is positive on the left interval and negative on the right interval, then the stationary point is a local maximum

- $f'(x)$ is negative on the left interval and positive on the right interval, then the stationary point is a local minimum

- $f'(x)$ is positive on both intervals or negative on both intervals, then the stationary point is a horizontal point of inflection.

This test is illustrated in Figure 43. The signs show whether the derivative is positive or negative on intervals immediately to the left and right of the stationary point.

Figure 43   The signs of the derivative to the left and right of different types of stationary point

Here's an example showing how you can use the first derivative test to determine the nature of the stationary points of a function. The example uses the technique of drawing up a table of signs, which you met in Unit 3.

Example 8   *Determining the nature of stationary points using the first derivative test*

Consider the function

$$f(x) = \tfrac{4}{3}x^3 + 5x^2 - 6x - 2.$$

(a) Find the stationary points of f.

(b) Determine whether each stationary point of f is a local maximum, local minimum or horizontal point of inflection.

Solution

(a) 🔍 Find $f'(x)$, and factorise it, if possible. 💭

The derivative is

$$f'(x) = 4x^2 + 10x - 6$$
$$= 2(2x^2 + 5x - 3)$$
$$= 2(2x - 1)(x + 3).$$

🔍 Solve the equation $f'(x) = 0$. 💭

Solving the equation $f'(x) = 0$ gives

$$2(2x - 1)(x + 3) = 0;$$

that is,

$$x = \tfrac{1}{2} \quad \text{or} \quad x = -3.$$

Hence the stationary points of f are -3 and $\tfrac{1}{2}$.

(b) 🔍 Construct a table of signs to help you find intervals on which $f'(x)$ is negative or positive. In the column headings, write the values where $f'(x) = 0$ (that is, the stationary points of f), in increasing order, and also the intervals to the left and right of, and between, these values. In the row headings, write the factors of $f'(x)$, and then $f'(x)$ itself. Find the signs in the way that you learned in Subsection 5.4 of Unit 3. 💭

x	$(-\infty, -3)$	-3	$(-3, \frac{1}{2})$	$\frac{1}{2}$	$(\frac{1}{2}, \infty)$
2	$+$	$+$	$+$	$+$	$+$
$2x - 1$	$-$	$-$	$-$	0	$+$
$x + 3$	$-$	0	$+$	$+$	$+$
$f'(x)$	$+$	0	$-$	0	$+$

Apply the first derivative test. You might find it helpful to add a further row to the table, in which you use the signs of f' to determine whether f is increasing, decreasing or stationary, and indicate this with sloping or horizontal lines, as shown.

slope of f	$\diagup$	$-$	$\diagdown$	$-$	$\diagup$

The stationary point -3 is a local maximum, and the stationary point $\frac{1}{2}$ is a local minimum.

Activity 17   Determining the nature of stationary points using the first derivative test

Consider the function
$$f(x) = 3x^4 - 2x^3 - 9x^2 + 7.$$

(a) Find the stationary points of f.
   Hint: to factorise $f'(x)$, first notice that it has x as a factor.

(b) Determine whether each stationary point of f is a local maximum, local minimum or horizontal point of inflection.

There's an alternative way to apply the first derivative test, which you can use instead of constructing a table of signs, if you prefer. It's described in the following box. The different possibilities in step 3 are illustrated in Figure 44.

Strategy:
To apply the first derivative test by choosing sample points

1. Choose two points (that is, two x-values) fairly close to the stationary point, one on each side.

2. Check that the function is differentiable at all points between the chosen points and the stationary point, and that there are no other stationary points between the chosen points and the stationary point.

3. Find the value of the derivative of the function at the two chosen points.

    *   If the derivative is positive at the left chosen point and negative at the right chosen point, then the stationary point is a local maximum.

    *   If the derivative is negative at the left chosen point and positive at the right chosen point, then the stationary point is a local minimum.

    *   If the derivative is positive at both chosen points or negative at both chosen points, then the stationary point is a horizontal point of inflection.

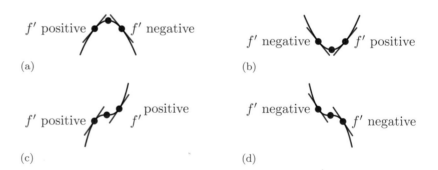

Figure 44   How to recognise, by considering points on each side of a stationary point, whether the stationary point is (a) a local maximum (b) a local minimum or (c), (d) a horizontal point of inflection

When you use this alternative way of applying the first derivative test, it doesn't matter how far the two points that you choose are from the stationary point, as long as the conditions in step 2 are satisfied. The reason why these conditions are important is explained after the next example. This example repeats Example 8, but uses the alternative way of applying the first derivative test.

Example 9 *Determining the nature of stationary points using the alternative way of applying the first derivative test*

Consider the function

$$f(x) = \tfrac{4}{3}x^3 + 5x^2 - 6x - 2.$$

(a) Find the stationary points of f.

(b) Determine whether each stationary point of f is a local maximum, local minimum or horizontal point of inflection.

Solution

(a) 🔍 This part is the same as in Example 8. 💬

The derivative is

$$\begin{aligned} f'(x) &= 4x^2 + 10x - 6 \\ &= 2(2x^2 + 5x - 3) \\ &= 2(2x - 1)(x + 3). \end{aligned}$$

Solving the equation $f'(x) = 0$ gives

$$2(2x - 1)(x + 3) = 0;$$

that is,

$$x = \tfrac{1}{2} \quad \text{or} \quad x = -3.$$

Hence the stationary points of f are -3 and $\tfrac{1}{2}$.

(b) 🔍 Apply the method in the box above. There are many possible choices of points in step 1; choose them to be simple as possible. 💬

Consider the values -4, 0 and 1. The values -4 and 0 lie on each side of the stationary point -3, and the values 0 and 1 lie on each side of the stationary point $\tfrac{1}{2}$.

The function f is differentiable at all values of x (as is every polynomial function). Also, there are no stationary points between -4 and -3 or between -3 and 0. Similarly, there are no stationary points between 0 and $\tfrac{1}{2}$ or between $\tfrac{1}{2}$ and 1.

Since $f'(x) = 4x^2 + 10x - 6$, we have

$$\begin{aligned} f'(-4) &= 4(-4)^2 + 10(-4) - 6 = 64 - 40 - 6 = 18, \\ f'(0) &= -6, \\ f'(1) &= 4 + 10 - 6 = 8. \end{aligned}$$

Since f' is positive at -4 and negative at 0, the stationary point -3 is a local maximum.

Since f' is negative at 0 and positive at 1, the stationary point $\tfrac{1}{2}$ is a local minimum.

Figure 45 illustrates the reasons for the restrictions mentioned in the strategy box above. Each of the three graphs shows a situation where you might be misled into thinking that a stationary point is a local minimum, whereas in fact it is a local maximum.

In Figure 45(a), the function isn't differentiable at all points between the chosen points and the stationary point, because it isn't even *defined* at all such points. It is undefined (and has vertical asymptotes) at $x = 4$ and $x = 8$.

In Figure 45(b), the function isn't differentiable at all points between the chosen points and the stationary point. It isn't differentiable at $x = 4$ and $x = 8$.

Finally, in Figure 45(c), there are further stationary points between the chosen points and the stationary point of interest. There are stationary points at $x = 4$ and $x = 8$.

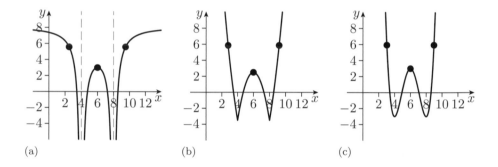

(a)   (b)   (c)

Figure 45   The graphs of three functions

You can try using the alternative way of applying the first derivative test in the next activity.

Activity 18   *Determining the nature of stationary points using the first derivative test, again*

Consider the function

$$f(x) = x^4 - 2x^3.$$

(a) Find the stationary points of f.
    Hint: to factorise $f'(x)$, first notice that it has x^2 as a factor.

(b) By finding the value of f' at appropriate points, determine whether each stationary point of f is a local maximum, local minimum or horizontal point of inflection.

4.3   Uses of finding stationary points

In this subsection you'll see some situations where it can be useful to find, and sometimes determine the nature of, the stationary points of a function.

Finding the vertex of a parabola

In Unit 2 you saw some methods for finding the vertex of a u-shaped or n-shaped parabola. An alternative method is to use the fact that the vertex of a parabola is a stationary point. You're asked to do this in the next activity, for a parabola that models a particular economic situation.

The type of economic graph in this activity is different from the type that you considered in the 'chocolate manufacturer' example in Subsection 3.2. There you considered graphs of total cost against quantity of product made, whereas here you'll consider a graph of total *profit* against quantity of product made.

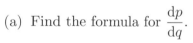

Activity 19   *Using differentiation to find the vertex of a parabola*

A bakery has found that its daily profit, p (in £), from making and selling cakes of a particular type can be modelled by the equation

$$p = -0.006q^2 + 3.3q,$$

where q is the quantity of cakes sold.

(Since the coefficient of q^2 is negative, the graph of p against q is an n-shaped parabola, so, as the quantity of cakes sold increases, the profit first increases and then decreases. The decrease might be caused by the fact that, when the quantity of cakes increases beyond a certain number, the limits of the bakery's facilities means that it becomes more expensive to make them – for example, the bakery may have to pay its staff at higher rates, for overtime or non-standard hours.)

Cakes

(a) Find the formula for $\dfrac{dp}{dq}$.

(b) Use your answer to part (a) to find the stationary point of the parabola that is the graph of p against q. Hence write down the number of cakes that the bakery should make and sell per day if it wants to earn the maximum profit.

(c) Find the daily profit earned by the bakery from these cakes if it sells the number of them found in part (b).

Sketching the graph of a function

Another situation where it can be useful to find, and in this case determine the nature of, the stationary points of a function is when you want to sketch its graph. If you plot the stationary points, and indicate their natures, then you can often draw a reasonable sketch of the graph.

It's a good idea to also include on your sketch any x- or y-intercepts that you can find and plot easily. It's usually straightforward to find the y-intercept, if there is one, but often not so easy to find any x-intercepts.

As an illustration, we'll consider **cubic functions**, that is, functions of the form

$$f(x) = ax^3 + bx^2 + cx + d,$$

where a, b, c and d are constants, with $a \neq 0$. The graph of every cubic function, in common with the graph of every polynomial function that isn't a constant function, tends to plus or minus infinity at the left and right. You can find its shape between these extremes by finding its stationary points, if it has any.

The derivative of every cubic function is a quadratic function, because when you differentiate the formula for a cubic function you reduce the power of x in each term by 1. So to find the stationary points of a cubic function you have to solve a quadratic equation, and hence there are at most two stationary points.

Example 10   *Sketching the graph of a cubic function*

Sketch the graph of the function $f(x) = \frac{1}{3}x^3 - x^2 - 3x + 2$.

Solution

🔍 Find the stationary points, including the y-coordinates. 💭

The derivative is

$$f'(x) = x^2 - 2x - 3 = (x+1)(x-3).$$

Solving the equation $f'(x) = 0$ gives

$$(x+1)(x-3) = 0;$$

that is,

$$x = -1 \quad \text{or} \quad x = 3.$$

When $x = -1$,

$$\begin{aligned}
y &= f(-1) \\
&= \tfrac{1}{3}(-1)^3 - (-1)^2 - 3(-1) + 2 \\
&= -\tfrac{1}{3} - 1 + 3 + 2 \\
&= \tfrac{11}{3}.
\end{aligned}$$

When $x = 3$,

$$y = f(3)$$
$$= \tfrac{1}{3} \times 3^3 - 3^2 - 3 \times 3 + 2$$
$$= 9 - 9 - 9 + 2$$
$$= -7.$$

So the stationary points are $(-1, \tfrac{11}{3})$ and $(3, -7)$.

🔍 Determine the nature of the stationary points. 💬

x	$(-\infty, -1)$	-1	$(-1, 3)$	3	$(3, \infty)$
$x + 1$	$-$	0	$+$	$+$	$+$
$x - 3$	$-$	$-$	$-$	0	$+$
$f'(x)$	$+$	0	$-$	0	$+$
slope of f	╱	—	╲	—	╱

By the first derivative test, $(-1, \tfrac{11}{3})$ is a local maximum, and $(3, -7)$ is a local minimum.

🔍 Find the y-intercept. Don't try to find the x-intercepts in this case, as this isn't easy, because it involves solving the equation $\tfrac{1}{3}x^3 - x^2 - 3x + 2 = 0$. 💬

When $x = 0$,

$$y = f(0) = 2.$$

🔍 Mark the stationary points and the y-intercept on a pair of labelled axes, and indicate the nature of the stationary points, as shown on the left below. Hence sketch the graph, as shown on the right. Label the points that you've marked with their coordinates, and label the graph with its equation. 💬

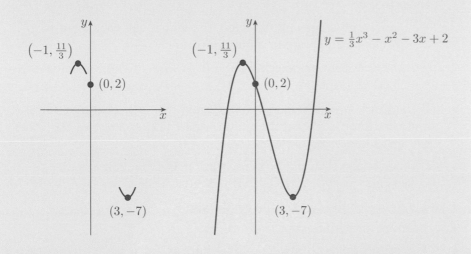

271

You've now seen the graphs of several cubic functions in this unit. These include the one in the example above, and the graphs of $f(x) = x^3$ and $g(x) = -x^3$ in Figure 40 on page 261. Before you go on, it's useful for you to get to know the general shapes of the graphs of cubic functions. You can do that in the next activity.

Activity 20   *Investigating the graphs of cubic functions*

Open the *Investigating cubic functions* applet. Experiment with changing the values of the constants a, b, c and d in the equation $y = ax^3 + bx^2 + cx + d$, and observe the shapes of the resulting graphs. Try to answer the following questions.

(a) How does the sign of a, the coefficient of x^3, affect the properties of the graph?

(b) How many x-intercepts can a cubic function have?

Finally, read through the list of properties of graphs of cubic functions given below this activity, and check that these properties seem to describe the graphs that you've seen.

In Activity 20 you should have seen evidence of the following facts.

Properties of graphs of cubic functions

The graph of every cubic function has the following properties.

- There are two, one or no stationary points.
- Apart from at any stationary points and in the interval between them if there are two,
    - the graph slopes up from left to right if the coefficient of x^3 in the rule of the function is positive
    - the graph slopes down from left to right if the coefficient of x^3 is negative.
- If there are two stationary points, then one is a local maximum and the other is a local minimum, and the graph slopes the other way in the interval between them.
- If there is one stationary point, then it is a horizontal point of inflection.
- There are three, two or one x-intercepts.
- There is one y-intercept.
- The graph tends to plus or minus infinity for large positive and large negative values of x.

Whether a cubic function has two, one or no stationary points depends on whether the quadratic equation that you solve to find the stationary points has two, one or no solutions.

It's useful to keep the properties in the box above in mind when you're sketching the graph of a cubic function.

Activity 21 *Sketching the graphs of cubic functions*

Sketch the graphs of the following cubic functions.

(a) $f(x) = -\frac{1}{3}x^3 - 4x^2 - 12x - 4$

(b) $f(x) = \frac{1}{9}x^3 - x^2 + 3x$

Hint for part (a): factorise the derivative $f'(x)$ into a product of *three* factors, one of which is -1.

Finding the greatest and least values of a function on an interval of the form $[a, b]$

A third situation where it can be useful to find the stationary points of a function is when you want to find the greatest or least value that a function takes on a particular interval of the form $[a, b]$, where a and b are real numbers. This is sometimes a helpful thing to do when the function models a real-life situation. You'll see some examples of this in Unit 7.

Usually the function that you're working with is **continuous** on the interval – this means that it has no discontinuities in the interval, or, informally, that you can draw its graph over the whole interval without taking your pen off the paper. (In particular, for a function to be continuous on an interval, it must also be *defined* for all values in the interval.)

If the function is also differentiable at all values in the interval except possibly the endpoints, then its greatest or least value on the interval occurs either at a stationary point in the interval or at an endpoint of the interval. For example, in Figure 46 the greatest value of the function on the interval shown occurs at the right endpoint of the interval, and the least value occurs at the local minimum in the interval.

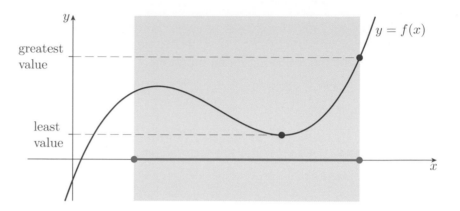

Figure 46   The greatest and least values of a particular function on a particular interval

This fact gives the following strategy, which is demonstrated in Example 11.

Strategy:
To find the greatest or least value of a function on an interval of the form $[a, b]$

(This strategy is valid when the function is continuous on the interval, and differentiable at all values in the interval except possibly the endpoints.)

1. Find the stationary points of the function.

2. Find the values of the function at any stationary points inside the interval, and at the endpoints of the interval.

3. Find the greatest or least of the function values found.

Example 11   *Finding the greatest and least values of a function on an interval of the form* $[a, b]$

Find the greatest and least values of the function

$$f(x) = -\tfrac{1}{3}x^3 + 2x^2 + 5x$$

on the interval $[-7, 7]$.

Solution

The function is

$$f(x) = -\tfrac{1}{3}x^3 + 2x^2 + 5x.$$

🔍 Find its stationary points. 💬

Its derivative is

$$\begin{aligned}
f'(x) &= -x^2 + 4x + 5 \\
&= -(x^2 - 4x - 5) \\
&= -(x - 5)(x + 1).
\end{aligned}$$

So its stationary points are -1 and 5.

🔍 Find the values of f at any stationary points inside the interval, and at the endpoints of the interval. 💬

Both stationary points are inside the interval, and the values of f at these points are

$$\begin{aligned}
f(-1) &= -\tfrac{1}{3}(-1)^3 + 2(-1)^2 + 5(-1) = -\tfrac{8}{3} = -2\tfrac{2}{3} \\
f(5) &= -\tfrac{1}{3} \times 5^3 + 2 \times 5^2 + 5 \times 5 = \tfrac{100}{3} = 33\tfrac{1}{3}.
\end{aligned}$$

The values of f at the endpoints of the interval are

$$\begin{aligned}
f(-7) &= -\tfrac{1}{3}(-7)^3 + 2(-7)^2 + 5(-7) = \tfrac{532}{3} = 177\tfrac{1}{3} \\
f(7) &= -\tfrac{1}{3} \times 7^3 + 2 \times 7^2 + 5 \times 7 = \tfrac{56}{3} = 18\tfrac{2}{3}.
\end{aligned}$$

🔍 Find the greatest and least of the values of f found. 💬

The greatest value of f on the interval $[-7, 7]$ is $177\tfrac{1}{3}$, and the least value is $-2\tfrac{2}{3}$.

The graph of the function in Example 11 is shown in Figure 47. You can see that its greatest and least values on the interval $[-7, 7]$ do seem to be the values found in the example, at least roughly.

When you use the strategy in the box above to find the greatest or least value of a function on an interval of the form $[a, b]$, it's important to make sure that any stationary points that you consider are *inside the interval*! For example, if Example 11 had asked for the greatest and least values of the function on the interval $[0, 7]$, rather than on $[-7, 7]$, then the solution would have considered the values of the function at the stationary point 5 and at the endpoints of the interval, and would have ignored the stationary point -1.

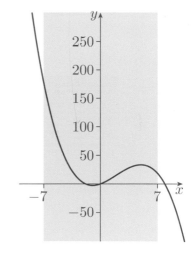

Figure 47   The graph of the function
$f(x) = -\tfrac{1}{3}x^3 + 2x^2 + 5x$

Find the greatest and least values of each of the following functions on the stated interval. Check that your answers seem reasonable by plotting the graphs of the functions using the module computer algebra system.

(a) $f(x) = \frac{1}{3}x^3 - x^2 - 8x + 1$ on the interval $[-3, 2]$

(b) $f(x) = 3x^2 - 2x + 5$ on the interval $[-1, 4]$

Activity 23   *Thinking about the strategy*

Give an example of a function and a closed interval such that the strategy in the box on page 274 doesn't work, because the function isn't differentiable (but is defined) at a value in the interval. Draw a sketch-graph to illustrate your answer.

Hint: some graphs of functions with values at which they aren't differentiable are given in Figure 9 on page 215.

5 Differentiating twice

In this section you'll learn what it means to differentiate a function more than once, and why this can be a helpful thing to do.

5.1 Second derivatives

As you've seen, the derivative of a function is itself a function, which is sometimes called the *derived function*. This means that the derivative of a function can itself be differentiated. The function that is obtained by differentiating a function twice in this way is called the **second derivative** (or **second derived function**) of the original function. In Lagrange notation, the second derivative of a function f is denoted by f'' (read as 'f double prime' or 'f double dash' or 'f double dashed').

For example, consider the function $f(x) = x^3$. The derivative of f is

$$f'(x) = 3x^2.$$

Differentiating this derivative gives the second derivative of f:

$$f''(x) = 6x.$$

Activity 24 *Finding a second derivative*

Find the second derivative of the function $f(x) = 2x^4 + 3x^2 + x$.

In Leibniz notation, the second derivative of y with respect to x is denoted by $\mathrm{d}^2y/\mathrm{d}x^2$ (read as 'd two y by d x squared'). For example, if $y = 4x^3 + 5x^2$, then

$$\frac{\mathrm{d}y}{\mathrm{d}x} = 12x^2 + 10x, \quad \text{and} \quad \frac{\mathrm{d}^2y}{\mathrm{d}x^2} = 24x + 10.$$

To see the thinking behind this notation for a second derivative, notice that the second derivative of y with respect to x can be written in Leibniz notation as

$$\frac{\mathrm{d}}{\mathrm{d}x}\left(\frac{\mathrm{d}}{\mathrm{d}x}y\right).$$

Historically, this was, rather loosely, abbreviated to

$$\left(\frac{\mathrm{d}}{\mathrm{d}x}\right)^2 y, \quad \text{and then to} \quad \frac{\mathrm{d}^2y}{\mathrm{d}x^2}.$$

The domain of the second derivative of a function consists of all the values of x at which its first derivative is differentiable. We say that the original function is **twice-differentiable** at such values of x.

Once you've differentiated a function twice, you can go on to differentiate it three times, and then four times, and so on. The derivatives obtained in this way are called the **third derivative**, the **fourth derivative**, and so on. In Lagrange notation, the third derivative is denoted by f''' or $f^{(3)}$, the fourth derivative is denoted by $f^{(4)}$, and the higher derivatives are denoted in the same way. In Leibniz notation, the third derivative is denoted by $\mathrm{d}^3y/\mathrm{d}x^3$, the fourth derivative is denoted by $\mathrm{d}^4y/\mathrm{d}x^4$, and so on.

The domain of the third derivative of a function consists of all the values of x at which the second derivative of the function is differentiable, that is, all the values of x at which the original function is **three times differentiable**. Similarly a function can be **four times differentiable** at a value of x, and so on. It can also be **differentiable infinitely many times** at a value of x. For example, every polynomial function is differentiable infinitely many times at every value of x.

In Unit 11 you'll see one reason why the third and higher derivatives of functions are useful, but for now you won't need to work with derivatives beyond second derivatives.

Activity 25   *Thinking about derivatives and second derivatives*

Try to work out which of the graphs B, C and D below shows the derivative of the function in graph A, and which shows its second derivative.

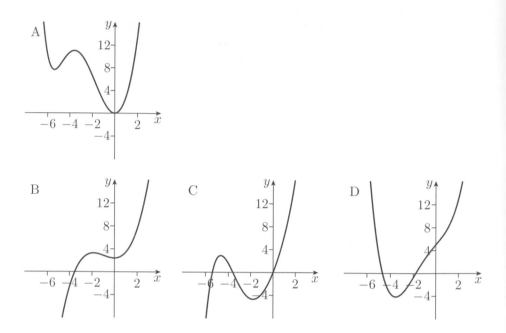

The derivative of a function is sometimes called its **first derivative**, to emphasise that it's not one of the higher derivatives. This is the reason for the word 'first' in the name 'first derivative test', which you met on page 263. Later in this subsection, you'll meet the *second derivative test*, which has the same purpose as the first derivative test – determining the nature of a stationary point – but involves the second derivative of a function.

You know that the derivative of a function tells you the gradients of the graph of the function. So the second derivative of a function tells you the gradients of the graph of the first derivative. This means that the second derivative also gives you information about the shape of the graph of the original function.

To see this, suppose, for example, that there is an interval on which the second derivative of a particular function is *positive*. By the increasing/decreasing criterion, this means that the first derivative is *increasing* on that interval. In other words, the gradient of the graph of the original function is increasing on that interval. This means that the shape of the graph of the original function on the interval must be something like one of the shapes shown in Figure 48. All of these shapes are sections of graphs with increasing gradient. For example, in the second shape the gradient increases from large negative values to small negative values.

Figure 48   Sections of graphs with increasing gradient

A section of a graph shaped like one of the diagrams in Figure 48 is said to be *concave up*. More precisely, a graph is **concave up** on an interval if the tangents to the graph on that interval lie *below* the graph, as illustrated in Figure 49. (Of course the tangents may cross the graph outside the interval.) Informally, a section of a graph is concave up if it looks like a cross-section of a bowl that's the right way up, or part of such a cross-section. One way to remember the meaning of 'concave up' is to think of the rhyme 'Concave up, like a cup'.

So, in summary, if the second derivative of a function is *positive* on an interval, then the graph of the function is concave up on the interval.

Figure 49   A section of a graph is concave up when the tangents lie below the graph

For example, Figure 50 shows the graphs of the function $f(x) = x^2$, its derivative $f'(x) = 2x$ and its second derivative $f''(x) = 2$. The domain of each of these functions consists of all of the real numbers. The second derivative f'' is positive on the whole domain, which tells you that the first derivative f' is increasing on the whole domain, which in turn tells you that the graph of the function f is concave up on its whole domain.

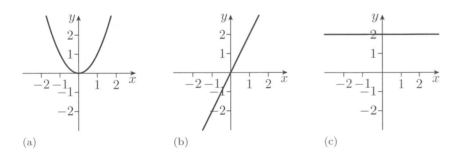

Figure 50   The graphs of (a) $f(x) = x^2$ (b) its derivative $f'(x) = 2x$ (c) its second derivative $f''(x) = 2$

Now suppose that there's an interval on which the second derivative of a particular function is *negative*. By the increasing/decreasing criterion, this means that the first derivative is *decreasing* on that interval. In other words, the gradient of the graph of the original function is decreasing on that interval. This means that the shape of the graph of the original function on the interval must be something like one of the shapes shown in Figure 51.

Figure 51   Sections of graphs with decreasing gradient

A section of a graph shaped like one of the diagrams in Figure 51 is said to be *concave down*. More precisely, a graph is **concave down** on an interval if the tangents to the graph on that interval lie *above* the graph, as illustrated in Figure 52. (Again the tangents may cross the graph outside the interval.) Informally, a section of a graph is concave down if it looks like a cross-section of a bowl that's the wrong way up, or part of such a cross-section. One way to remember the meaning of 'concave down' is to think of the rhyme 'Concave down, like a frown'.

So, in summary, if the second derivative of a function is *negative* on an interval, then the graph of the function is concave down on the interval.

For example, Figure 53 shows the graphs of the function $f(x) = x^3$, its derivative $f'(x) = 3x^2$ and its second derivative $f''(x) = 6x$. The domain of each of these functions consists of all of the real numbers. The second derivative f'' is negative on the interval $(-\infty, 0)$ and positive on the interval $(0, \infty)$, which tells you that the first derivative f' is decreasing on the interval $(-\infty, 0)$ and increasing on the interval $(0, \infty)$, which in turn tells you that the function f is concave down on the interval $(-\infty, 0)$ and concave up on the interval $(0, \infty)$.

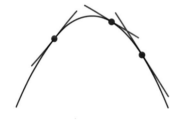

Figure 52   A section of a graph is concave down when the tangents lie above the graph

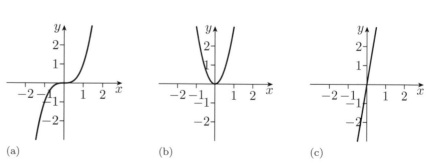

Figure 53   The graphs of (a) $f(x) = x^3$ (b) its derivative $f'(x) = 3x^2$ (c) its second derivative $f''(x) = 6x$

In some texts, the words *convex* and *concave* are used instead of concave up and concave down, respectively.

A point where a graph changes from concave up to concave down or vice versa is called a **point of inflection**. For example, the graph of $f(x) = x^3$ has a point of inflection at the origin. The tangents to a graph on one side of a point of inflection lie above the graph, and the tangents to the graph on the other side lie below the graph, as illustrated in Figure 54. The tangent at the point of inflection itself crosses the graph at that point. You can determine whether a point on the graph of a function is a point of inflection by checking whether its second derivative changes sign at that point.

If the gradient of a graph at a point of inflection is zero, then the point is a **horizontal** point of inflection – this is a type of stationary point that you met earlier. Otherwise the point is a **slant** point of inflection. For example, the graph of $y = x^3$ and the graph in Figure 55(a) have horizontal points of inflection, and the graphs in Figures 55(b) and (c) have slant points of inflection.

Figure 54   Tangents to a graph at and near a point of inflection

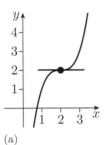 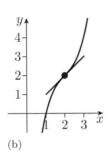 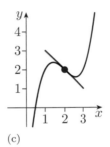

(a)   (b)   (c)

Figure 55   The graphs of (a) $y = x^3 - 6x^2 + 12x - 6$ (b) $y = x^3 - 6x^2 + 11x - 4$ (c) $y = x^3 - 6x^2 + 13x - 8$

If the graph of a function is concave up or concave down on an interval, then we also say that the function itself is concave up or concave down on the interval, respectively. (In general, for simplicity we often say that a function has a certain property if its graph has that property, and vice versa.) So the relationship between the sign of the second derivative of a function and the shape of the graph of the function can be summarised as follows.

Concave up/concave down criterion

If $f''(x)$ is positive for all x in an interval I, then f is concave up on I.

If $f''(x)$ is negative for all x in an interval I, then f is concave down on I.

Consider the function $f(x) = \frac{1}{6}x^4 - 2x^3 + 11x^2 - 18x$.

(a) Find the second derivative of this function.

(b) Hence show that this function is concave up on the whole of its domain (all the real numbers).

Hint for part (b): start by completing the square in your answer to part (a).

Activity 27 *Using the concave up/concave down criterion again*

Consider the function $f(x) = \frac{1}{12}x^4 - 2x^2$.

(a) Find the second derivative of this function.

(b) Hence show that this function is concave down on the interval $(-2, 2)$.

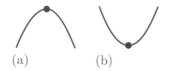

(a)   (b)

Figure 56 (a) A local maximum (b) a local minimum

The connection between the sign of the second derivative of a function and the shape of the graph of the function gives a useful test, called the *second derivative test*, for determining the nature of some stationary points. This test can often, but not always, be used as an alternative to the first derivative test. It's based on the fact that the graph of a function is concave down at and around a local maximum, and concave up at and around a local minimum, as illustrated in Figure 56. In other words, by the concave up/concave down criterion, the second derivative of a function is negative at and around a local maximum, and positive at and around a local minimum.

> **Second derivative test (for determining the nature of a stationary point)**
>
> If, at a stationary point of a function, the value of the second derivative of the function is
>
> - negative, then the stationary point is a local maximum
> - positive, then the stationary point is a local minimum.

One way to remember the second derivative test is to keep in mind that a negative sign corresponds to a frown shape (a negative mood) and a positive sign corresponds to a smile shape (a positive mood). You might like to think of the emoticons ☹ and ☺.

Alternatively, you might prefer simply to remember that a local maximum corresponds to *decreasing gradient*, and hence a negative second derivative, whereas a local minimum corresponds to *increasing gradient*, and hence a positive second derivative. This is illustrated in Figure 57.

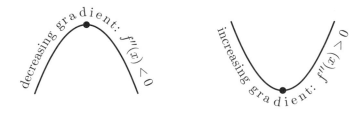

Figure 57 The change in the gradient at and around a local maximum and a local minimum

---

Example 12 *Determining the nature of stationary points using the second derivative test*

Consider the function

$$f(x) = x^3 - 3x^2 + 1.$$

(a) Find the stationary points of f.

(b) Use the second derivative test to determine the nature of each stationary point of f.

Solution

(a) We have

$$f'(x) = 3x^2 - 6x$$
$$= 3x(x - 2).$$

Solving the equation $f'(x) = 0$ gives

$$3x(x - 2) = 0;$$

that is,

$$x = 0 \quad \text{or} \quad x = 2.$$

Hence the stationary points of f are 0 and 2.

(b) The second derivative is
$$f''(x) = 6x - 6.$$
For the stationary point 0,
$$f''(0) = 6 \times 0 - 6 = -6.$$
💬 The second derivative is negative: ☹. 💭

Hence, by the second derivative test, the stationary point 0 is a local maximum.

For the stationary point 2,
$$f''(2) = 6 \times 2 - 6 = 6.$$
💬 The second derivative is positive: ☺. 💭

Hence, by the second derivative test, the stationary point 2 is a local minimum.

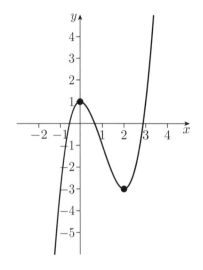

Figure 58 The graph of $f(x) = x^3 - 3x^2 + 1$

The graph of the function in Example 12 is shown in Figure 58. You can see that its stationary points are of the types determined in the example.

Activity 28 *Determining the nature of stationary points using the second derivative test*

Consider the function
$$f(x) = \tfrac{2}{3}x^3 - \tfrac{5}{2}x^2 + 2x.$$

(a) Find the stationary points of f, including the y-coordinates.

(b) Use the second derivative test to determine the nature of each stationary point.

(c) Using your answers to parts (a) and (b), sketch the graph of f.

Unfortunately, if the value of the second derivative of a function at a stationary point is *zero*, rather than either negative or positive, then you can't use the second derivative test to determine the nature of the stationary point. The stationary point might be a local maximum, a local minimum, a horizontal point of inflection, or none of these.

For example, Figure 59 shows the graphs of the functions $f(x) = x^4$, $g(x) = -x^4$, $h(x) = x^3$ and $k(x) = -x^3$. Each of these four functions has a stationary point at the origin, and at each of these stationary points the value of the second derivative is zero, as you might like to check. The stationary points on the four graphs are a local minimum, a local maximum and two horizontal points of inflection, respectively.

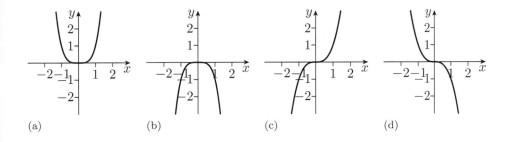

(a)   (b)   (c)   (d)

Figure 59   The graphs of (a) $f(x) = x^4$ (b) $g(x) = -x^4$ (c) $h(x) = x^3$ (d) $k(x) = -x^3$

So the second derivative test isn't as widely applicable as the first derivative test. If you're trying to use it to find the nature of a stationary point, and find that you can't because the value of the second derivative at the stationary point is zero, then try the first derivative test instead.

5.2   Rates of change of rates of change

Earlier in the unit you saw that if two variables x and y are related, then the derivative dy/dx is the rate of change of y with respect to x. In the same way, the second derivative d^2y/dx^2 is the rate of change of dy/dx with respect to x.

You saw that it's particularly useful to think of derivatives as rates of change when you're dealing with mathematical models of real-life situations.

For example, consider the graph in Figure 60, which is a repeat of Figure 32(b) on page 249. It's the displacement–time graph for a man walking along a straight path, and has equation

$$s = 6t - \tfrac{5}{8}t^2,$$

where t is the time in hours that the man has been walking, and s is his displacement in kilometres from his starting point.

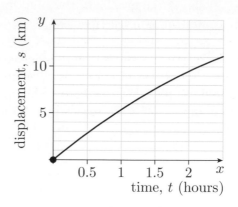

Figure 60   A displacement–time graph, with equation $s = 6t - \frac{5}{8}t^2$, for a man's walk along a straight path

As you know, the gradient of the displacement–time graph of an object is the object's velocity. So, as you saw in Example 5 on page 251, the man's velocity is given by the equation

$$v = \frac{\mathrm{d}s}{\mathrm{d}t};$$

that is,

$$v = 6 - \tfrac{5}{4}t.$$

The graph of this equation is shown in Figure 61. A graph like this, which shows an object's velocity plotted against time, is known as a **velocity–time graph**.

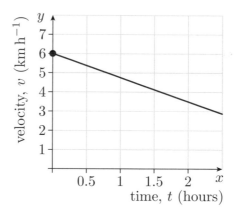

Figure 61   The velocity–time graph, with equation $v = 6 - \frac{5}{4}t$, corresponding to Figure 60

The velocity–time graph in Figure 61 shows that the man's velocity decreases as time goes on, as expected. For example, his velocity at the start of his walk is $6\,\mathrm{km\,h^{-1}}$, and his velocity one hour later is $4.75\,\mathrm{km\,h^{-1}}$.

The gradient of the velocity–time graph is the rate of change of the man's velocity with respect to time. The velocity–time graph is a straight line, so its gradient is the same at all points, and you can see from its equation, $v = 6 - \frac{5}{4}t$, that the numerical value of the gradient is $-\frac{5}{4} = -1.25$. Because the quantity on the horizontal axis (time) is measured in hours, and the quantity on the vertical axis (velocity) is measured in kilometres per hour, the gradient is measured in kilometres per hour per hour. So the gradient is -1.25 kilometres per hour per hour. This means that in each hour that passes, the man's velocity decreases by 1.25 kilometres per hour.

The units 'kilometres per hour per hour' are more usually called 'kilometres per hour squared', and are usually abbreviated as km/h^2 or $km\,h^{-2}$ (both read as 'kilometres per hour squared'). Similarly, 'metres per second per second' are known as 'metres per second squared' and abbreviated as m/s^2 or $m\,s^{-2}$, and so on.

The rate of change of velocity with respect to time is called **acceleration**, and is usually denoted by the variable a. Like displacement and velocity, acceleration can be constant, or it can take different values at different times. For example, you've just seen that the man on his walk has a constant acceleration of $-1.25\,km\,h^{-2}$. Also like displacement and velocity, the values that acceleration takes can be positive, negative or zero. The fact that the man's acceleration is *negative* at all times corresponds to the fact that his velocity is *decreasing* throughout his walk. Similarly, a positive acceleration would correspond to *increasing* velocity.

Because the gradient of the velocity–time graph of an object is the acceleration of the object, the important facts in the box on page 250 can be extended as follows.

Relationships between displacement, velocity and acceleration

Suppose that an object is moving in a straight line. If t is the time that has elapsed since some chosen point in time, and s, v and a are the displacement, velocity and acceleration of the object, respectively, then

$$v = \frac{ds}{dt}, \quad a = \frac{dv}{dt} \quad \text{and} \quad a = \frac{d^2 s}{dt^2}.$$

(Time, displacement, velocity and acceleration can be measured in any suitable units, as long as they are consistent.)

An example of a set of consistent units is seconds for time, metres for displacement, metres per second for velocity, and metres per second squared for acceleration.

In the discussion above, the value of the man's acceleration was found by using the fact that the equation relating his velocity to time is the equation of a straight line. An alternative way to find his acceleration is to use differentiation, as illustrated in the example below. The advantage of this method is, of course, that it can be used even when the acceleration isn't constant.

Example 13 *Using differentiation to find an acceleration*

Suppose that a man walks along a straight path, and his displacement s (in kilometres) from his starting point at time t (in hours) after he began his walk is given by the equation $s = 6t - \frac{5}{8}t^2$. Use differentiation to show that the man's acceleration is constant, and to find its value.

Solution

The man's displacement s (in km) at time t (in hours) is given by

$$s = 6t - \tfrac{5}{8}t^2.$$

Hence his velocity v (in $\mathrm{km\,h^{-1}}$) at time t (in hours) is given by

$$
\begin{aligned}
v &= \frac{\mathrm{d}s}{\mathrm{d}t}\\
&= 6 - \tfrac{5}{8} \times 2t\\
&= 6 - \tfrac{5}{4}t.
\end{aligned}
$$

It follows that his acceleration a (in $\mathrm{km\,h^{-2}}$) at time t (in hours) is given by

$$a = \frac{\mathrm{d}v}{\mathrm{d}t} = -\tfrac{5}{4} = -1.25.$$

That is, the man's acceleration is constant, with value $-1.25\ \mathrm{km\,h^{-2}}$.

When you're working with displacement, velocity and acceleration along a straight line, it's important to keep in mind that *displacement* is different from *distance*, and *velocity* is different from *speed*. As you know, distance is the magnitude of displacement, and speed is the magnitude of velocity. For example, an object that has a displacement of -10 metres from some reference point has a distance of 10 metres from that point, and, similarly, an object that has a velocity of $-2\,\mathrm{m\,s^{-1}}$ has a speed of $2\,\mathrm{m\,s^{-1}}$. Unfortunately, the magnitude of acceleration is also known as acceleration, but this doesn't usually cause any confusion in practice.

Consider the graph in Figure 62, which is the displacement–time graph for an object falling from rest, where the positive direction along the line of motion has been taken to be upwards and the reference point has been taken to be the point from which the object falls. Notice that the object's displacement from its starting point is decreasing, but its *distance* from its starting point is *increasing*. In general, if an object's displacement from a chosen reference point is always negative over some time interval, then saying that its displacement is decreasing over the time interval is the same as saying that its distance from the reference point is increasing over the time interval, and vice versa.

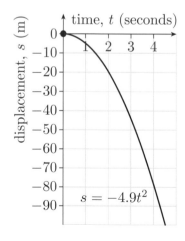

Figure 62 The displacement–time graph for an object falling from rest

Similarly, if an object's velocity is always negative over some time interval, then saying that its velocity is decreasing over the time interval is the same as saying that its speed is increasing, and vice versa. For example, in Figure 62 the velocity (the gradient of the graph) is decreasing, but the speed of the object is increasing.

Activity 29 *Using differentiation to find an acceleration*

Suppose that the displacement of an object along a straight line is given by the equation

$$s = \tfrac{1}{3}t^3 - 5t^2 + 16t + 8,$$

where t is the time in seconds and s is the displacement in metres.

(a) Find an equation giving the object's velocity in terms of time, and an equation giving the object's acceleration in terms of time.

(b) Is the object's acceleration constant? Explain how you know.

(c) Find the object's velocity and acceleration at time 6 seconds.

(d) This part of the question is about the time interval from 5 seconds to 8 seconds (not including the endpoints of this time interval).

(i) Over this time interval, is the object's velocity increasing, decreasing or neither? Explain how you know.

(ii) Over the time interval, is the object's velocity always positive, always negative or neither?

(iii) Over the time interval, is the object's speed increasing, decreasing or neither? Explain how you know.

Activity 30 *Using differentiation to find another acceleration*

In Subsection 3.1 you saw that the displacement of an object falling from rest is given by the equation

$$s = -4.9t^2,$$

where t is the time in seconds that the object has been falling, and s is its displacement in metres from its starting point (where the positive direction is upwards). This is assuming that the effect of air resistance is negligible.

Show that the acceleration of the object is constant, and find its value.

Activity 30 shows that the model for the motion of a falling object given in Subsection 3.1 is based on *constant acceleration*. It's a good model for the motion of any object falling from rest, provided that the effect of air resistance is negligible (which it is if the object is fairly compact and the fall is fairly short). The constant acceleration of a falling object in the absence of air resistance is known as the **acceleration due to gravity**.

If the falling object is near the surface of the Earth, then its acceleration due to gravity is approximately the value found in Activity 30. However, the value of the acceleration due to gravity varies slightly depending on the location of the object on the surface of the Earth. This is because of variations in the shape and density of the Earth. For example, the magnitude of the acceleration due to gravity in London is $9.812 \, \text{m s}^{-2}$, to three decimal places, whereas in Sydney it is $9.797 \, \text{m s}^{-2}$.

> In the fall of 1972 President Nixon announced that the rate of increase of inflation was decreasing. This was the first time a sitting president used the third derivative to advance his case for reelection.
>
> (Hugo Rossi (1996) 'Mathematics is an edifice, not a toolbox', *Notices of the American Mathematical Society*, vol. 43, no. 10.)

Learning outcomes

After studying this unit, you should be able to:

- understand the meaning of differentiation
- understand the idea of differentiation from first principles
- use both Lagrange and Leibniz notation for derivatives
- differentiate power functions
- use the constant multiple rule and the sum rule for derivatives
- use differentiation to determine whether a function is increasing, or decreasing, on an interval
- find the stationary points of some functions
- determine the nature of some stationary points using either the first or second derivative test
- use differentiation to determine whether a function is concave up, or concave down, on an interval
- understand and work with derivatives as rates of change in mathematical models
- understand and work with the relationships between displacement, velocity and acceleration.

Solutions to activities

Solution to Activity 1

In the first half-hour the man walks about three kilometres, and in the final half-hour he walks about one and a half kilometres.

Solution to Activity 2

(a) Large negative gradient: graph E.

(b) Small negative gradient: graph C.

(c) Zero gradient: graph A.

(d) Small positive gradient: graph B.

(e) Large positive gradient: graph D.

Solution to Activity 3

The point on the graph with x-coordinate 0.9 has y-coordinate $0.9^2 = 0.81$. The gradient of the line through $(1, 1)$ and $(0.9, 0.81)$ is

$$\frac{\text{rise}}{\text{run}} = \frac{0.81 - 1}{0.9 - 1} = \frac{-0.19}{-0.1} = 1.9.$$

So another approximate value for the gradient of the graph at $(1, 1)$ is 1.9.

Solution to Activity 4

(What you should have found in this activity is discussed in the text after the activity.)

Solution to Activity 5

By formula (1), the gradient of the graph of $y = x^2$ at the point with x-coordinate 3 is

$$2 \times 3 = 6.$$

Similarly, the gradient at the point with x-coordinate -1.5 is

$$2 \times (-1.5) = -3.$$

Solution to Activity 6

(a) Multiplying out $(x + h)^4$ gives

$$\begin{aligned}
(x + h)^4 \\
&= (x + h)(x + h)^3 \\
&= (x + h)(x^3 + 3x^2h + 3xh^2 + h^3) \\
&= x(x^3 + 3x^2h + 3xh^2 + h^3) \\
&\quad + h(x^3 + 3x^2h + 3xh^2 + h^3) \\
&= x^4 + 3x^3h + 3x^2h^2 + \ xh^3 \\
&\quad + \ x^3h + 3x^2h^2 + 3xh^3 + h^4 \\
&= x^4 + 4x^3h + 6x^2h^2 + 4xh^3 + h^4.
\end{aligned}$$

(b) The difference quotient for the function $f(x) = x^4$ at x is

$$\frac{f(x + h) - f(x)}{h} = \frac{(x + h)^4 - x^4}{h}.$$

By part (a),

$$\begin{aligned}
&\frac{f(x + h) - f(x)}{h} \\
&= \frac{x^4 + 4x^3h + 6x^2h^2 + 4xh^3 + h^4 - x^4}{h} \\
&= \frac{4x^3h + 6x^2h^2 + 4xh^3 + h^4}{h} \\
&= 4x^3 + 6x^2h + 4xh^2 + h^3.
\end{aligned}$$

Each of the terms in the final expression above, except the first term, contains the factor h. Hence, as h gets closer and closer to zero, each of the terms except the first term gets closer and closer to zero. So the value of the whole expression gets closer and closer to the value of the first term, $4x^3$. That is, the formula for the derivative is

$$f'(x) = 4x^3.$$

(c) By the formula found in part (b), the gradient of the graph of the function $f(x) = x^4$ at the point with x-coordinate $\frac{1}{4}$ is

$$4 \times \left(\tfrac{1}{4}\right)^3 = 4 \times \tfrac{1}{64} = \tfrac{1}{16}.$$

(The graph of $f(x) = x^4$ is shown below.)

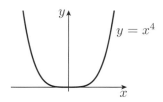

Solution to Activity 7

(a) $f(x) = x^8$, so

$$f'(x) = 8x^7.$$

(b) $f(x) = x^5$, so

$$f'(x) = 5x^4.$$

(c) $f(x) = \dfrac{1}{x^3} = x^{-3}$, so

$$f'(x) = -3x^{-4} = -\frac{3}{x^4}.$$

(d) $f(x) = x^{3/2}$, so
$$f'(x) = \tfrac{3}{2}x^{1/2} = \tfrac{3}{2}\sqrt{x}.$$

(e) $f(x) = \dfrac{1}{x} = x^{-1}$, so
$$f'(x) = -1 \times x^{-2} = -\dfrac{1}{x^2}.$$

(f) $f(x) = x^{5/2}$, so
$$f'(x) = \tfrac{5}{2}x^{3/2}.$$
(This derivative can also be written as $f'(x) = \tfrac{5}{2}\sqrt{x^3}$.)

(g) $f(x) = x^{4/3}$, so
$$f'(x) = \tfrac{4}{3}x^{1/3}.$$
(This form of the derivative is preferable to $f'(x) = \tfrac{4}{3}\sqrt[3]{x}$, which could be misread as $f'(x) = \tfrac{43}{3}\sqrt{x}$.)

(h) $f(x) = \dfrac{1}{x^8} = x^{-8}$, so
$$f'(x) = -8x^{-9} = -\dfrac{8}{x^9}.$$

(i) $y = \dfrac{1}{x^{1/4}} = x^{-1/4}$, so
$$\dfrac{dy}{dx} = -\dfrac{1}{4}x^{-5/4} = -\dfrac{1}{4} \times \dfrac{1}{x^{5/4}} = -\dfrac{1}{4x^{5/4}}.$$

(j) $y = x^{1/3}$, so
$$\dfrac{dy}{dx} = \dfrac{1}{3}x^{-2/3} = \dfrac{1}{3x^{2/3}}.$$

(k) $y = \dfrac{1}{\sqrt{x}} = \dfrac{1}{x^{1/2}} = x^{-1/2}$, so
$$\dfrac{dy}{dx} = -\dfrac{1}{2}x^{-3/2} = -\dfrac{1}{2} \times \dfrac{1}{x^{3/2}} = -\dfrac{1}{2x^{3/2}}.$$

(l) $y = \sqrt[3]{x^5} = x^{5/3}$, so
$$\dfrac{dy}{dx} = \tfrac{5}{3}x^{2/3}.$$

(m) $y = x^{2/7}$, so
$$\dfrac{dy}{dx} = \dfrac{2}{7}x^{-5/7} = \dfrac{2}{7} \times \dfrac{1}{x^{5/7}} = \dfrac{2}{7x^{5/7}}.$$

(n) $f(x) = x^{-2}$, so
$$f'(x) = -2x^{-3} = -\dfrac{2}{x^3}.$$

(o) $f(x) = \dfrac{1}{x^{1/3}} = x^{-1/3}$, so
$$f'(x) = -\dfrac{1}{3}x^{-4/3} = -\dfrac{1}{3} \times \dfrac{1}{x^{4/3}} = -\dfrac{1}{3x^{4/3}}.$$

(p) $f(x) = \dfrac{1}{x^4} = x^{-4}$, so
$$f'(x) = -4x^{-5} = -\dfrac{4}{x^5}.$$

Solution to Activity 8

By the solution to Example 2(c), the derivative of $y = \sqrt{x}$ is
$$\dfrac{dy}{dx} = \dfrac{1}{2\sqrt{x}}.$$
So the gradient of the graph at the point with x-coordinate 4 is
$$\dfrac{1}{2\sqrt{4}} = \dfrac{1}{2 \times 2} = \dfrac{1}{4}.$$
(Check: the gradient of the line in Figure 22, in the margin beside this activity, appears to be about $\tfrac{1}{4}$.)

Solution to Activity 9

(a) $f(x) = 5x^3$, so
$$f'(x) = 5 \times 3x^2 = 15x^2.$$

(b) $f(x) = -x^7$, so
$$f'(x) = -7x^6.$$

(c) $f(x) = 2\sqrt{x} = 2x^{1/2}$, so
$$f'(x) = 2 \times \dfrac{1}{2}x^{-1/2}$$
$$= \dfrac{1}{x^{1/2}}$$
$$= \dfrac{1}{\sqrt{x}}.$$

(d) $f(x) = 6x$, so
$$f'(x) = 6 \times 1 = 6.$$

(e) $f(x) = \dfrac{x}{4} = \dfrac{1}{4}x$, so
$$f'(x) = \dfrac{1}{4} \times 1 = \dfrac{1}{4}.$$

(f) $f(t) = \dfrac{2}{t} = 2t^{-1}$, so
$$f'(t) = 2 \times (-1)t^{-2}$$
$$= -\dfrac{2}{t^2}.$$

(g) $g(u) = -7u$, so
$$g'(u) = -7 \times 1 = -7.$$

(h) $y = \dfrac{\sqrt{x}}{3} = \dfrac{1}{3}x^{1/2}$, so

$$\begin{aligned}\frac{dy}{dx} &= \frac{1}{3} \times \frac{1}{2}x^{-1/2}\\ &= \frac{1}{6} \times \frac{1}{x^{1/2}}\\ &= \frac{1}{6\sqrt{x}}.\end{aligned}$$

(i) $y = \dfrac{8}{x^2} = 8x^{-2}$, so

$$\begin{aligned}\frac{dy}{dx} &= 8 \times (-2)x^{-3}\\ &= -\frac{16}{x^3}.\end{aligned}$$

(j) $y = -\dfrac{5}{x} = -5x^{-1}$, so

$$\begin{aligned}\frac{dy}{dx} &= -5 \times (-1)x^{-2}\\ &= \frac{5}{x^2}.\end{aligned}$$

(k) $y = \dfrac{4}{\sqrt{x}} = \dfrac{4}{x^{1/2}} = 4x^{-1/2}$, so

$$\begin{aligned}\frac{dy}{dx} &= 4 \times \left(-\frac{1}{2}\right)x^{-3/2}\\ &= -\frac{2}{x^{3/2}}.\end{aligned}$$

(l) $y = 4x^{3/2}$, so

$$\begin{aligned}\frac{dy}{dx} &= 4 \times \tfrac{3}{2}x^{1/2}\\ &= 6\sqrt{x}.\end{aligned}$$

(m) $p = \dfrac{1}{3\sqrt{u}} = \dfrac{1}{3u^{1/2}} = \dfrac{1}{3}u^{-1/2}$, so

$$\begin{aligned}\frac{dp}{du} &= \frac{1}{3} \times \left(-\frac{1}{2}\right)u^{-3/2}\\ &= -\frac{1}{6} \times \frac{1}{u^{3/2}}\\ &= -\frac{1}{6u^{3/2}}.\end{aligned}$$

(n) $q = -12r^{1/3}$, so

$$\begin{aligned}\frac{dq}{dr} &= -12 \times \frac{1}{3}r^{-2/3}\\ &= -4 \times \frac{1}{r^{2/3}}\\ &= -\frac{4}{r^{2/3}}.\end{aligned}$$

Solution to Activity 10

The derivative of the function $f(x) = 3x^2$ is

$$f'(x) = 3 \times 2x = 6x.$$

So the gradient of this function f at the point with x-coordinate 2 is

$$6 \times 2 = 12.$$

Solution to Activity 11

(a) $f(x) = 6x^2 - 2x + 1$, so

$$f'(x) = 12x - 2.$$

(b) $f(x) = \tfrac{2}{3}x^3 + 2x^2 + x - \tfrac{1}{2}$, so

$$\begin{aligned}f'(x) &= \tfrac{2}{3} \times 3x^2 + 2 \times 2x + 1\\ &= 2x^2 + 4x + 1.\end{aligned}$$

(c) $f(x) = 5x + 1$, so

$$f'(x) = 5.$$

(Notice that in general the derivative of $f(x) = mx + c$ is $f'(x) = m$, as you'd expect.)

(d) $g(t) = \tfrac{1}{2}t + \sqrt{t} = \tfrac{1}{2}t + t^{1/2}$, so

$$\begin{aligned}f'(t) &= \frac{1}{2} + \frac{1}{2}t^{-1/2}\\ &= \frac{1}{2} + \frac{1}{2} \times \frac{1}{t^{1/2}}\\ &= \frac{1}{2} + \frac{1}{2} \times \frac{1}{\sqrt{t}}\\ &= \frac{1}{2}\left(1 + \frac{1}{\sqrt{t}}\right).\end{aligned}$$

(e) $f(x) = (1 + x^2)(1 + 3x)$
$$= 1 + 3x + x^2 + 3x^3,$$
so
$$f'(x) = 3 + 2x + 9x^2.$$

(f) $k(u) = (u + 3)^2$
$$= u^2 + 6u + 9,$$
so
$$k'(u) = 2u + 6.$$

(g) $f(x) = 30(x^{3/2} - x)$, so

$$\begin{aligned}f'(x) &= 30\left(\tfrac{3}{2}x^{1/2} - 1\right)\\ &= 30\left(\tfrac{3}{2}\sqrt{x} - 1\right)\\ &= 45\sqrt{x} - 30\\ &= 15(3\sqrt{x} - 2).\end{aligned}$$

(h) $f(x) = x(x^{3/2} - x) = x^{5/2} - x^2$, so

$$f'(x) = \tfrac{5}{2}x^{3/2} - 2x.$$

(Note that this function can't be differentiated in a similar way to the function in part (g), because the multiplier of the brackets, x, isn't a *constant*, and hence the constant multiple rule doesn't apply.)

(i) $v = \dfrac{(t-2)(t+5)}{t}$

$$= \dfrac{t^2 + 3t - 10}{t}$$

$$= t + 3 - 10t^{-1},$$

so

$$\dfrac{\mathrm{d}v}{\mathrm{d}t} = 1 - 10 \times (-1)t^{-2}$$

$$= 1 + 10t^{-2}$$

$$= 1 + \dfrac{10}{t^2}.$$

(The final answer can also be expressed as $\dfrac{t^2 + 10}{t^2}$.)

(j) $y = \dfrac{x + \sqrt{x}}{x^2}$

$$= \dfrac{x + x^{1/2}}{x^2}$$

$$= x^{-1} + x^{-3/2},$$

so

$$\dfrac{\mathrm{d}y}{\mathrm{d}x} = -x^{-2} - \tfrac{3}{2}x^{-5/2}$$

$$= -\dfrac{1}{x^2} - \dfrac{3}{2x^{5/2}}.$$

(The final answer can be expressed in various ways. For example, you could combine the fractions and simplify the result like this:

$$-\dfrac{1}{x^2} - \dfrac{3}{2x^{5/2}} = -\dfrac{2x}{2x^3} - \dfrac{3x^{1/2}}{2x^3}$$

$$= -\dfrac{2x + 3\sqrt{x}}{2x^3}.)$$

(k) $y = (x^{1/3} + 1)(x^{1/3} + 5x)$

$$= x^{2/3} + 5x^{4/3} + x^{1/3} + 5x,$$

so

$$\dfrac{\mathrm{d}y}{\mathrm{d}x} = \tfrac{2}{3}x^{-1/3} + \tfrac{20}{3}x^{1/3} + \tfrac{1}{3}x^{-2/3} + 5$$

$$= \dfrac{2}{3x^{1/3}} + \dfrac{20x^{1/3}}{3} + \dfrac{1}{3x^{2/3}} + 5.$$

Solution to Activity 12

(a) The displacement s (in metres) of the object at time t (in seconds) is

$$s = -4.9t^2.$$

Hence the velocity v (in $\mathrm{m\,s}^{-1}$) of the object at time t (in seconds) is

$$v = \dfrac{\mathrm{d}s}{\mathrm{d}t}$$

$$= -9.8t.$$

(b) When $t = 3$,

$$v = -9.8 \times 3 = -29.4.$$

So the velocity of the object 3 seconds into its fall is $-29.4\,\mathrm{m\,s}^{-1}$.

(c) When the object has a speed of $15\,\mathrm{m\,s}^{-1}$, it has a velocity of $-15\,\mathrm{m\,s}^{-1}$. So the time t at which the object is moving at this speed is given by

$$-15 = -9.8t.$$

This equation has solution

$$t = \dfrac{-15}{-9.8} = 1.5 \text{ (to 1 d.p.)}.$$

So the object takes about 1.5 seconds to reach a speed of $15\,\mathrm{m\,s}^{-1}$.

(As a check on parts (b) and (c), you can see that the gradients of the graph of the equation $s = -4.9t^2$, which is given in Figure 34 and repeated below, at the points with time-coordinates 1.5 and 3 seconds are about $-15\,\mathrm{m\,s}^{-1}$ and about $-30\,\mathrm{m\,s}^{-1}$, respectively. The tangents at these points are shown below.)

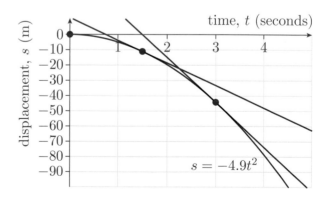

Solution to Activity 13

(a) The equation for c in terms of q is
$$c = 3000 + 4q + \tfrac{1}{125}q^2.$$
Hence
$$m = \frac{dc}{dq} = 4 + \tfrac{2}{125}q.$$
That is, an equation for m in terms of q is
$$m = 4 + \tfrac{2}{125}q.$$

(b) Substituting $q = 300$ into the equation found in part (a) gives
$$m = 4 + \tfrac{2}{125} \times 300 = 8.8.$$
So the marginal cost per kilogram of making extra chocolate when the amount of chocolate already being made is 300 kilograms is £8.80.

(c) The marginal cost is equal to the selling price when
$$m = 16.$$
By part (a), the value of q for which this happens is given by
$$4 + \tfrac{2}{125}q = 16.$$
Solving this equation gives
$$\tfrac{2}{125}q = 12;$$
that is,
$$q = 750.$$
So the company should make 750 kg of chocolate per week.

(As a check on parts (b) and (c), you can see that the gradients of the graph in Figure 36 at the points with q-coordinates 300 and 750 kilograms are about £9 per kilogram and about £16 per kilogram, respectively. The tangents at these points are shown below.)

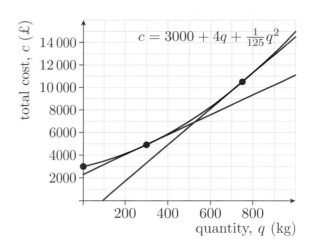

Solution to Activity 14

(a) $f(x) = \tfrac{2}{3}x^3 - 8x^2 + 30x - 36$, so
$$\begin{aligned} f'(x) &= 2x^2 - 16x + 30 \\ &= 2(x^2 - 8x + 15) \\ &= 2(x - 3)(x - 5). \end{aligned}$$

(b) When x is less than 3, the values of $x - 3$ and $x - 5$ are both negative, and hence the value of $f'(x) = 2(x - 3)(x - 5)$ is positive.

Similarly, when x is greater than 5, the values of $x - 3$ and $x - 5$ are both positive, and hence the value of $f'(x) = 2(x - 3)(x - 5)$ is also positive.

Therefore, by the increasing/decreasing criterion, the function f is increasing on each of the intervals $(-\infty, 3)$ and $(5, \infty)$.

(c) When x is in the interval $(3, 5)$, the value of $x - 3$ is positive and the value of $x - 5$ is negative, and hence the value of $f'(x) = 2(x - 3)(x - 5)$ is negative.

Therefore, by the increasing/decreasing criterion, the function f is decreasing on the interval $(3, 5)$.

(The graph of $f(x) = \tfrac{2}{3}x^3 - 8x^2 + 30x - 36$ is as follows.)

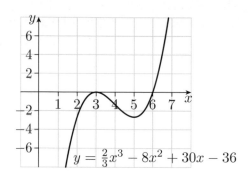

$$y = \tfrac{2}{3}x^3 - 8x^2 + 30x - 36$$

Solution to Activity 15

(a) $f(x) = x^3 - 3x^2 + 4x + 3$, so
$$\begin{aligned} f'(x) &= 3x^2 - 6x + 4 \\ &= 3(x^2 - 2x) + 4 \\ &= 3\left((x-1)^2 - 1\right) + 4 \\ &= 3(x-1)^2 + 1. \end{aligned}$$

(b) For every value of x, the expression $(x-1)^2$ is non-negative, and hence the expression $3(x-1)^2 + 1$ is positive.

That is, the derivative $f'(x)$ is positive on the interval $(-\infty, \infty)$. Therefore, by the increasing/decreasing criterion, the function f is increasing on the interval $(-\infty, \infty)$.

(The graph of $f(x) = x^3 - 3x^2 + 4x + 3$ is shown below.)

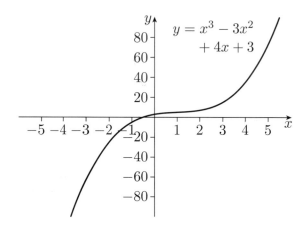

$$y = x^3 - 3x^2 + 4x + 3$$

Solution to Activity 16

Here $f(x) = x^3 - x^2 - 2x$, so
$$f'(x) = 3x^2 - 2x - 2.$$
The expression for $f'(x)$ cannot be factorised easily, so we solve the equation $f'(x) = 0$ using the

quadratic formula. This gives
$$\begin{aligned} x &= \frac{-(-2) \pm \sqrt{(-2)^2 - 4 \times 3 \times (-2)}}{2 \times 3} \\ &= \frac{2 \pm \sqrt{28}}{6} \\ &= \frac{2 \pm 2\sqrt{7}}{6} \\ &= \frac{1 \pm \sqrt{7}}{3} \\ &= 1.22 \text{ or } -0.55 \text{ (to 2 d.p.)}. \end{aligned}$$
That is, the stationary points are 1.22 and -0.55, to two decimal places.

Solution to Activity 17

(a) Here $f(x) = 3x^4 - 2x^3 - 9x^2 + 7$, so
$$\begin{aligned} f'(x) &= 12x^3 - 6x^2 - 18x \\ &= 6x(2x^2 - x - 3) \\ &= 6x(2x - 3)(x + 1). \end{aligned}$$
Solving the equation $f'(x) = 0$ gives
$$6x(2x - 3)(x + 1) = 0;$$
that is,
$$x = 0 \quad \text{or} \quad x = \tfrac{3}{2} \quad \text{or} \quad x = -1.$$
Hence the stationary points of f are 0, $\tfrac{3}{2}$ and -1.

(b) A table of signs for $f'(x) = 6x(2x - 3)(x + 1)$ is given below. (The table is split to make it fit in a narrow text column.)

x	$(-\infty, -1)$	-1	$(-1, 0)$
$6x$	$-$	$-$	$-$
$2x - 3$	$-$	$-$	$-$
$x + 1$	$-$	0	$+$
$f'(x)$	$-$	0	$+$
slope of f	$\searrow$	$-$	$\nearrow$

0	$(0, \tfrac{3}{2})$	$\tfrac{3}{2}$	$(\tfrac{3}{2}, \infty)$
0	$+$	$+$	$+$
$-$	$-$	0	$+$
$+$	$+$	$+$	$+$
0	$-$	0	$+$
$-$	$\searrow$	$-$	$\nearrow$

The table shows that -1 is a local minimum, 0 is a local maximum, and $\frac{3}{2}$ is a local minimum. (You can see these stationary points on the graph below.)

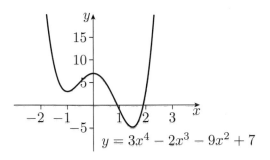
$$y = 3x^4 - 2x^3 - 9x^2 + 7$$

Since the derivative is negative at 1 and positive at 2, the stationary point $\frac{3}{2}$ is a local minimum. (You can see these stationary points on the graph below.)

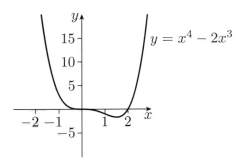
$$y = x^4 - 2x^3$$

Solution to Activity 18

(a) $f(x) = x^4 - 2x^3$, so
$$f'(x) = 4x^3 - 6x^2$$
$$= 2x^2(2x - 3),$$
Solving the equation $f'(x) = 0$ gives
$$2x^2(2x - 3) = 0;$$
that is,
$$x = 0 \quad \text{or} \quad x = \tfrac{3}{2}.$$
Hence the stationary points of f are 0 and $\frac{3}{2}$.

(b) To determine the nature of the stationary points, apply the method described on page 266.

Consider the values -1, 1 and 2. The values -1 and 1 lie on each side of the stationary point 0, and the values 1 and 2 lie on each side of the stationary point $\frac{3}{2}$.

The function f is differentiable at all values of x (as is every polynomial function).

Also, there are no stationary points between -1 and 0 or between 0 and 1. Similarly, there are no stationary points between 1 and $\frac{3}{2}$ or between $\frac{3}{2}$ and 2.

Since $f'(x) = 2x^2(2x - 3)$, we have
$$f'(-1) = 2(-1)^2(2(-1) - 3) = 2(-2 - 3) = -10$$
$$f'(1) = 2 \times 1^2(2 \times 1 - 3) = 2(2 - 3) = -2$$
$$f'(2) = 2 \times 2^2(2 \times 2 - 3) = 8(4 - 3) = 8.$$
Since the derivative is negative at both -1 and 1, the stationary point 0 is a horizontal point of inflection.

Solution to Activity 19

(a) Here
$$p = -0.006q^2 + 3.3q,$$
so
$$\frac{dp}{dq} = -0.012q + 3.3.$$

(b) The stationary point q is given by
$$\frac{dp}{dq} = 0;$$
that is,
$$-0.012q + 3.3 = 0,$$
so
$$q = \frac{3.3}{0.012} = 275.$$

So if the bakery wants to earn the maximum profit, then it should make and sell 275 cakes per day.

(c) Substituting $q = 275$ into the formula for p gives
$$p = -0.006 \times 275^2 + 3.3 \times 275 = 453.75,$$
so the daily profit is £453.75.

(The graph of the equation $p = -0.006q^2 + 3.3q$ is shown below. You can see that the stationary point appears to be roughly $(275, 450)$, which accords with the results found above.)

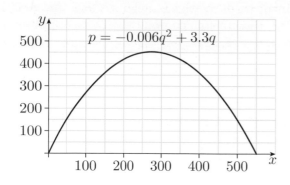

$p = -0.006q^2 + 3.3q$

Solution to Activity 20

(a) If the coefficient of x^3 is positive, then the graph tends to infinity for large positive values of x, and tends to minus infinity for large negative values of x.

If the coefficient of x^3 is negative, then the graph tends to minus infinity for large positive values of x, and tends to infinity for large negative values of x.

(This is because for large positive and large negative values of x, the value of the term in x^3, the dominant term, overwhelms the values of the other terms.)

(b) A cubic function can have one, two or three x-intercepts, as illustrated below.

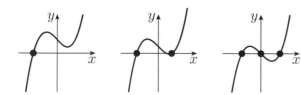

Solution to Activity 21

(a) The function is
$$f(x) = -\tfrac{1}{3}x^3 - 4x^2 - 12x - 4.$$
So the derivative is
$$\begin{aligned} f'(x) &= -x^2 - 8x - 12 \\ &= -(x^2 + 8x + 12) \\ &= -(x + 6)(x + 2). \end{aligned}$$
Solving the equation $f'(x) = 0$ gives
$$-(x + 6)(x + 2) = 0;$$
that is,
$$x = -6 \quad \text{or} \quad x = -2.$$

When $x = -6$,
$$\begin{aligned} y &= f(-6) \\ &= -\tfrac{1}{3}(-6)^3 - 4(-6)^2 - 12(-6) - 4 \\ &= 72 - 144 + 72 - 4 \\ &= -4. \end{aligned}$$
When $x = -2$,
$$\begin{aligned} y &= f(-2) \\ &= -\tfrac{1}{3}(-2)^3 - 4(-2)^2 - 12(-2) - 4 \\ &= \tfrac{8}{3} - 16 + 24 - 4 \\ &= \tfrac{20}{3}. \end{aligned}$$
So the stationary points are $(-6, -4)$ and $(-2, \tfrac{20}{3})$.

A table of signs for $f'(x) = -(x + 6)(x + 2)$ is given below. (The table is split to make it fit in a narrow text column.)

x	$(-\infty, -6)$	-6
-1	$-$	$-$
$x + 6$	$-$	0
$x + 2$	$-$	$-$
$f'(x)$	$-$	0
slope of f	$\searrow$	$-$

$(-6, -2)$	-2	$(-2, \infty)$
$-$	$-$	$-$
$+$	$+$	$+$
$-$	0	$+$
$+$	0	$-$
$\nearrow$	$-$	$\searrow$

By the first derivative test, $(-6, -4)$ is a local minimum, and $(-2, \tfrac{20}{3})$ is a local maximum.

When $x = 0$,
$$y = f(0) = -4.$$

A sketch of the graph is shown below.

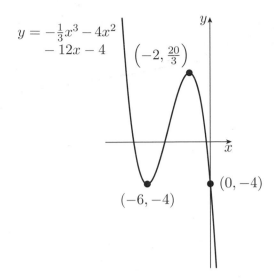

$y = -\frac{1}{3}x^3 - 4x^2 - 12x - 4$

$\left(-2, \frac{20}{3}\right)$

$(0, -4)$

$(-6, -4)$

(b) The function is
$$f(x) = \tfrac{1}{9}x^3 - x^2 + 3x.$$
So the derivative is
$$f'(x) = \tfrac{1}{3}x^2 - 2x + 3$$
$$= \tfrac{1}{3}(x^2 - 6x + 9)$$
$$= \tfrac{1}{3}(x - 3)^2.$$
Solving the equation $f'(x) = 0$ gives
$$\tfrac{1}{3}(x - 3)^2 = 0;$$
that is,
$$x = 3.$$
When $x = 3$,
$$y = f(3) = \tfrac{1}{9} \times 3^3 - 3^2 + 3 \times 3 = 3.$$
So there is just one stationary point, $(3, 3)$.

Since $f'(x)$ is positive everywhere except at $x = 3$, it follows, by the first derivative test, that $(3, 3)$ is a horizontal point of inflection and also, by the increasing/decreasing criterion, that f is increasing to the left and the right of the stationary point.

When $x = 0$,
$$y = f(0) = 0.$$

A sketch of the graph is shown below.

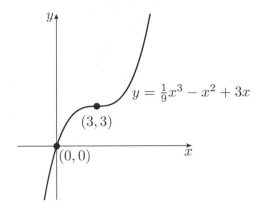

$y = \tfrac{1}{9}x^3 - x^2 + 3x$

$(3, 3)$

$(0, 0)$

Solution to Activity 22

(a) Here
$$f(x) = \tfrac{1}{3}x^3 - x^2 - 8x + 1.$$
This gives
$$f'(x) = x^2 - 2x - 8 = (x - 4)(x + 2),$$
so the stationary points are -2 and 4.

Only the stationary point -2 is inside the interval, and the value of f at this point is
$$f(-2) = \tfrac{1}{3}(-2)^3 - (-2)^2 - 8(-2) + 1$$
$$= -\tfrac{8}{3} - 4 + 16 + 1$$
$$= \tfrac{31}{3} = 10\tfrac{1}{3}.$$
The values of f at the endpoints of the interval are
$$f(-3) = \tfrac{1}{3}(-3)^3 - (-3)^2 - 8(-3) + 1$$
$$= -\tfrac{27}{3} - 9 + 24 + 1$$
$$= 7$$
and
$$f(2) = \tfrac{1}{3} \times 2^3 - 2^2 - 8 \times 2 + 1$$
$$= \tfrac{8}{3} - 4 - 16 + 1$$
$$= -\tfrac{49}{3} = -16\tfrac{1}{3}.$$
The greatest value of f on the interval $[-3, 2]$ is $10\tfrac{1}{3}$, and the least value is $-16\tfrac{1}{3}$.

(The graph of f is below.)

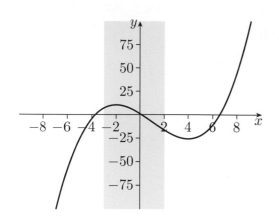

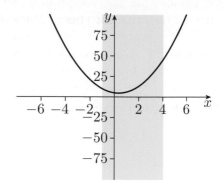

(b) Here
$$f(x) = 3x^2 - 2x + 5.$$
This gives
$$f'(x) = 6x - 2 = 2(3x - 1),$$
so the only stationary point is $\frac{1}{3}$.

This stationary point is inside the interval, and the value of f at this point is
$$f\left(\tfrac{1}{3}\right) = 3\left(\tfrac{1}{3}\right)^2 - 2\left(\tfrac{1}{3}\right) + 5$$
$$= \tfrac{1}{3} - \tfrac{2}{3} + 5$$
$$= 4\tfrac{2}{3}.$$

The values of f at the endpoints of the interval are
$$f(-1) = 3(-1)^2 - 2(-1) + 5$$
$$= 3 + 2 + 5$$
$$= 10$$
and
$$f(4) = 3 \times 4^2 - 2 \times 4 + 5$$
$$= 48 - 8 + 5$$
$$= 45.$$

The greatest value of f on the interval $[-1, 4]$ is 45, and the least value is $4\tfrac{2}{3}$.

(The graph of f is below.)

Solution to Activity 23

An example is the function $f(x) = |x|$ and the interval $[-1, 1]$. This function is continuous on this interval. Its least value on the interval is 0, which occurs when $x = 0$, but 0 is neither a stationary point of the function nor an endpoint of the interval. The function is not differentiable when $x = 0$.

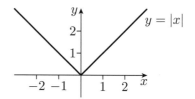

Solution to Activity 24

Here
$$f(x) = 2x^4 + 3x^2 + x,$$
so
$$f'(x) = 8x^3 + 6x + 1,$$
and
$$f''(x) = 24x^2 + 6.$$

Solution to Activity 25

The derivative of the function in graph A is shown in graph C.

The second derivative of the function in graph A is shown in graph D.

(There are various ways to work this out. For example, notice that the function in graph A has a stationary point when x is approximately 0. So the graph of its derivative must cross or touch the x-axis when x is approximately 0, which tells you that the derivative must be the function in graph C. Alternatively, notice that the function in graph A is decreasing for values of x just less than 0. So its derivative must be negative for these values of x, which again tells you that the derivative must be the function in graph C. You can use similar arguments to work out that the derivative of the function in graph C is the function in graph D.)

(Graph B shows the third derivative of the function in graph A.)

Solution to Activity 26

(a) We have
$$f(x) = \tfrac{1}{6}x^4 - 2x^3 + 11x^2 - 18x,$$
so
$$f'(x) = \tfrac{2}{3}x^3 - 6x^2 + 22x - 18,$$
and
$$f''(x) = 2x^2 - 12x + 22.$$

(b) To show that f is concave up on all of its domain, which is all the real numbers, we show that f'' is positive on the interval $(-\infty, \infty)$. One way to do that is by completing the square, as follows.
$$
\begin{aligned}
f''(x) &= 2x^2 - 12x + 22 \\
&= 2(x^2 - 6x) + 22 \\
&= 2\left((x-3)^2 - 9\right) + 22 \\
&= 2(x-3)^2 - 18 + 22 \\
&= 2(x-3)^2 + 4.
\end{aligned}
$$

The first term in this expression for $f''(x)$ is greater than or equal to zero for every value of x, and the second term is positive, so $f''(x)$ is positive for every value of x.

It follows, by the concave up/concave down criterion, that f is concave up on $(-\infty, \infty)$.

(The graph of f is shown below.)

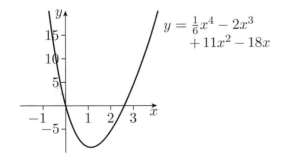

$$y = \tfrac{1}{6}x^4 - 2x^3 + 11x^2 - 18x$$

Solution to Activity 27

(a) We have
$$f(x) = \tfrac{1}{12}x^4 - 2x^2,$$
so
$$f'(x) = \tfrac{1}{3}x^3 - 4x,$$
and
$$f''(x) = x^2 - 4.$$

(b) Factorising the expression for $f''(x)$ found in part (a) gives
$$f''(x) = (x+2)(x-2).$$
When x is in the interval $(-2, 2)$, the value of $x + 2$ is positive and the value of $x - 2$ is negative, so the value of $f''(x)$ is negative.

It follows, by the concave up/concave down criterion, that f is concave down on $(-2, 2)$.

(The graph of f is shown below.)

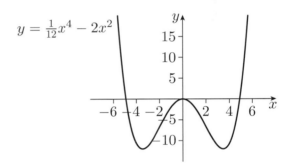

$$y = \tfrac{1}{12}x^4 - 2x^2$$

Solution to Activity 28

(a) We have
$$f(x) = \tfrac{2}{3}x^3 - \tfrac{5}{2}x^2 + 2x,$$
so
$$
\begin{aligned}
f'(x) &= 2x^2 - 5x + 2 \\
&= (2x - 1)(x - 2).
\end{aligned}
$$
Hence the stationary points of f are $\tfrac{1}{2}$ and 2.

The y-coordinate of the stationary point $\tfrac{1}{2}$ is given by
$$
\begin{aligned}
y &= \tfrac{2}{3}\left(\tfrac{1}{2}\right)^3 - \tfrac{5}{2}\left(\tfrac{1}{2}\right)^2 + 2 \times \tfrac{1}{2} \\
&= \tfrac{2}{24} - \tfrac{5}{8} + 1 \\
&= \tfrac{11}{24}.
\end{aligned}
$$

The y-coordinate of the stationary point 2 is given by
$$y = \tfrac{2}{3} \times 2^3 - \tfrac{5}{2} \times 2^2 + 2 \times 2$$
$$= \tfrac{16}{3} - 10 + 4$$
$$= -\tfrac{2}{3}.$$
Hence the stationary points are $(\tfrac{1}{2}, \tfrac{11}{24})$ and $(2, -\tfrac{2}{3})$.

(b) We have
$$f''(x) = 4x - 5,$$
so
$$f''(\tfrac{1}{2}) = 4 \times \tfrac{1}{2} - 5 = 2 - 5 = -3$$
and
$$f''(2) = 4 \times 2 - 5 = 8 - 5 = 3.$$
Hence, by the second derivative test, $(\tfrac{1}{2}, \tfrac{11}{24})$ is a local maximum and $(2, -\tfrac{2}{3})$ is a local minimum.

(c) The y-intercept of f is 0.

A sketch of the graph of f is shown below.

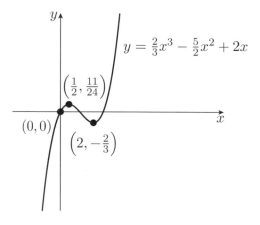

$y = \tfrac{2}{3}x^3 - \tfrac{5}{2}x^2 + 2x$

$(\tfrac{1}{2}, \tfrac{11}{24})$

$(0,0)$

$(2, -\tfrac{2}{3})$

Solution to Activity 29

(a) The displacement s metres of the object at time t seconds is given by
$$s = \tfrac{1}{3}t^3 - 5t^2 + 16t + 8.$$
Hence the velocity $v\,\mathrm{m\,s^{-1}}$ of the object at time t seconds is given by
$$v = \frac{\mathrm{d}s}{\mathrm{d}t} = t^2 - 10t + 16,$$
and the acceleration $a\,\mathrm{m\,s^{-2}}$ of the object at time t seconds is given by
$$a = \frac{\mathrm{d}v}{\mathrm{d}t} = 2t - 10.$$

(b) The object's acceleration is not constant, because the expression that gives the object's acceleration in terms of time is $2t - 10$, which is not a constant (it contains the variable t).

(c) When $t = 6$,
$$v = 6^2 - 10 \times 6 + 16 = -8,$$
and
$$a = 2 \times 6 - 10 = 2.$$
So at time 6 seconds, the velocity of the object is $-8\,\mathrm{m\,s^{-1}}$ and its acceleration is $2\,\mathrm{m\,s^{-2}}$.

(d) (i) When t is between 5 and 8 (exclusive), the value of $a = 2t - 10$ is always positive. Hence the acceleration of the object is always positive in the given time interval, so its velocity is increasing over this time interval.

(ii) We have $v = t^2 - 10t + 16 = (t - 2)(t - 8)$. When t is between 5 and 8 (exclusive), the value of $t - 2$ is always positive and the value of $t - 8$ is always negative, so the value of $v = (t - 2)(t - 8)$ is always negative. That is, the velocity of the object is always negative over the given time interval.

(iii) By parts (b)(i) and (b)(ii), over the given time interval the object's velocity is always negative, and always increasing. So its speed is decreasing over this time interval.

(The object's displacement, velocity and acceleration are shown in the graphs below. Notice in particular that over the time interval from 5 seconds to 8 seconds (excluding the endpoints), the object's velocity is negative and increasing. So the magnitude of its velocity is decreasing; that is, its speed is decreasing.)

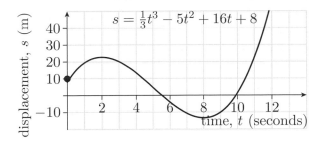

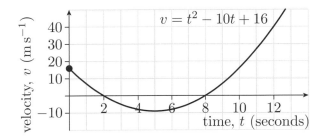

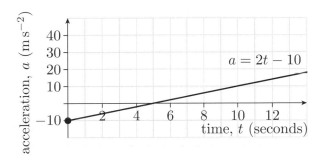

(The object's displacement, velocity and acceleration are shown in the graphs below. Notice in particular that although the velocity of the object is decreasing, its speed is increasing, because its velocity is negative.)

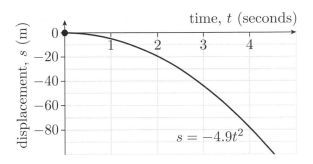

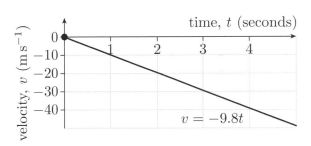

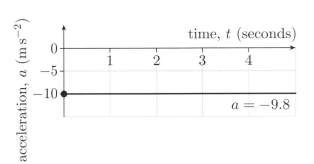

Solution to Activity 30

The displacement s metres of the falling object at time t seconds is given by

$$s = -4.9t^2.$$

Hence the velocity $v\,\mathrm{m\,s^{-1}}$ of the object at time t seconds is given by

$$v = \frac{\mathrm{d}s}{\mathrm{d}t} = -9.8t,$$

and the acceleration $a\,\mathrm{m\,s^{-2}}$ of the object at time t seconds is given by

$$a = \frac{\mathrm{d}v}{\mathrm{d}t} = -9.8.$$

So the acceleration of the object is constant, with value $-9.8\,\mathrm{m\,s^{-2}}$.

Index

Index